The Campus History Series

FLORIDA STATE UNIVERSITY

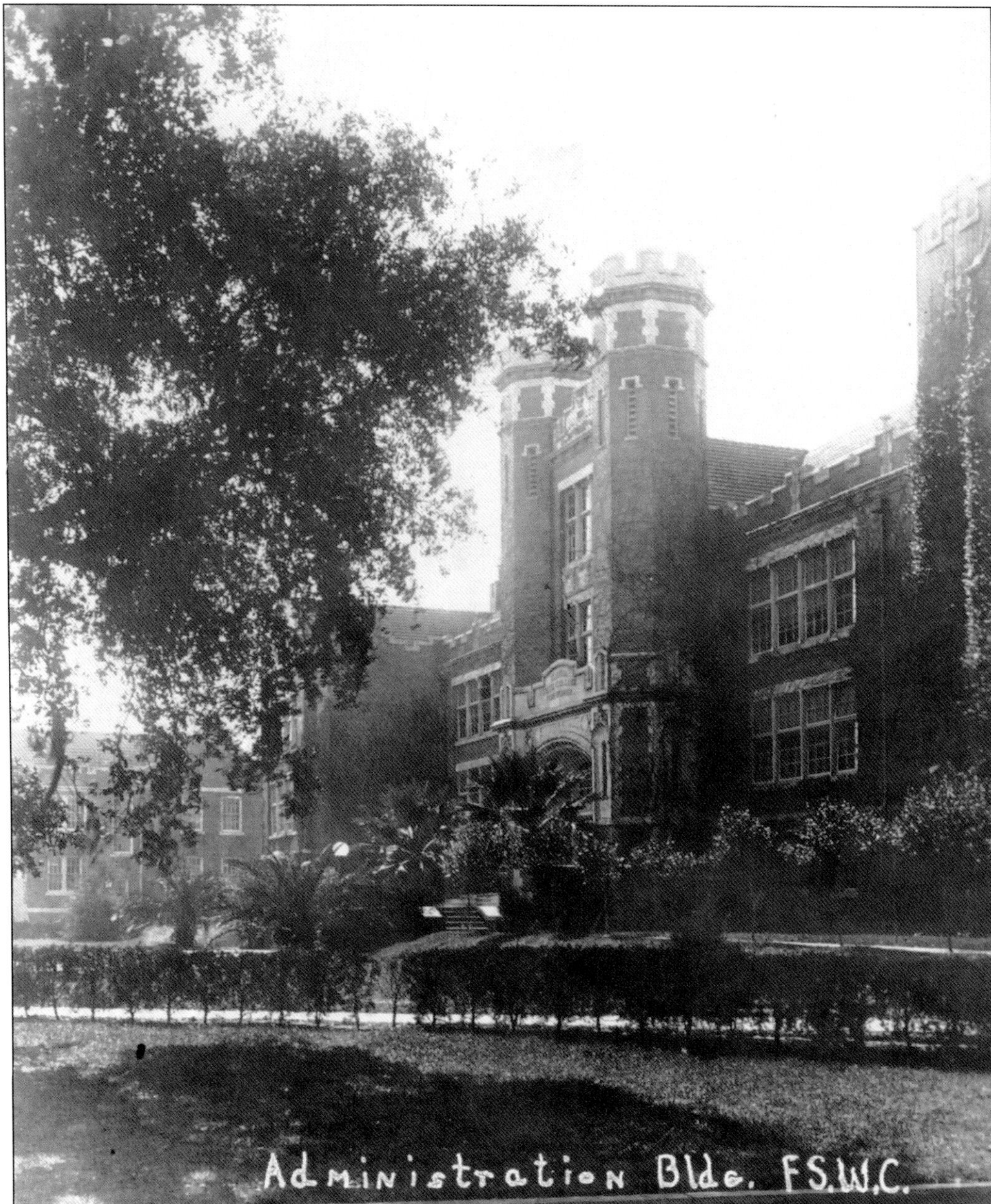

Constructed at the Florida State College for Women between 1909 and 1911 and originally known as the Administration Building, the Westcott Building, then as today, serves as the main building for the school and is an iconic image of the strength and permanence of Florida State University as an institution. (Historic Photograph Collection, Special Collections and Archives, Strozier Library, Florida State University, Tallahassee, Florida.)

ON THE COVER: The Florida State University Westcott Building and Fountain is pictured around 1952. (Historic Photograph Collection, Special Collections and Archives, Strozier Library, Florida State University, Tallahassee, Florida.)

The Campus History Series

FLORIDA STATE UNIVERSITY

EDDIE WOODWARD

ARCADIA PUBLISHING

ISBN 978-0-7385-9203-9

Published by Arcadia Publishing
Charleston, South Carolina

Printed in the United States of America

Library of Congress Catalog Card Number: 2011930211

For all general information, please contact Arcadia Publishing:
Telephone 843-853-2070
Fax 843-853-0044
E-mail sales@arcadiapublishing.com
For customer service and orders:
Toll-Free 1-888-313-2665

Visit us on the Internet at www.arcadiapublishing.com

In memory of Mary Lou Norwood (class of 1947), the driving force behind the creation of the Heritage Protocol program and its efforts to document and preserve the history of Florida State University

Contents

ACKNOWLEDGMENTS

The creation of this book would not have been possible without the support of Julia Zimmerman, dean of University Libraries at Florida State University (FSU). All of the author proceeds generated from the sale of this book will go to the FSU University Libraries. Unless otherwise noted, all images are from the FSU Heritage Protocol Photograph Collection and the Historic Photograph Collection in the Special Collections and Archives in Robert Manning Strozier Library at Florida State University.

Those from outside the university community who have provided assistance include John Coski and Ann Drury Wellford with the Museum of the Confederacy; Kieran M. Orr with the Museum of Florida History; Lindsey Harrington, Jody Norman, and Adam Watson with the State Archives of Florida; Geoffery Stark with Special Collections at the University of Arkansas Libraries; and John Nemmers and Carl Van Ness with Special Collections at the University of Florida's George A. Smathers Libraries.

Those from within the university community who have provided assistance include Jessica Rosenthal with the Alumni Association; Rob Wilson with FSU Athletics Department; Kay Cordle with the FSU Foundation; Michele Edmunds with FSU Photography Services; Ryals Lee, FSU sports photographer; David Thayer with FSU Facilities Department; Donna McHugh with FSU University Relations; Willa Patterson, Plato Smith, and Giesele Towels with the Digital Library Center in Robert Manning Strozier Library; Malcolm Shackelford with Scholars Commons in Strozier Library; Billy Glasco, Gina Woodward, and Benjamin Yadon with Special Collections and Archives in Strozier Library; and Heritage Protocol graduate assistants and interns Christine Bethke, Casey Christopher, Andrew Hautau, Lindsay Ogles, and Anya Owens.

Alumni, current and former faculty and staff, and friends of Florida State University who provided assistance include Bill Bolton, Alicia Crew, Steve Edwards, Gerald Ensley, Frankie Hall, James and Betty Lou Joanos, James P. Jones, Kris Knab, Guyte P. McCord III, Susie Skinner Moore, Bob O'Lary, Bob Perrone, Dick Puckett, Mike Rupp, Jerry Sexton, Nancy Smilowitz, Janet Stoner, Tommy Waits, Tommy Warren, Janet Wells, and Shirley and Eddie Woodward Sr.

This book would not have been possible without the historical research of Dr. William G. Dodd, Dr. Robin Sellers, Maxine Stern, and others. Special thanks to Fran Conaway for going above and beyond with her "magic editing" skills. Selecting the photographs to document FSU's history was a difficult task. Some may find themes or photographs that they believe to be out of proportion with the history of the university. In telling the story of FSU through photographs, it is my intention to show some aspects of FSU history that may not be so familiar, especially with regard to the early years. Many thanks again to all those who have provided assistance; all errors are my own.

INTRODUCTION

In 1851, the Florida State Legislature established two seminaries, one to the east and one west of the Suwannee River. Tallahassee was chosen as the site for the western school, to be known as the State Seminary West of the Suwannee River, or simply West Florida Seminary. The school opened its doors in 1857. The following year, the seminary absorbed the Leon Female Academy along with its schoolhouse. The institution then functioned as a coeducational school with separate male and female departments. With the commencement of the Civil War, the legislature authorized the organization of the male department of the seminary on a collegiate and military basis. On March 6, 1865, the cadets of West Florida Seminary were called to defend Tallahassee, the state capital, from a Federal advance from the Gulf Coast. At the Battle of Natural Bridge, they played a significant role in the defeat of the Union army. After the war, the seminary struggled for existence.

The 1880s proved a formative decade. In 1882, the separate male and female departments merged, and boys and girls were taught in the same classrooms. With the appointment of George M. Edgar as the first president in 1887, the institution took steps to reorganize into a complete college on par with its southeastern counterparts. On Edgar's recommendation, a totally new curriculum was developed, transforming the seminary into a competitive, four-year liberal arts college. At the same time, the military component was phased out. In 1901, the school's name was changed to Florida State College, which was more reflective of its strong liberal arts program. After a restructuring of the school's colleges and departments and the addition of student clubs and organizations, athletic and sports teams, and dormitories, the school took on the feeling of a full-fledged college, especially from the students' perspective.

It was all to be short-lived, however, because in 1905, in an effort to reduce duplication and consolidate higher education, the state legislature passed the Buckman Act, transforming Florida State College into Florida Female College. In 1909, school president Albert A. Murphree, who had been with the college through the transition, left and was replaced by Edward Conradi, who would hold that post for the next 32 years. The name change to Florida State College for Women (FSCW) that same year was cosmetic only and had no effect on the school's mission. Conradi faced the challenge of fulfilling the traditional expectations of an all-women's college while at the same time moving the curriculum forward and attempting to redefine traditional educational boundaries. The institution's strong liberal arts emphasis continued as the foundation on to which the curriculum would be structured. FSCW was ahead of its time in training and turning out women for such nontraditional professions as journalism and the sciences, with a remarkable number going on to graduate schools across the country. In 1935, FSCW became the first college or university in Florida to establish a chapter of Phi Beta Kappa. The FSCW era was decisive in the history and development of today's university, and during its existence, it was one of the premier women's colleges in the country. By every standard, the school strived to produce *femina perfecta*, or the "complete woman." The era was a period of extensive planning, growth, and development for the campus. Most importantly, the FSCW years were significant because of the traditions established by students and administration and the nurturing environment fostered by the nature of the all-female student body and its relationship with the staff, faculty, and administration. This intimate and collegial environment has carried through and is notably present in today's university.

After World War II and because of the newly established GI Bill of Rights and the flood of veterans returning home, the all-male University of Florida was unprepared for a deluge of applications for admission. Tallahassee-area veterans petitioned school president Doak Campbell asking that they be permitted to attend Florida State College for Women. It was determined that the law, which prevented men from attending FSCW, could be circumvented by permitting the men to attend the women's school under the authority of the University of Florida, as if a branch campus existed in Tallahassee. Accordingly, the Tallahassee Branch of University of Florida (TBUF) was established in 1946, permitting between 500 and 1,000 male students to attend FSCW.

The next year, new legislation transformed the college back to coeducational, renaming FSCW as Florida State University. The well-established, nationally recognized liberal arts program of the women's college was the institutional foundation for the new expanded curriculum. The school chose the Seminole Indian as its symbol, and intercollegiate athletic teams were established. The 1950s was a decade of unprecedented growth for the new university. The campus expanded to the west with construction of more classrooms, a new student union, an athletic stadium, and numerous dormitories for both men and women.

FSU's second decade saw a great expansion in the curriculum, especially the sciences, beginning with the establishment of the Institute of Molecular Biophysics in 1960. In 1966, the College of Law was established, and the study-abroad program began in Florence, Italy. The arts also continued to flourish. The social changes that were affecting the rest of the South were reflected on campus when Maxwell Courtney became the first African American to graduate from FSU in 1965. During this era, the football team achieved a new level of national prominence, going to four bowl games and beating the University of Florida (UF) Gators for the first time ever in 1964. Reflecting national events, FSU had a vocal contingent of activists, and campus dissent and protest reached its peak at the end of the 1960s. There were numerous demonstrations but no violence, thanks in part to Pres. Stanley Marshall's administration.

Prolific growth and achievement have continued through the decades. In 1976, Marshall resigned, and Bernie Sliger replaced him, serving until 1991, and then again as interim president in 1994. During the Sliger administration, enrollment increased by one-third, and the university acquired three supercomputers and its Panama City campus. During this time, FSU became a recognized leader in intercollegiate athletics, winning two national championships in football and joining the prestigious Atlantic Coast Conference (ACC). Sliger was followed by Talbot "Sandy" D'Alemberte in 1994, who continued the progress in academic excellence and research. During his tenure, the FSU College of Medicine was established, and the university became the headquarters of the National High Magnetic Field Laboratory, the largest and most powerful facility of its kind in the world. With the turn of the 20th century, the university continued its extraordinary growth, both physically and intellectually. Under the leadership of Pres. T.K. Wetherell, who took office in 2003, the university experienced $800 million in campus construction and renovations, while FSU students received unprecedented national academic recognition, including three Rhodes Scholars. Current president Eric Barron, an FSU alumnus like Wetherell, took office in 2010 with the mission of increasing private funding and building academic excellence within all aspects of the curriculum, making FSU a recognized leader in academic research not only in the country, but in the world.

One

West Florida Seminary 1851–1901

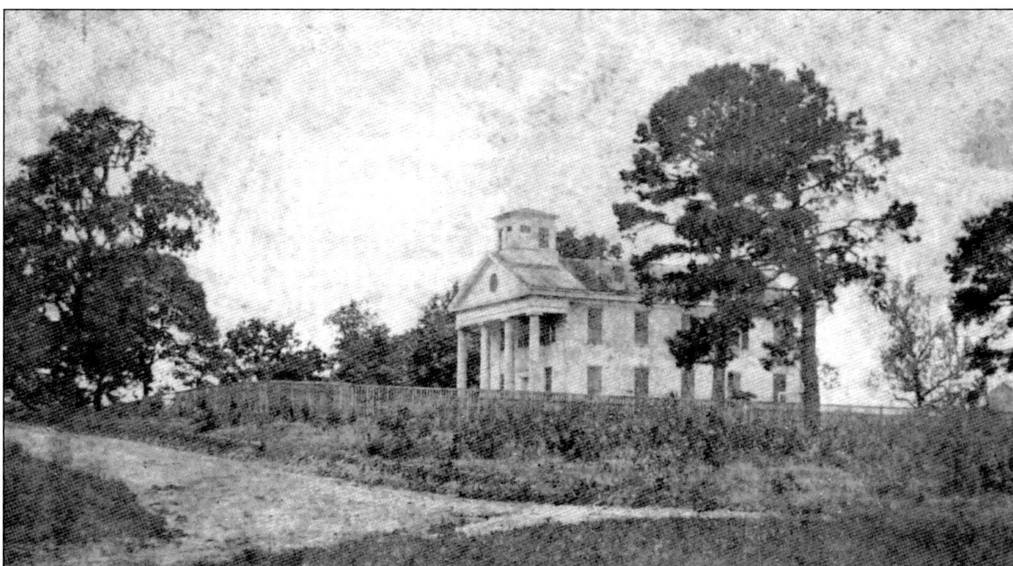

Near the southeast corner of the current Florida State University campus, four city lots were selected as the location for the new State Seminary West of the Suwannee River. The site at the very western outskirts of town was known as "Gallow's Hill" and was considered an unsavory neighborhood with its approaches inconvenient and unpleasant. After its construction in 1854, the new "City School House" was regarded not only as an unusually well-built and substantial structure but also "the handsomest edifice" in Tallahassee. (Archives of Florida.)

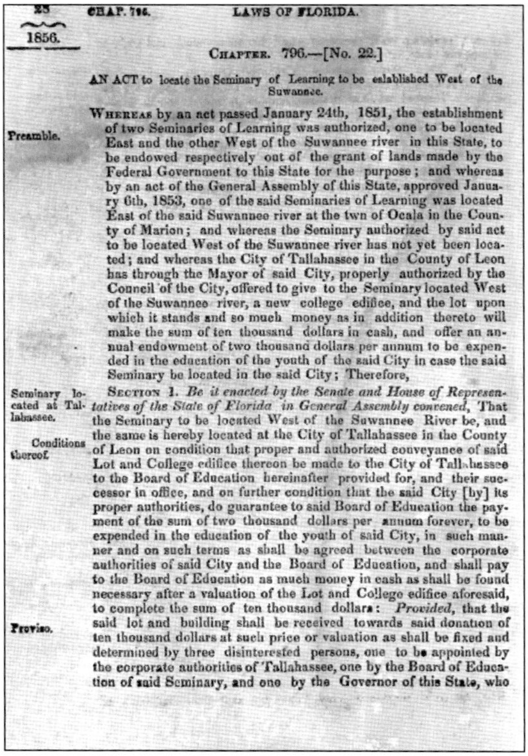

28 CHAP. 796. LAWS OF FLORIDA.

1856.

CHAPTER. 796.—[No. 22.]

AN ACT to locate the Seminary of Learning to be established West of the Suwannee.

Preamble. WHEREAS by an act passed January 24th, 1851, the establishment of two Seminaries of Learning was authorized, one to be located East and the other West of the Suwannee river in this State, to be endowed respectively out of the grant of lands made by the Federal Government to this State for the purpose; and whereas by an act of the General Assembly of this State, approved January 6th, 1853, one of the said Seminaries of Learning was located East of the said Suwannee river at the twn of Ocala in the County of Marion; and whereas the Seminary authorized by said act to be located West of the Suwannee river has not yet been located; and whereas the City of Tallahassee in the County of Leon has through the Mayor of said City, properly authorized by the Council of the City, offered to give to the Seminary located West of the Suwannee river, a new college edifice, and the lot upon which it stands and so much money as in addition thereto will make the sum of ten thousand dollars in cash, and offer an annual endowment of two thousand dollars per annum to be expended in the education of the youth of the said City in case the said Seminary be located in the said City; Therefore,

Seminary located at Tallahassee. SECTION 1. *Be it enacted by the Senate and House of Representatives of the State of Florida in General Assembly convened*, That the Seminary to be located West of the Suwannee River be, and the same is hereby located at the City of Tallahassee in the County of Leon on condition that proper and authorized conveyance of said Lot and College edifice thereon be made to the City of Tallahassee to the Board of Education hereinafter provided for, and their successor in office, and on further condition that the said City [by] its proper authorities, do guarantee to said Board of Education the payment of the sum of two thousand dollars per annum forever, to be expended in the education of the youth of said City, in such manner and on such terms as shall be agreed between the corporate authorities of said City and the Board of Education, and shall pay to the Board of Education as much money in cash as shall be found necessary after a valuation of the Lot and College edifice aforesaid, to complete the sum of ten thousand dollars: *Provided*, that the said lot and building shall be received towards said donation of ten thousand dollars at such price or valuation as shall be fixed and determined by three disinterested persons, one to be appointed by the corporate authorities of Tallahassee, one by the Board of Education of said Seminary, and one by the Governor of this State, who

Conditions thereof.

Proviso.

The Act of January 24, 1851, called for the establishment of two seminaries of learning, one to the east and the other to the west of the Suwannee River, to be awarded to the localities that offered the most suitable inducements in land, buildings, and money. Ocala was chosen as the site of the eastern school, and Tallahassee became the site for the Florida State Seminary West of the Suwannee River.

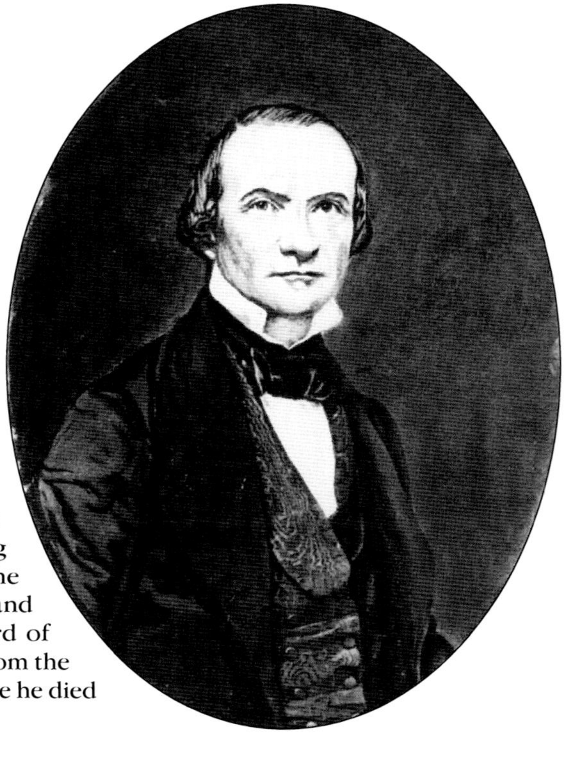

Born in Virginia in 1801, Francis Eppes, the grandson of Thomas Jefferson, moved to Tallahassee in 1829 where he spent much of his life in public service, including two terms as mayor. He spearheaded the efforts to lure the school to Tallahassee and served as the first president of its board of education. Shortly after his resignation from the board in 1868, he moved to Orlando, where he died on May 30, 1881. (Archives of Florida.)

The new West Florida Seminary building stood just in front of the present Westcott Building. The 60-foot-long-by-40-foot-wide, two-story structure had heavy brick walls covered with stucco. Inside, the ceilings were 12 feet high, and each floor had a "school room" and two small recitation rooms. This would be the school's main building until it was remodeled and enlarged in 1891.

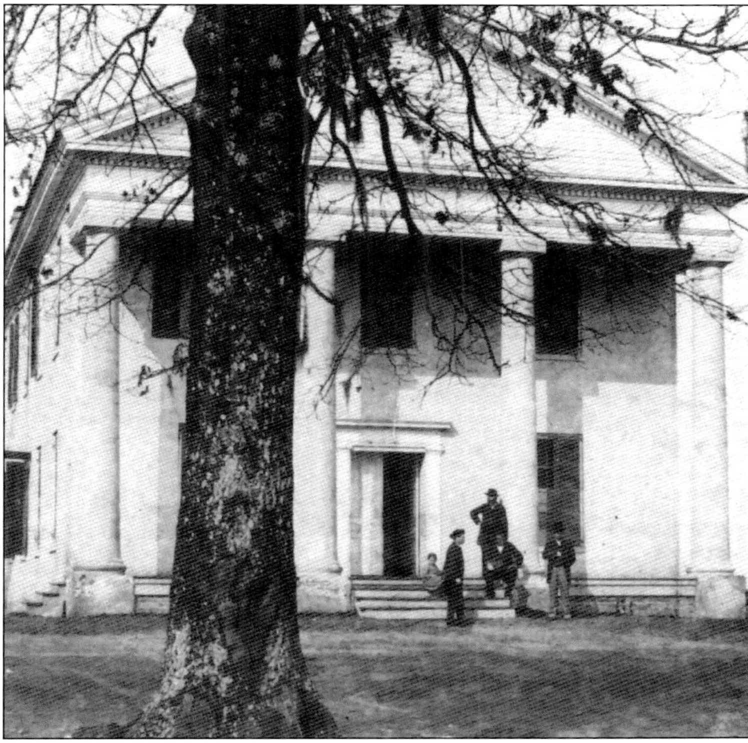

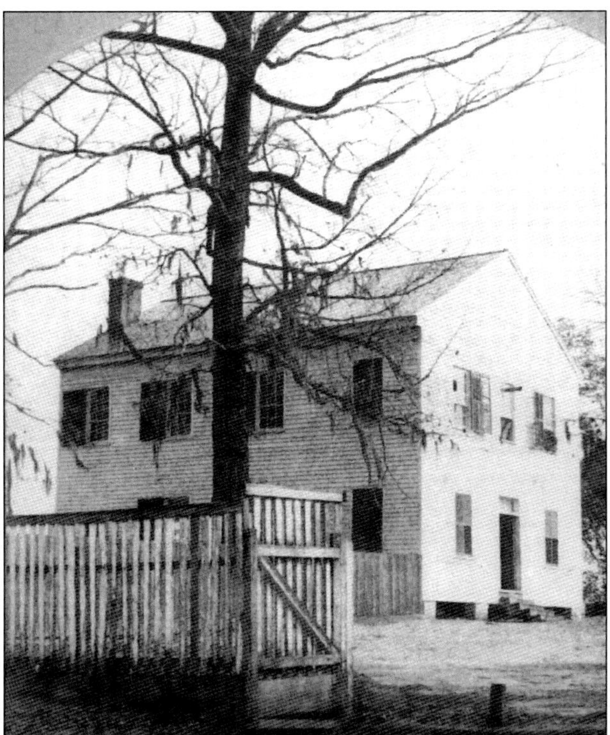

Established in 1844, the Leon Female Academy offered an unusually complete education for girls. In 1858, the trustees of the academy conveyed the property of the school to West Florida Seminary with the understanding that the seminary would provide an equitable education for the female students. In October of that year, the academy was absorbed into the seminary and was thereafter known as the Female Department of West Florida Seminary.

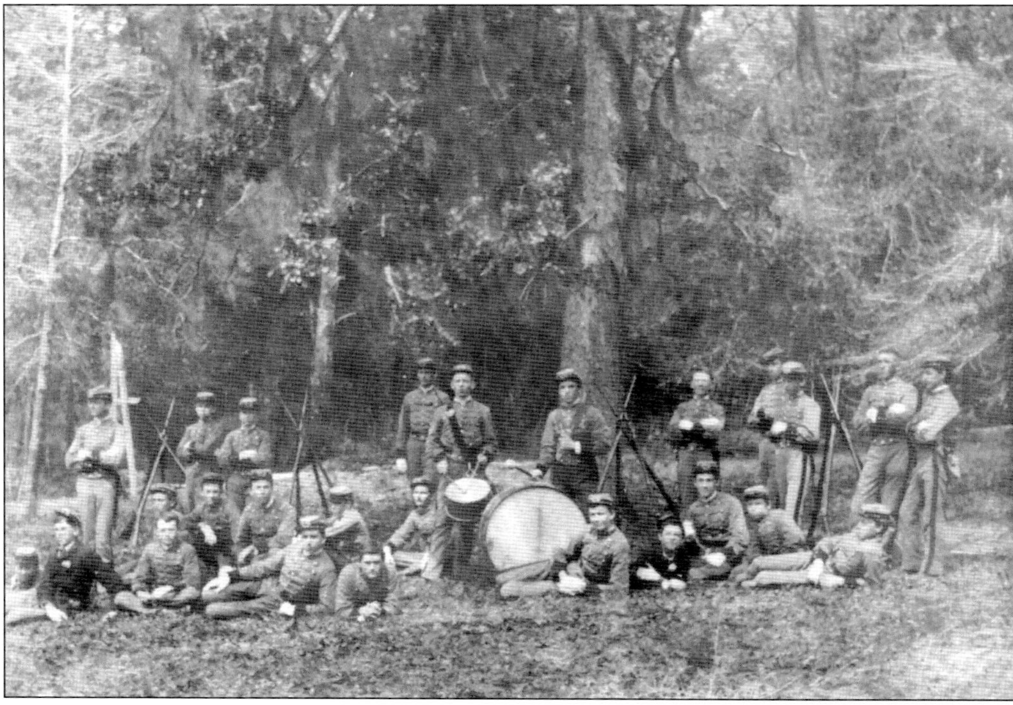

From its inception, a military component was to be a part of the Male Department of West Florida Seminary. In the summer of 1859, principal Duncan McNeill Turner spent several weeks visiting schools in which military training was an active part of the student curriculum. After that, and over the course of the seminary's history, various instructors held the title of professor of mathematics and tactics.

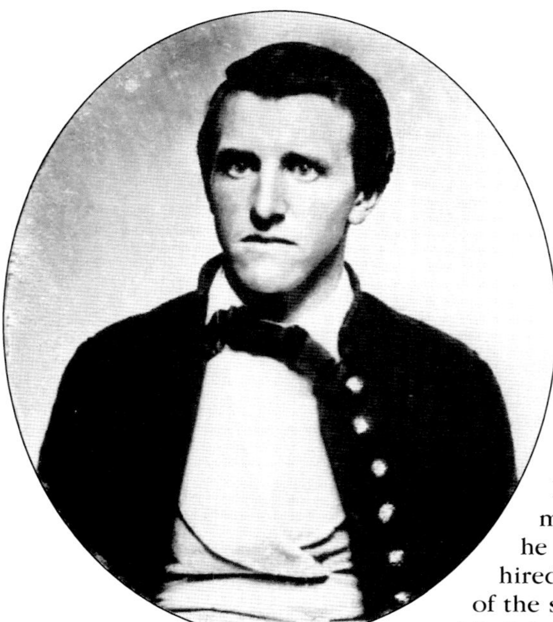

Valentine Mason Johnson, an 1860 Virginia Military Institute (VMI) graduate, was on his way to take a teaching position at West Florida Seminary when the Civil War broke out. After rising to the rank of captain with the 30th Virginia Volunteer Infantry Regiment, he was forced to leave military service for health reasons. In 1863, he again headed to Tallahassee where he was hired as assistant principal and then principal of the seminary. This photograph is from 1859, while Johnson was still a cadet at VMI.

With the commencement of the Civil War in 1861, the legislature drafted a law officially designating West Florida Seminary as the Florida Collegiate and Military Institute and authorizing the organization of the Male Department on a collegiate and military basis. Because of the near impossibility of keeping instructors with military experience during the war, attempts to establish a first-class military academy became more and more difficult. (Archives of Florida.)

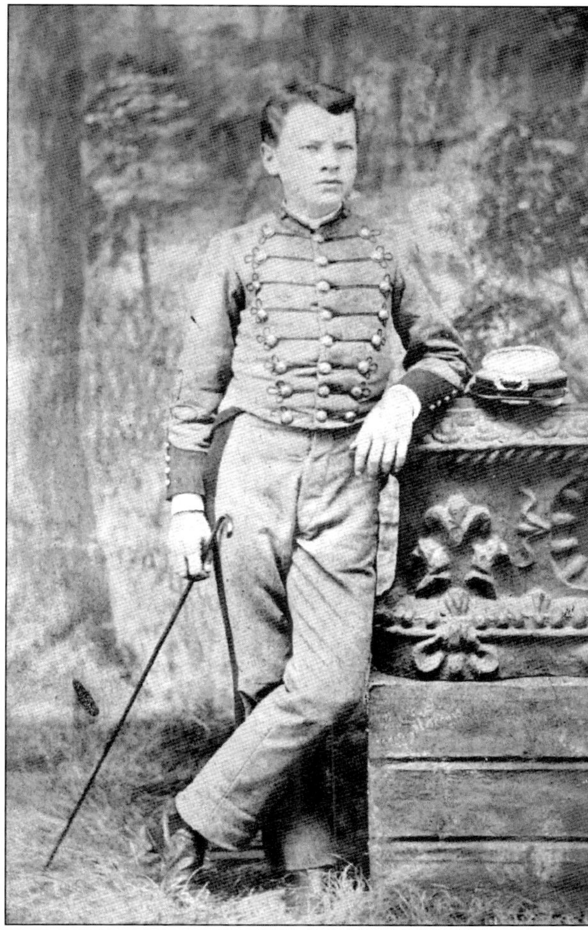

On March 6, 1865, an emergency call for the older students to defend the capital went out. At the Battle of Natural Bridge, which halted the Federal advance from the south, a company of West Florida Seminary cadets took a significant role, and by their bravery and gallant behavior won the praise of townspeople as well as older, more seasoned fighters. This 1924 photograph looks across the St. Marks River toward the battlefield. (Archives of Florida.)

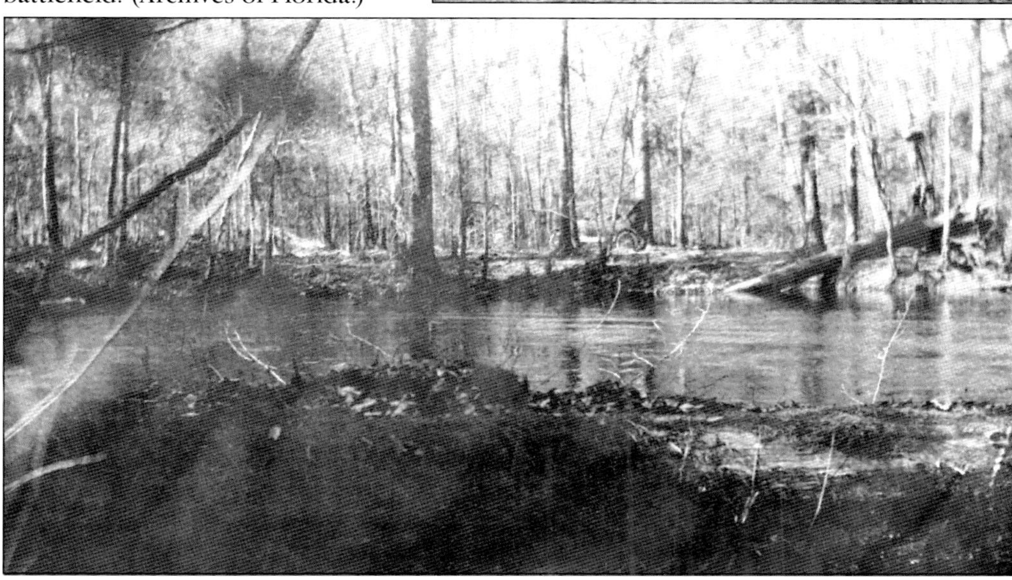

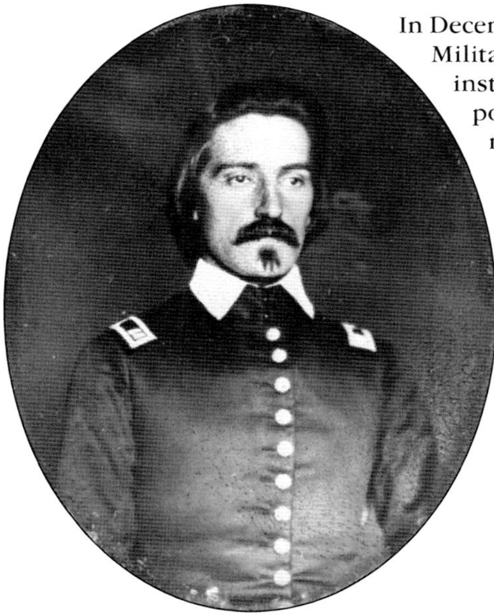

In December 1860, West Florida Seminary hired Virginia Military Institute graduate James Lucius Cross, an instructor with an excellent reputation, to fill the post of professor of mathematics and tactics. The next year, he was appointed principal but soon resigned to fight for the Confederacy. After the war, he worked at the school until 1870, first as superintendent of the Florida Collegiate and Military Institute and later as assistant principal of the seminary.

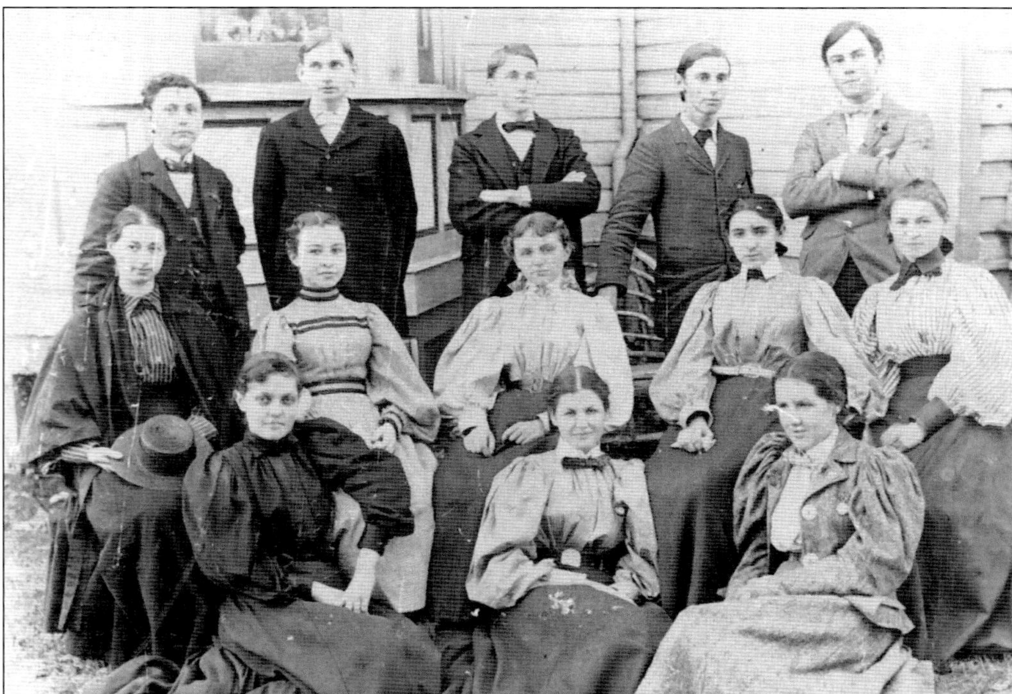

Until 1882, the boys and girls at the coeducational West Florida Seminary were taught separately. That year, the seminary abolished its male and female departments, after which, all the students were taught together in the same classes. Closer association of the sexes was considered conducive to good study and improved deportment, but the board had a more practical reason: coeducation was less expensive than segregated classrooms. This 1897 photograph is of the Naturalists Club. (Archives of Florida.)

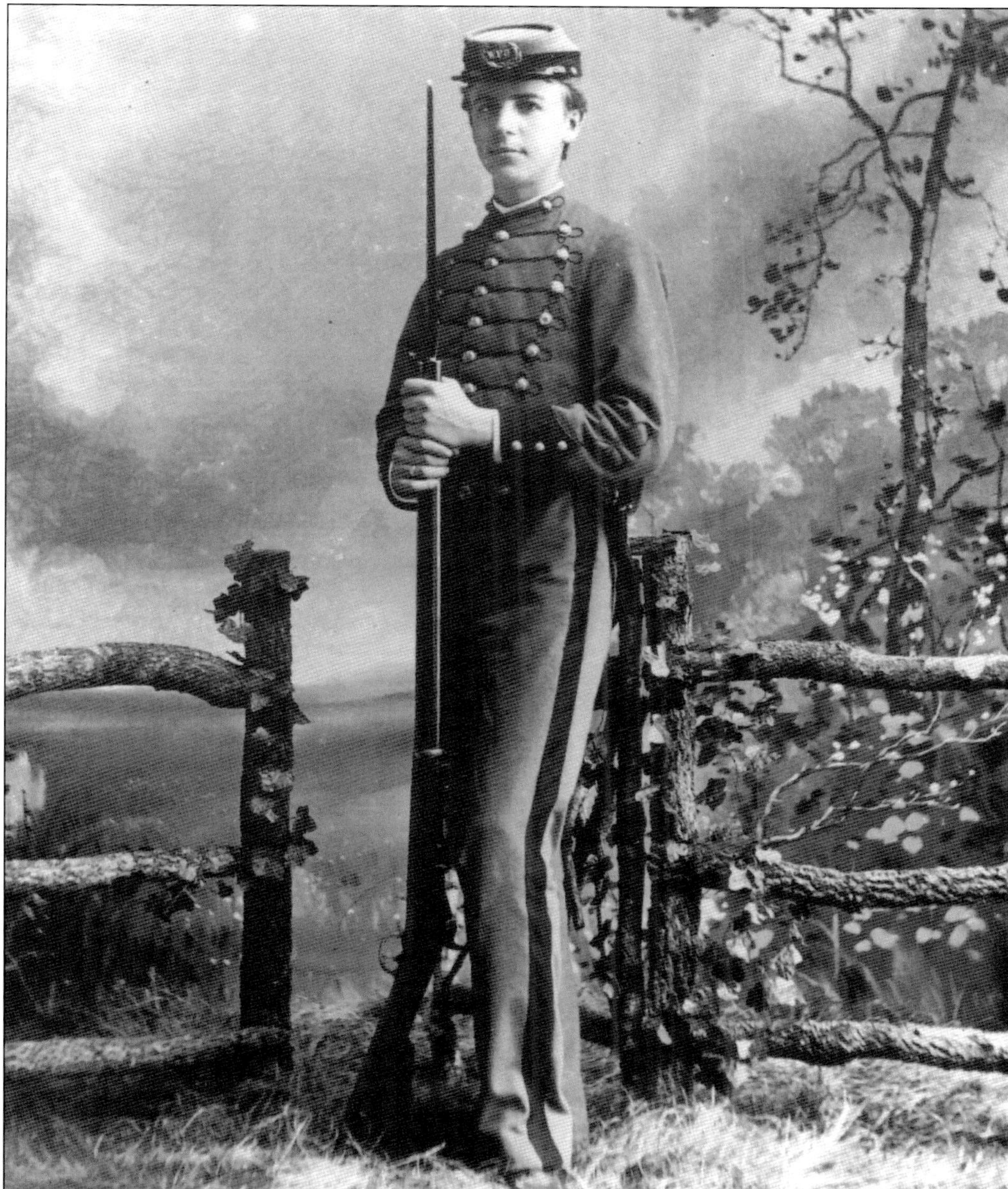

The cadet corps and military training continued well into the 1880s. Each cadet was responsible for his rifle, bayonet with scabbard, and cartridge box and belt; officers were issued swords or sabers with scabbards. A gun rack and a bass and snare drum were also supplied for the use of the corps. A uniform of Confederate gray with regulation blouse and cap, costing $15 per cadet, was approved, however, in warm weather, cadets were permitted to wear a lighter fatigue suit. All male students who were able were required to wear their uniforms during school hours and on parade. Drill was held each school day from 9:00 a.m. to 10:00 a.m., and public appearances by the corps were a source of great community pride. It was not uncommon for the governor, adjutant general, and other notable guests to review their maneuvers in the Capitol Square.

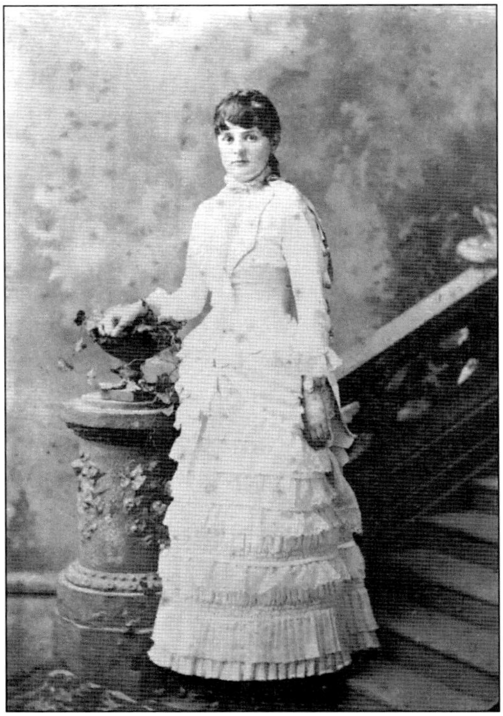

Although empowered to grant them since 1861, West Florida Seminary first awarded diplomas on June 24, 1880. The first recipients were Eugenia C. "Jennie" Tatum and Jessie T. Bernard. The photograph at left is purported to be that of Tatum in a graduation dress made for her by her grandmother. Below is the graduation certification of Bernard. The diploma is a part of the University Archives in the Florida State University's Strozier Library's Special Collections and Archives Department. (Left, Archives of Florida.)

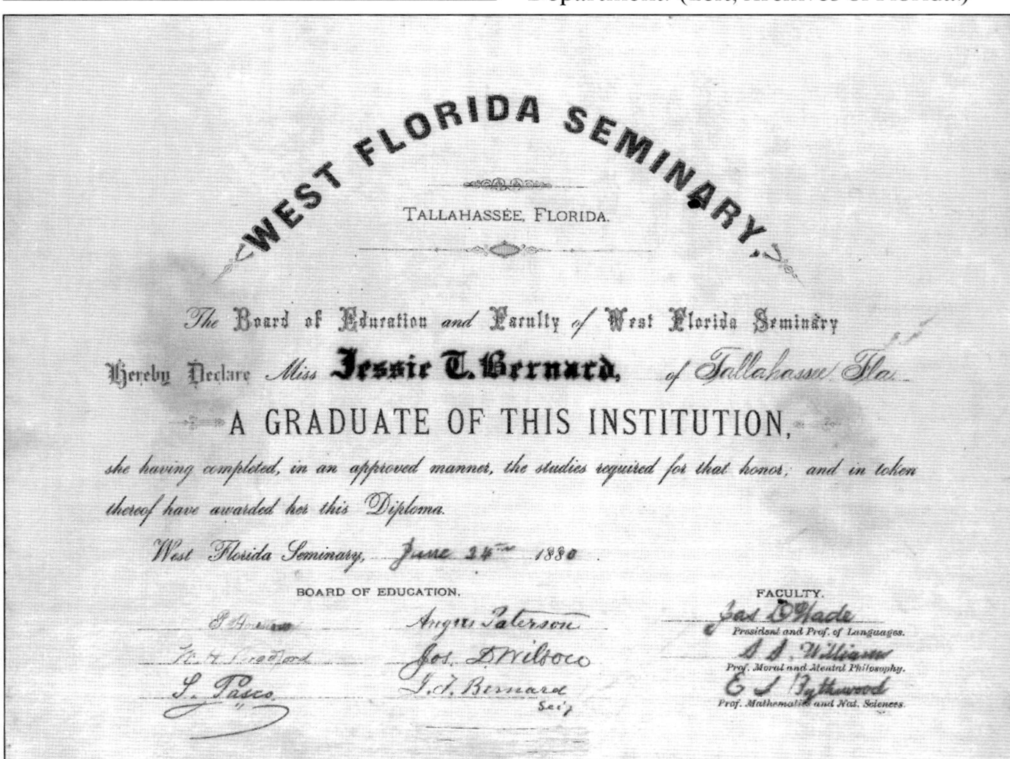

WEST FLORIDA SEMINARY,

TALLAHASSEE, FLORIDA.

The Board of Education and Faculty of West Florida Seminary

Hereby Declare Miss **Jessie T. Bernard,** of Tallahassee Fla.

A GRADUATE OF THIS INSTITUTION,

she having completed, in an approved manner, the studies required for that honor; and in token thereof have awarded her this Diploma.

West Florida Seminary, June 24th 1880.

BOARD OF EDUCATION.

Angus Paterson

Jos. D. Wilcox

S. Pasco

J. T. Bernard Sec'y

FACULTY.

Jas D. Wade
President and Prof. of Languages.

Prof. Moral and Mental Philosophy.

E. S. Bythwood
Prof. Mathematics and Nat. Sciences.

James D. Westcott Jr. attended West Florida Seminary and later served as a state legislator, attorney general, and associate justice of the state supreme court before he died in 1887 at the age of 48. According to his will, a major portion of his estate was to be held in trust for the benefit of West Florida Seminary. The will stipulated that the money was to be used to pay for teachers' salaries, and none of it was to be used for buildings or improvements. (Archives of Florida.)

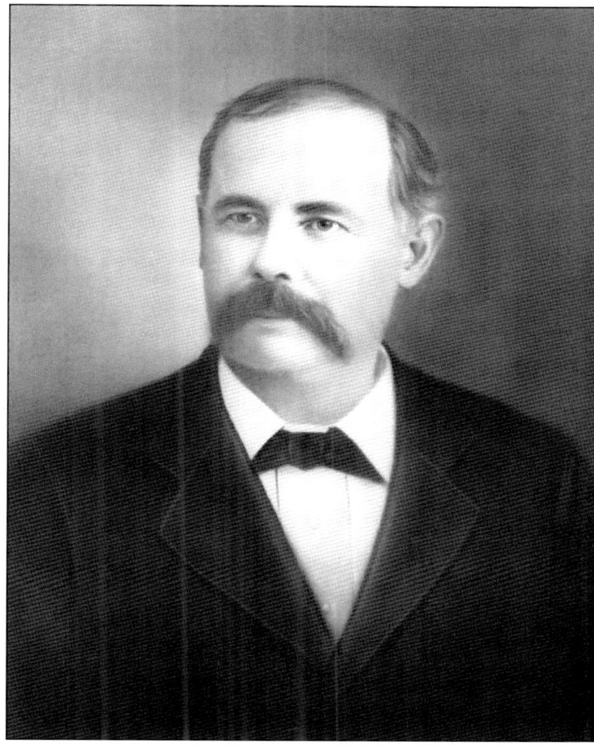

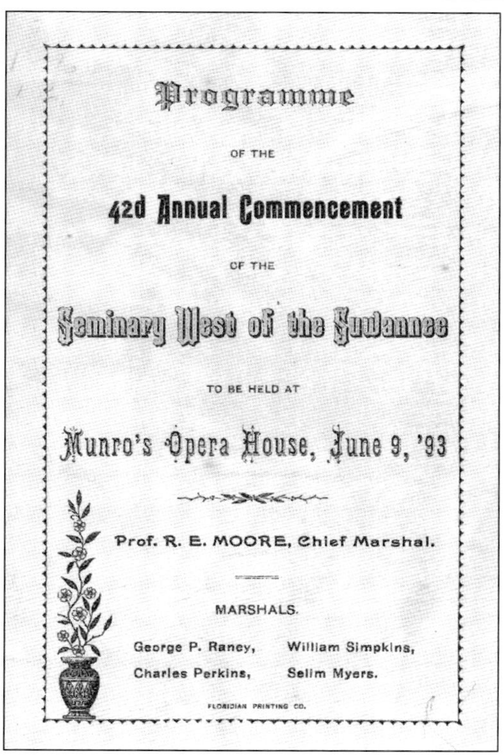

Programme

OF THE

42d Annual Commencement

OF THE

Seminary West of the Suwannee

TO BE HELD AT

Munro's Opera House, June 9, '93

Prof. R. E. MOORE, Chief Marshal.

MARSHALS.

George P. Raney, William Simpkins,
Charles Perkins, Selim Myers.

FLORIDIAN PRINTING CO.

The first commencement ceremony at West Florida Seminary took place on June 10–12, 1891. In those early days, the programs varied from year to year. Generally speaking, they were multiday events that included a sermon, followed by readings and orations, at least one debate featuring the campus literary societies, music recitals, a commencement address, and the conferring of the degrees to the graduates. The program at left is from the 1893 commencement ceremony.

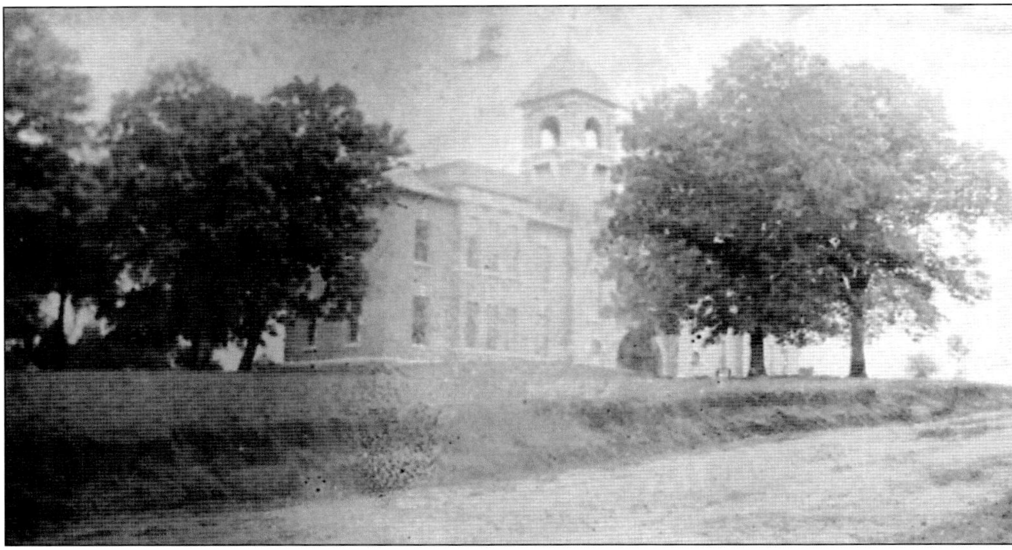

In 1891, the main school building was remodeled and enlarged with two projecting wings joined at a new two-story redbrick facade. The pure classic architecture of the previous structure was replaced by the eclectic style much in favor at the time. Seminary president George M. Edgar declared the new College Hall "one of the prettiest and most substantially constructed public buildings in the State." The photograph above was taken soon after its renovation.

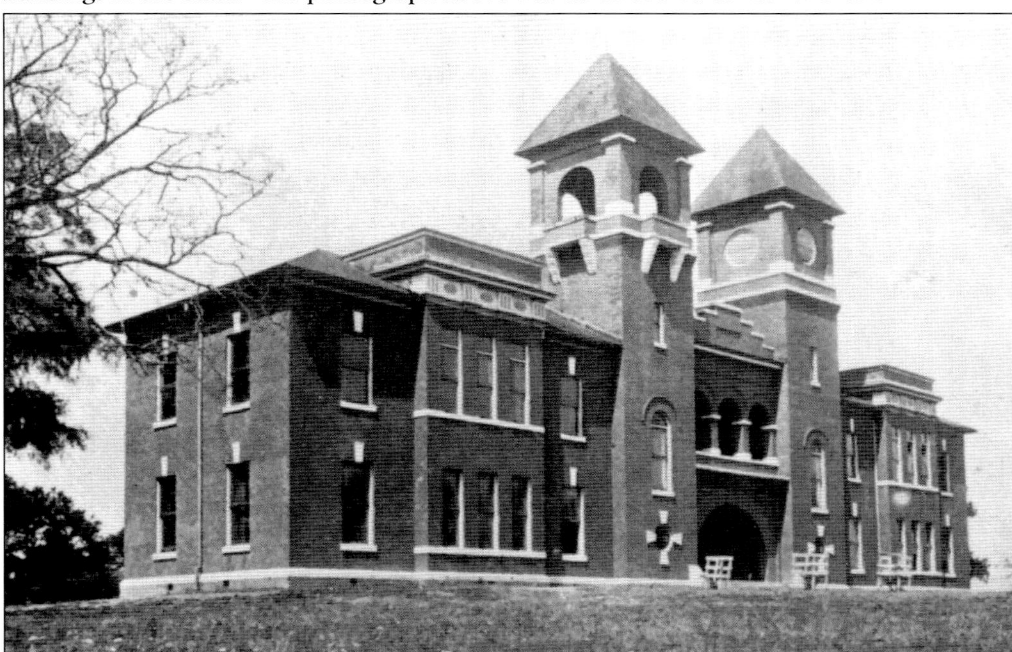

The most prominent features of the new facade were the two quadrangular towers near the center. After doubling the floor space, the building held most of the college's liberal arts classes in its 13 lecture rooms, four study halls, and four scientific laboratories. College Hall also contained a chapel and library, which were actually small lecture rooms converted for those purposes.

Virginia Military Institute graduate and Confederate veteran George M. Edgar was hired as a military instructor at West Florida Seminary beginning in 1859, but he left at the start of the Civil War. In August 1887, he returned, this time to serve as the seminary's first president. With his establishment of a totally new four-year curriculum, Edgar's administration proved to be a turning point in the history of the institution and its strong liberal arts tradition. (University of Arkansas Special Collections.)

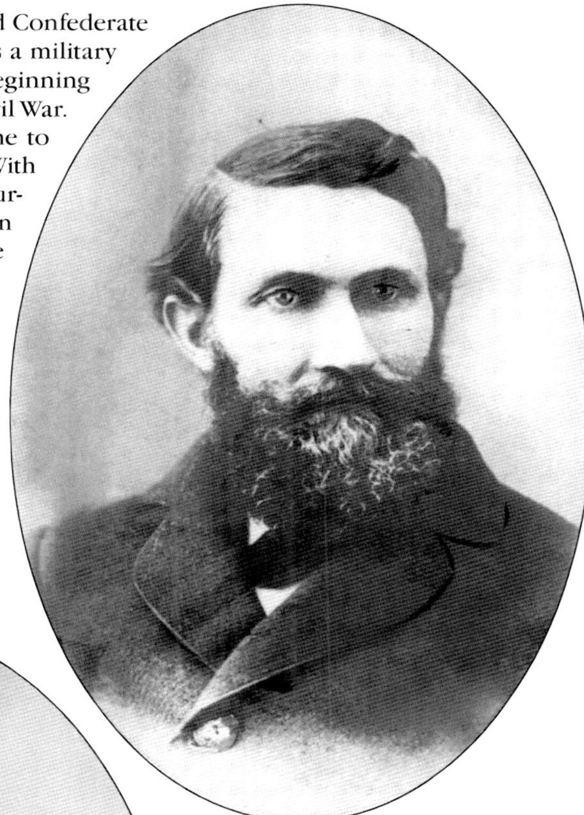

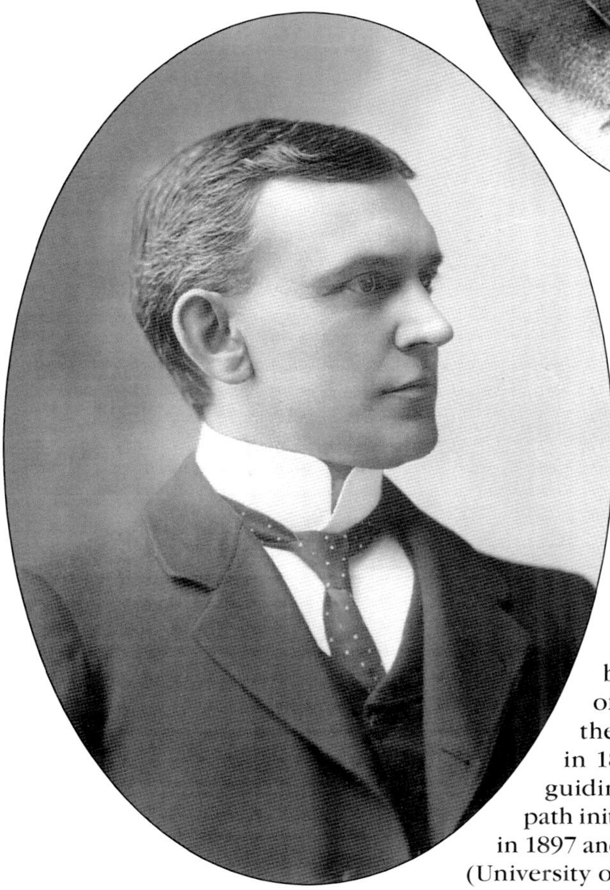

Alvin Fayette Lewis moved to Tallahassee in 1887 where he served as an assistant teacher during the seminary's reorganization under George M. Edgar. Leaving to earn his doctorate degree at Johns Hopkins, Lewis then served briefly on the faculty at the University of Arkansas before being appointed the second president of the seminary in 1892. Lewis's tenure was notable for guiding the school along the progressive path initiated by his predecessor. He resigned in 1897 and was replaced by Albert A. Murphree. (University of Arkansas Special Collections.)

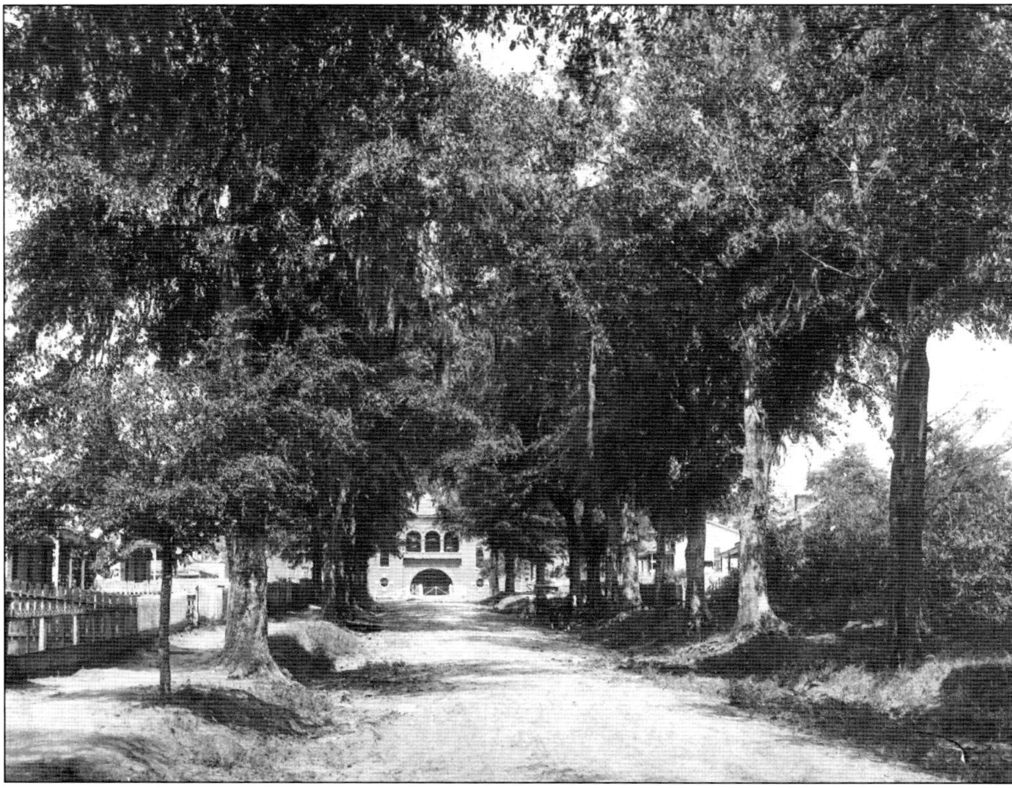

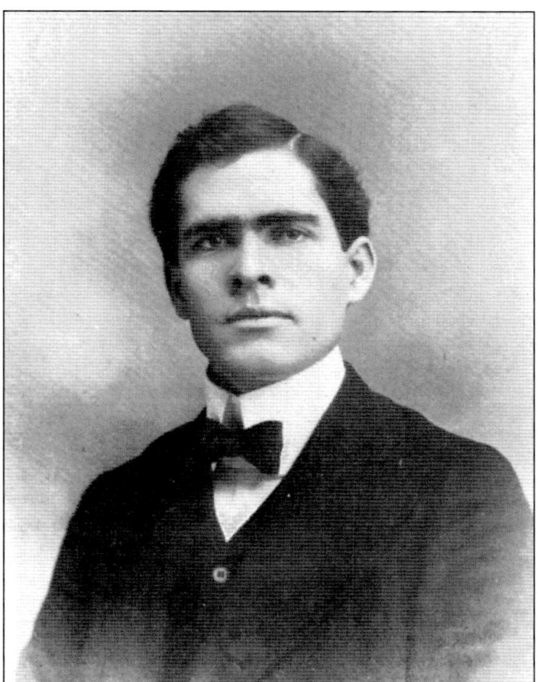

Clinton Street, renamed College Avenue in 1916, was a broad avenue lined with majestic oaks, running from Tallahassee's downtown to the seminary. First paved in 1912, the road was slated to be only 24 feet wide, however, city officials later agreed to make the street 30 feet wide. The photograph shows College Hall at the end of the road.

In 1897, faculty member Dr. Albert Alexander Murphree was appointed president of West Florida Seminary. Just 27 years old, Murphree's success as a teacher, his popularity on campus and in town, and his overall personality were factors that led to his appointment. His gift of winning the confidence and admiration of his students was one of his most valuable assets. The photograph at left is from the 1901 yearbook, the *Argo*.

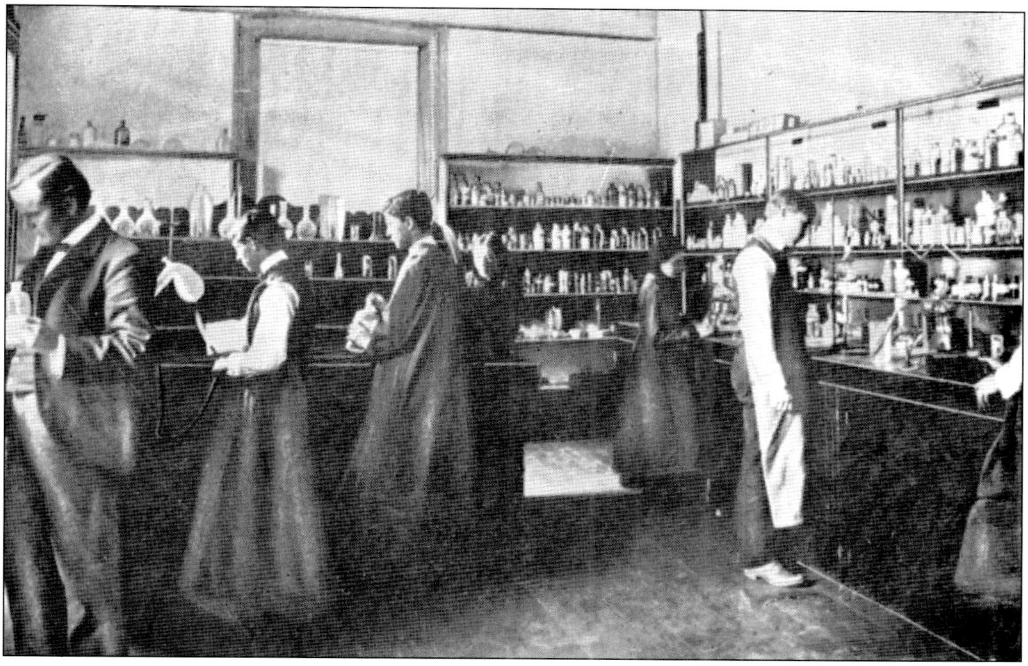

Albert A. Murphree appreciated the progress made by predecessors Presidents Edgar and Lewis, and he strived to continue where they had left off. To him, the natural development of the seminary included the maintenance and expansion of resources and equipment, the strengthening of the curriculum, and the enlargement of the campus to include dormitories. He made significant progress outfitting laboratories with the most up-to-date scientific equipment. Murphree was especially proud of the new biological and histological laboratories, which he asserted had no superior in the state. These improvements prepared the institution to offer a science curriculum leading to a bachelor's of science degree for the first time in the fall of 1898. With this, Murphree felt that the course of study at West Florida Seminary was comparable to any other college in the South. These photographs depict the chemistry lab (above) and biology lab (below) and are both from the College Catalog.

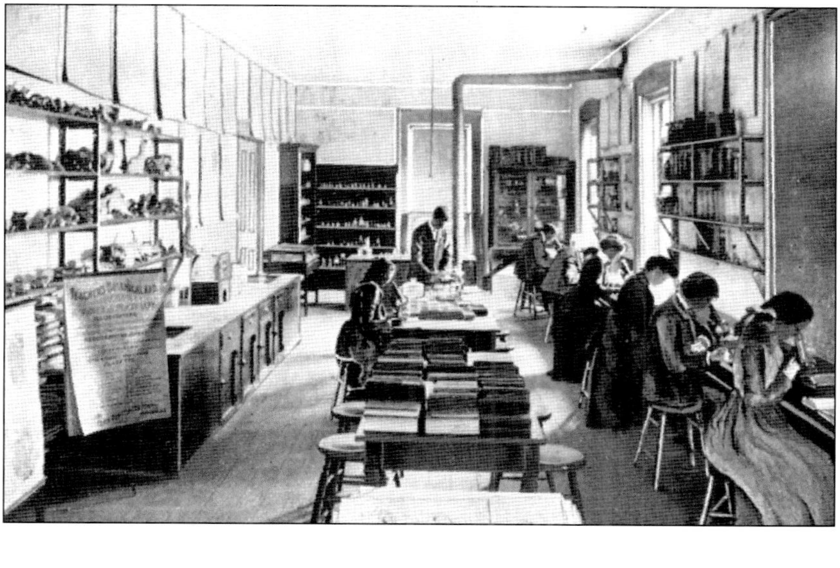

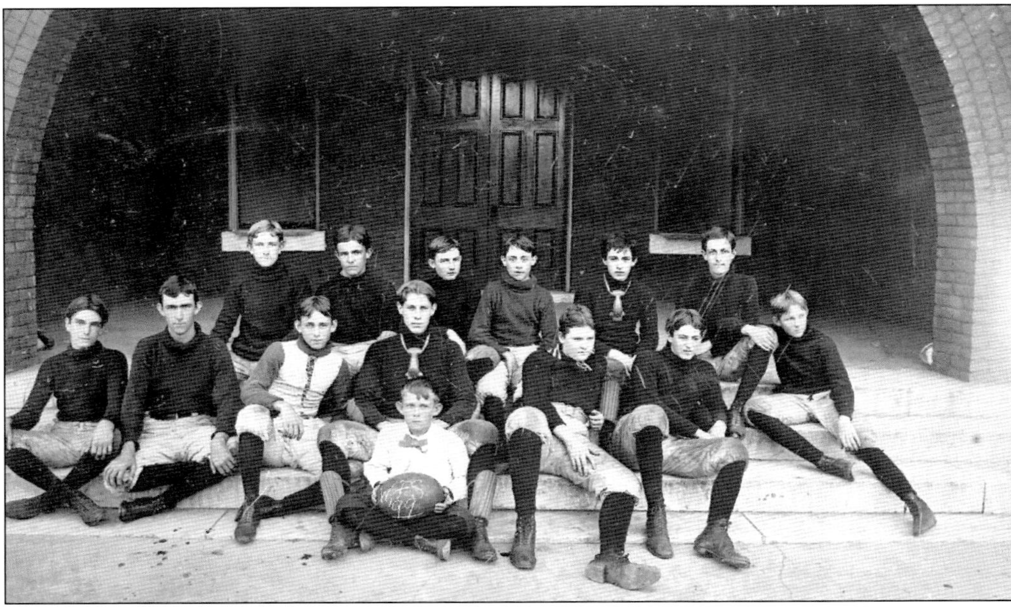

As student enrollment increased during the 1890s, the institution began to develop typical extracurricular collegiate activities like literary societies and debate clubs. Throughout its history, West Florida Seminary offered only intramural sports, and not until 1902 did the institution first field a football team that played other collegiate teams. The photograph of the team above shows a football with "W.F.S. '99" written on it. This may have been a subcollegiate (or high school) squad. (Archives of Florida.)

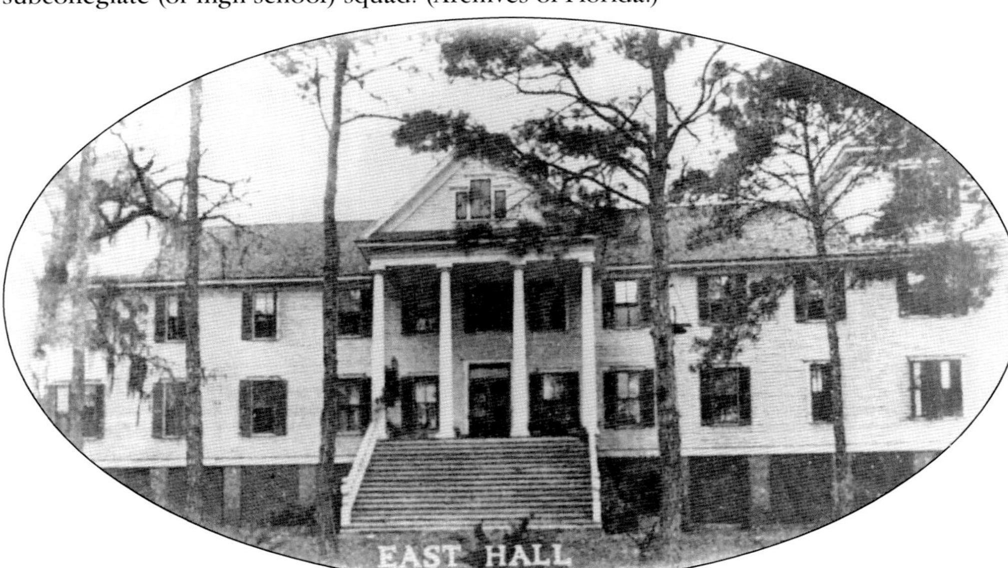

As the college continued to grow, it was always understood that without on-campus housing, student activities would be hamstrung and development of West Florida Seminary into a full-fledged college would be hampered. That all changed after the construction of the first two dormitories, East and West Halls, in June 1901—just in time for the transition to Florida State College. The photograph above is of East Hall, the women's dormitory.

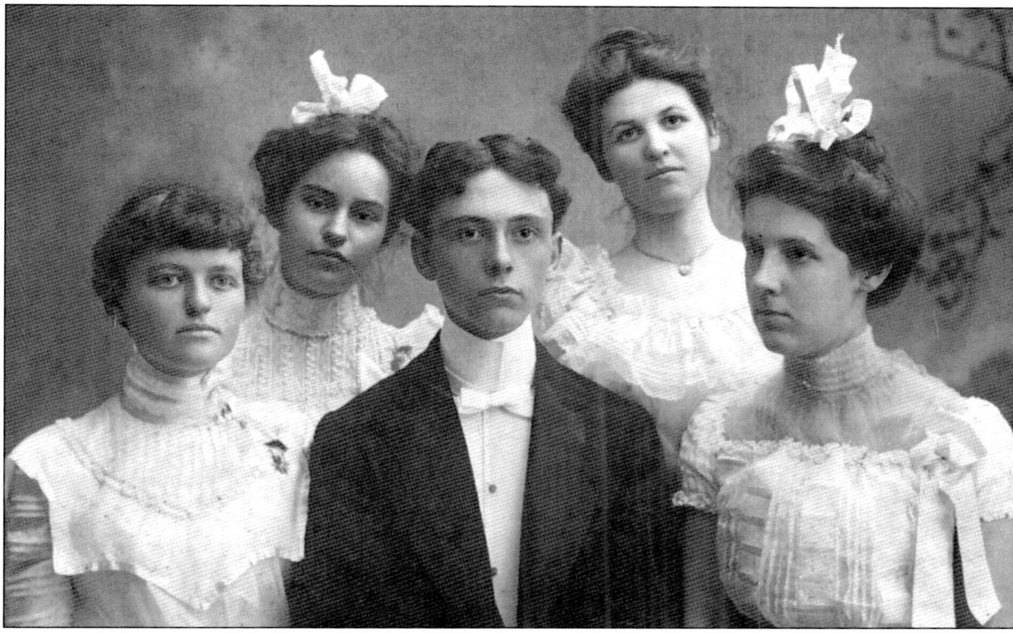

West Florida Seminary's 1900 graduating class includes, from left to right, Edith Elliot, Kate Moor, Lindsey Papy, Annie Rawls, and Evelyn C. Lewis. In an interview 40 years later, Papy, who became the auditor in the business office at the Florida State College for Women, acknowledged wearing his three-inch stiff collar and best coat for the photograph. From the waist down, however, "they were dressed in everyday clothes."

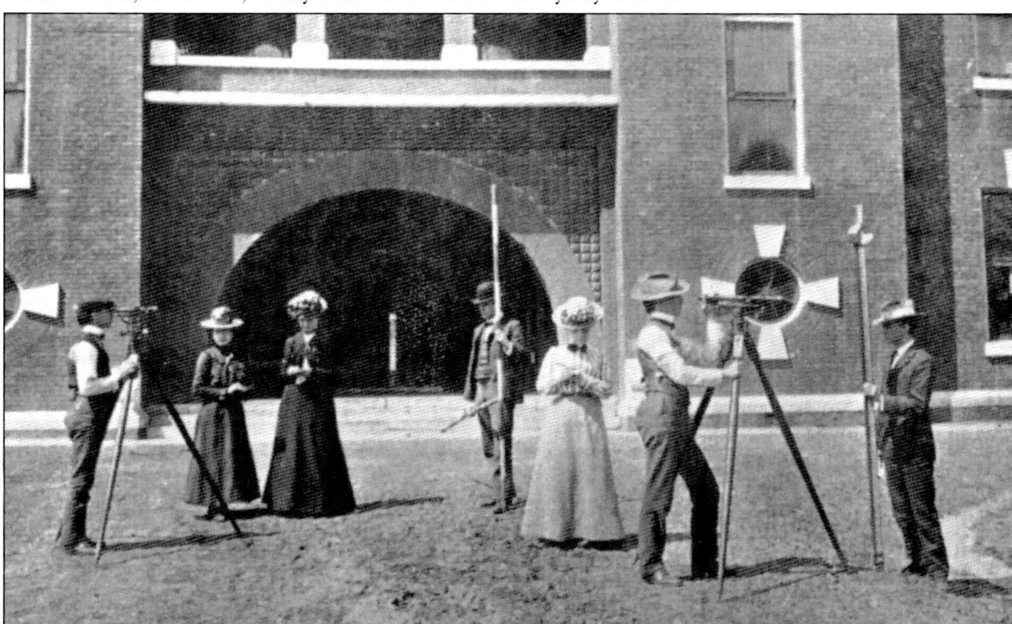

This 1900 photograph from the College Catalog depicts West Florida Seminary students in the front of College Hall, "Ready for Field Work in Surveying and Engineering." In 1900, practical surveying was taught at the beginning of the students' junior year.

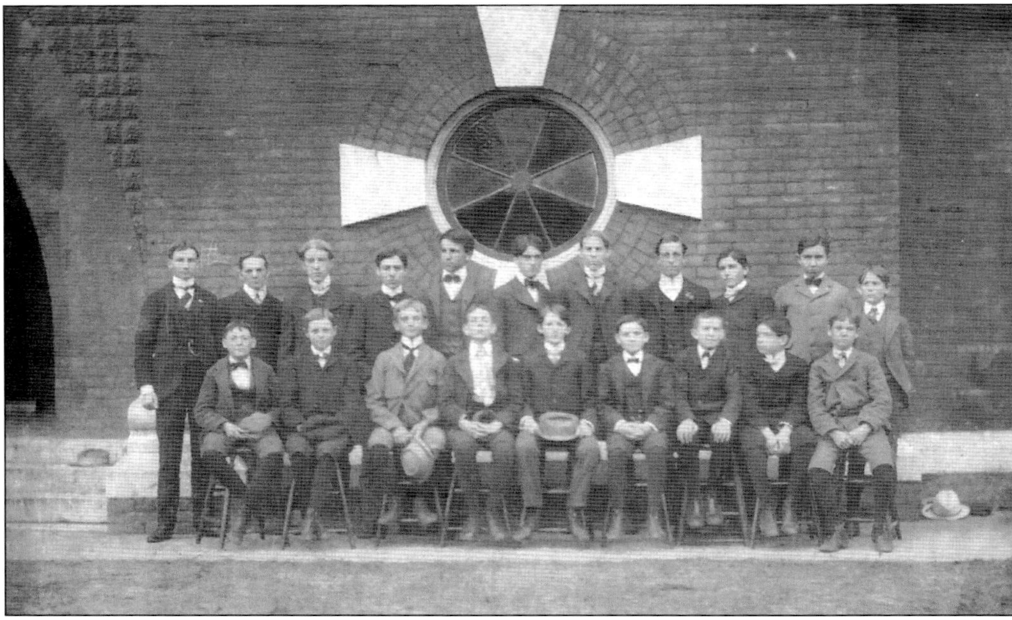

West Florida Seminary president Albert A. Murphree and the faculty encouraged the growth and development of extracurricular campus activities, such as the Dramatic Club, Natural History Association, the YWCA and YMCA, the Platonic Debating (Literary) Society, and Anaxagorean Literary Society (later the Gordon Literary Society). All male students were required to join one of the two literary societies. The women had their own literary group called the Murphreean Society in honor of their president. The photograph above is of the 1900–1901 Platonic Debating Society. The 1900–1901 photograph below is of the Anaxagorean Literary Society. President Murphree was an honorary member and is seated in the middle row, third from the right.

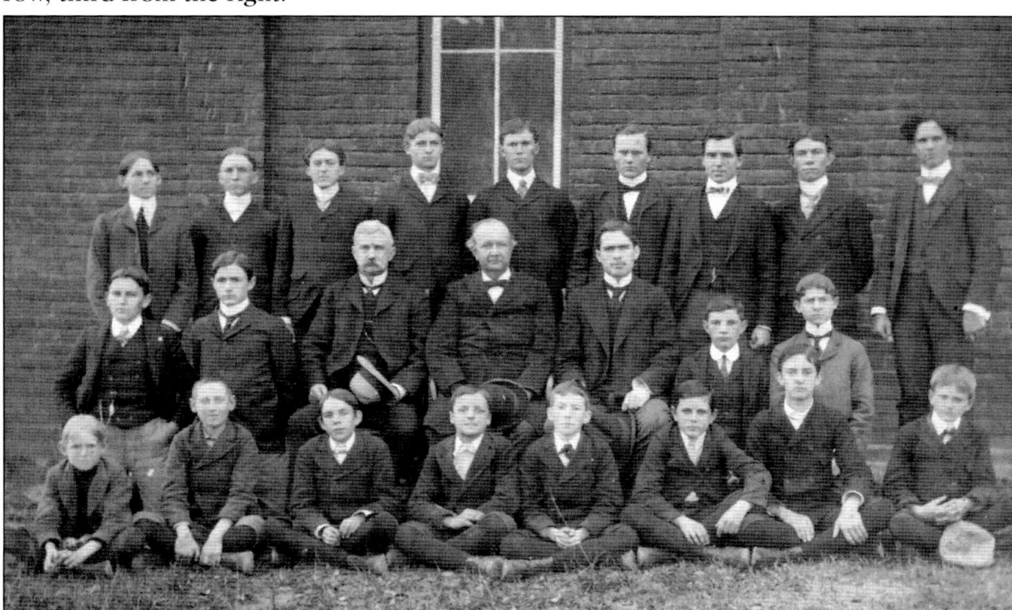

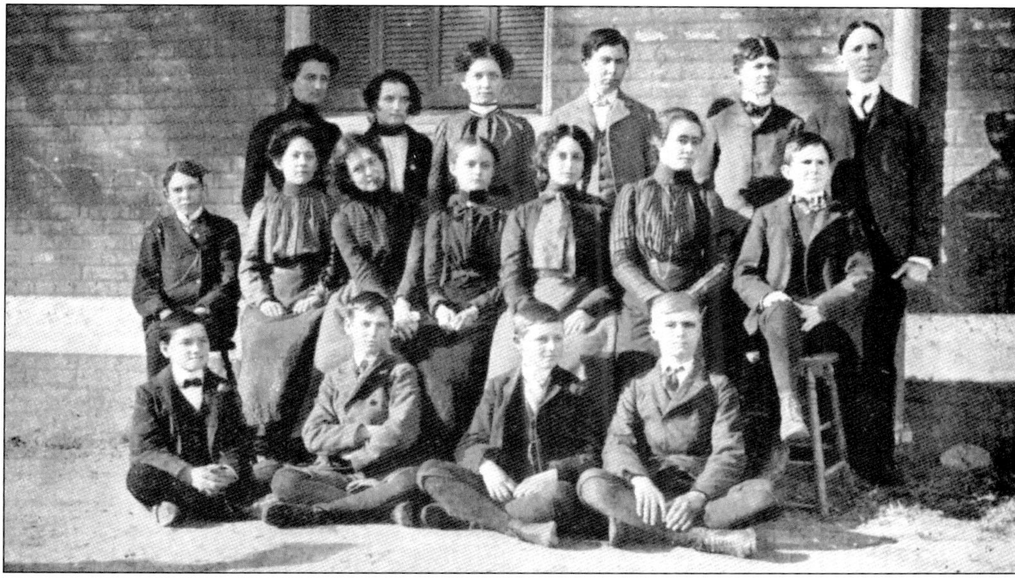

At any one time, seven levels of school were being taught at West Florida Seminary. In addition to the four-year college curriculum, the school provided classes for first-, second-, and third-year high school students, sometimes referred to as sub-freshmen or subcollegiate. Above is the West Florida Seminary third-year class of high school, shown around 1900–1901.

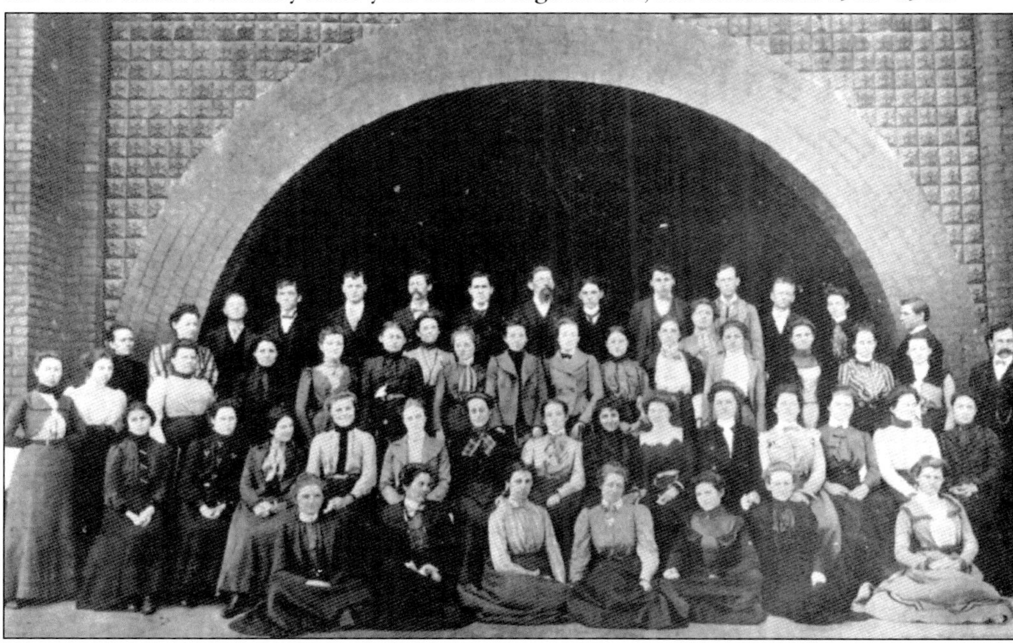

Fundamental to the purpose of many state-supported institutions of higher education was the training of teachers for the public school system. During President Edgar's administration, West Florida Seminary discontinued teacher training. In 1900, the normal department was reactivated, and a regular, two-year normal curriculum was inaugurated as the Teacher's Training Department under the direction of Prof. L.W. Buchholz in 1901. Above is West Florida Seminary Normal Class for Teachers, shown around 1900–1901.

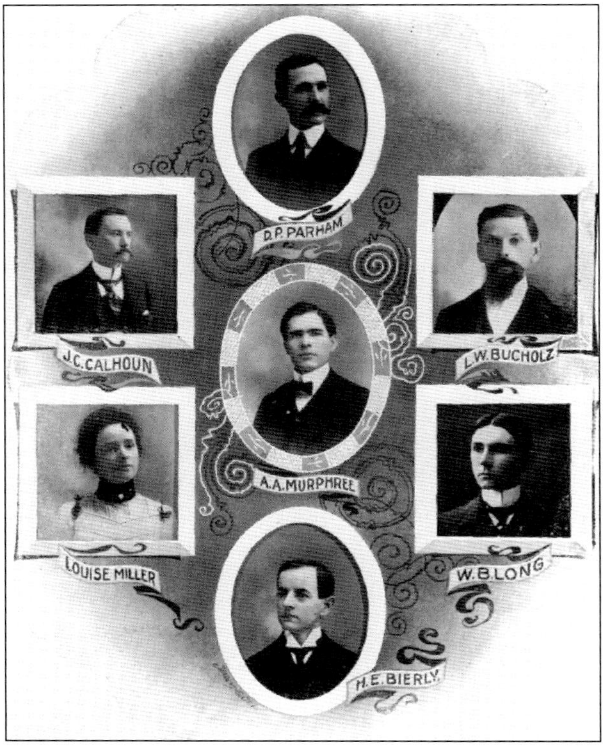

The photograph to the left of Pres. Albert A. Murphree and the 1901 faculty of West Florida Seminary is from the school's yearbook, the *Argo*. Murphree served as president of the college from 1897 to 1909 and taught higher mathematics, astronomy, and sociology. Below, from another page in the same yearbook, Murphree is listed as the "Chief Meerschaum" in the "Faculty Pipe Club." According to the yearbook, the club held semiweekly meetings in room 610 of the Science Building. "The standard tobacco used, as adopted by the Club, is Duke's 'Misery.'" The club used that brand of tobacco "to set a good example for the students in economy."

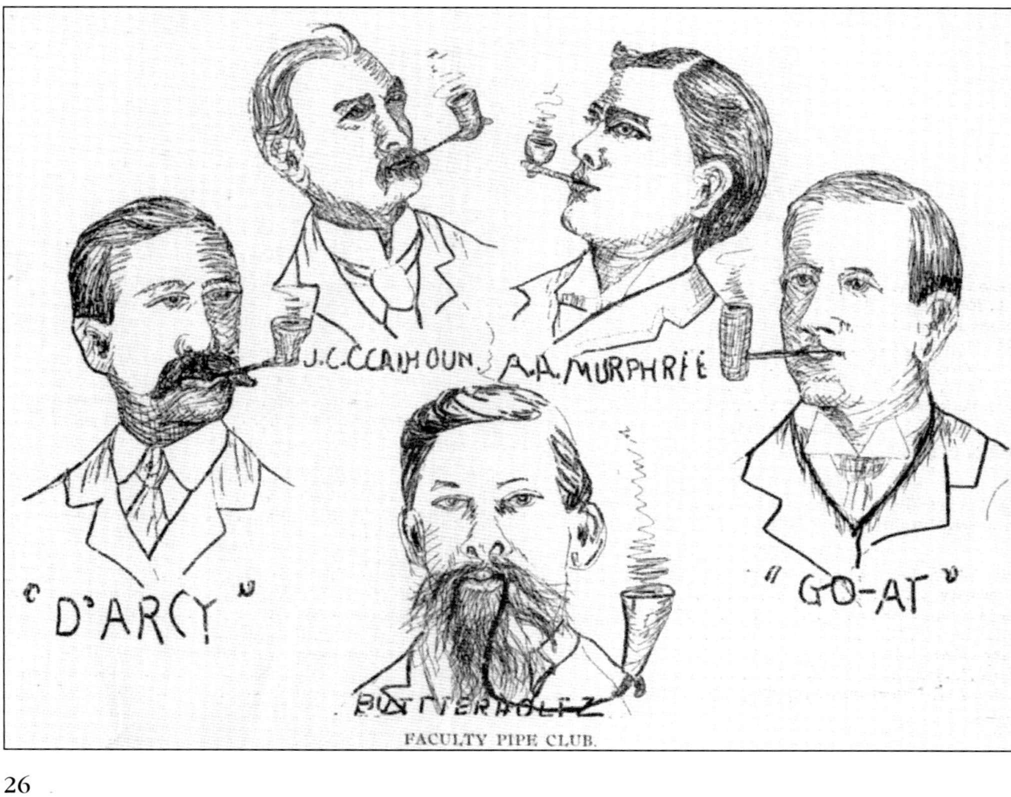

FACULTY PIPE CLUB.

The page to the right from the West Florida Seminary yearbook, the *Argo*, shows the school's five juniors, scheduled to graduate the following year. The accompanying history states that the junior class began in 1893 with an enrollment of 44 "bright boys and girls, each with the highest determination of graduating with the first honors of their class." Sadly, the essay continues, the class decreased to an enrollment of only five: "three big ugly boys and two lovely young ladies who are not afraid of syllogism and mathematics." Although the photograph below is purported to be of their 1902 graduating class, the next yearbook only lists three graduates: F.A. Hathaway (standing to the right), Mary Shutan (standing to the left), and Gaston Day (seated to the right). E.G. Johnston (seated to the left) is not listed as graduating, and that also appears to be the fate of Pauline Costa. (Below, Archives of Florida.)

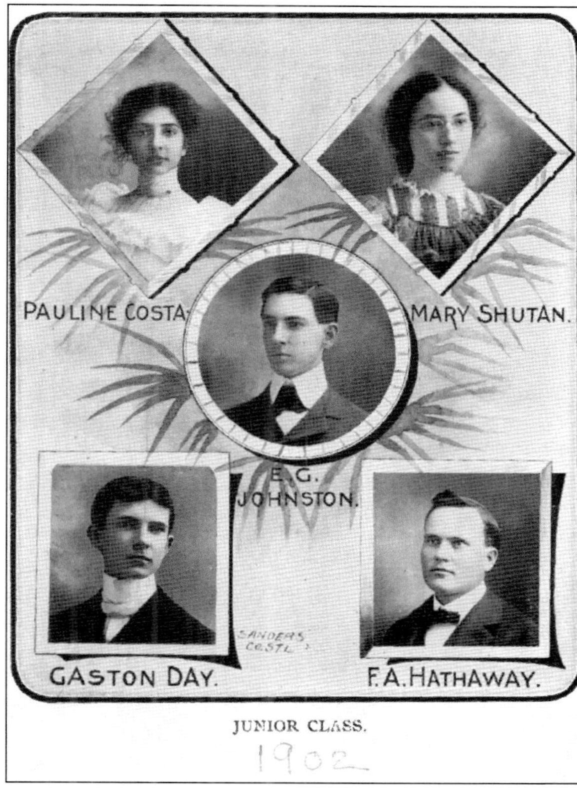

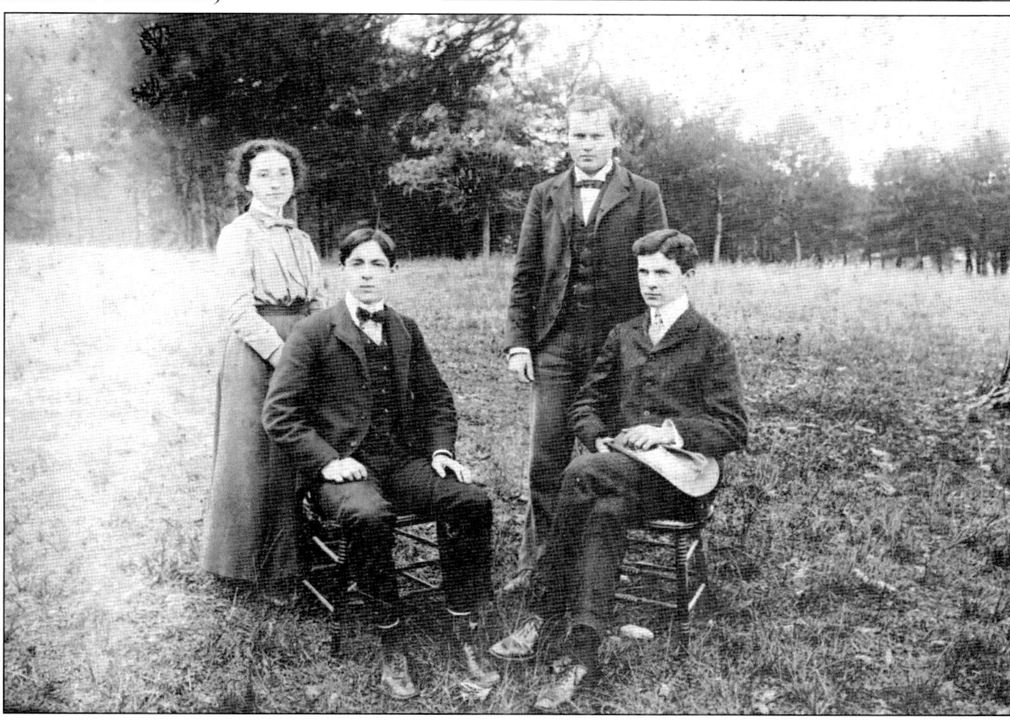

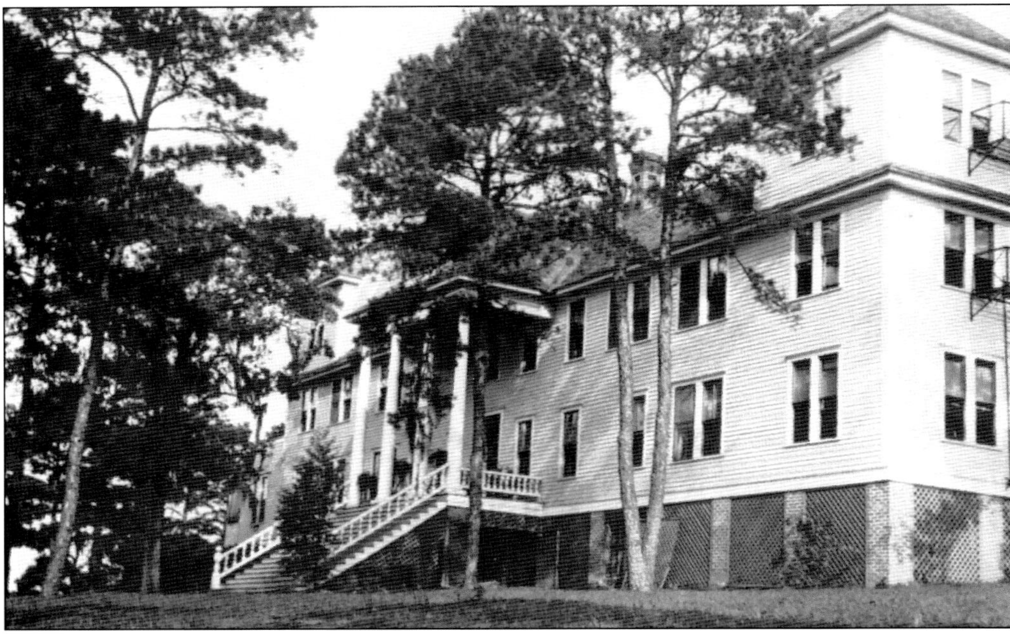

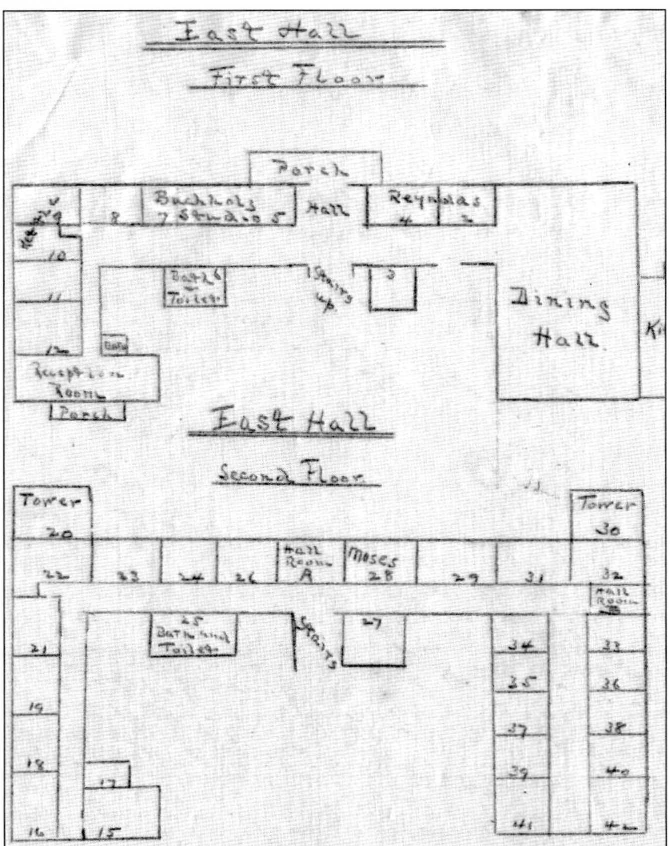

In the fall of 1901, two much-needed dormitories on the south side of the campus were ready for occupancy. Because of their locations and proximity to each other, they were referred to as East and West Halls. Both were similar in design, approximately 84 feet by 124 feet, and two and a half stories in height. The women's dorm, East Hall, also contained a reception area, 200-seat dining room, and kitchen large enough to serve all the resident and nonresident students, both men and women. The dormitory could accommodate 60 students plus the matron and one female faculty member in its 32 small rooms, each containing a double bed, washstand, and clothes cupboard. With its parlor, reception, and dining rooms, East Hall was the social center of the campus.

Two

FLORIDA STATE COLLEGE 1901–1905

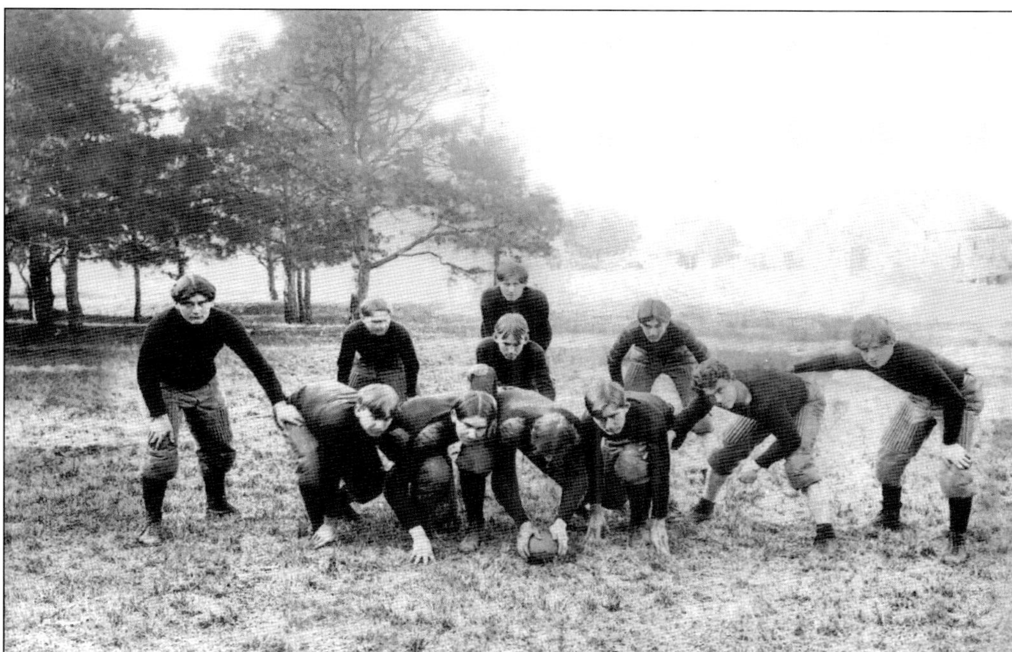

In June 1901, West Florida Seminary was renamed Florida State College. The most important transformation, however, was not in the name, but in the pride the students felt in the emergent Florida State College and its activities. Soon, the students and faculty, led by Pres. Albert A. Murphree, began clamoring for a football team to represent the college. The photograph above is of the 1903 squad. (Guyte P. McCord III.)

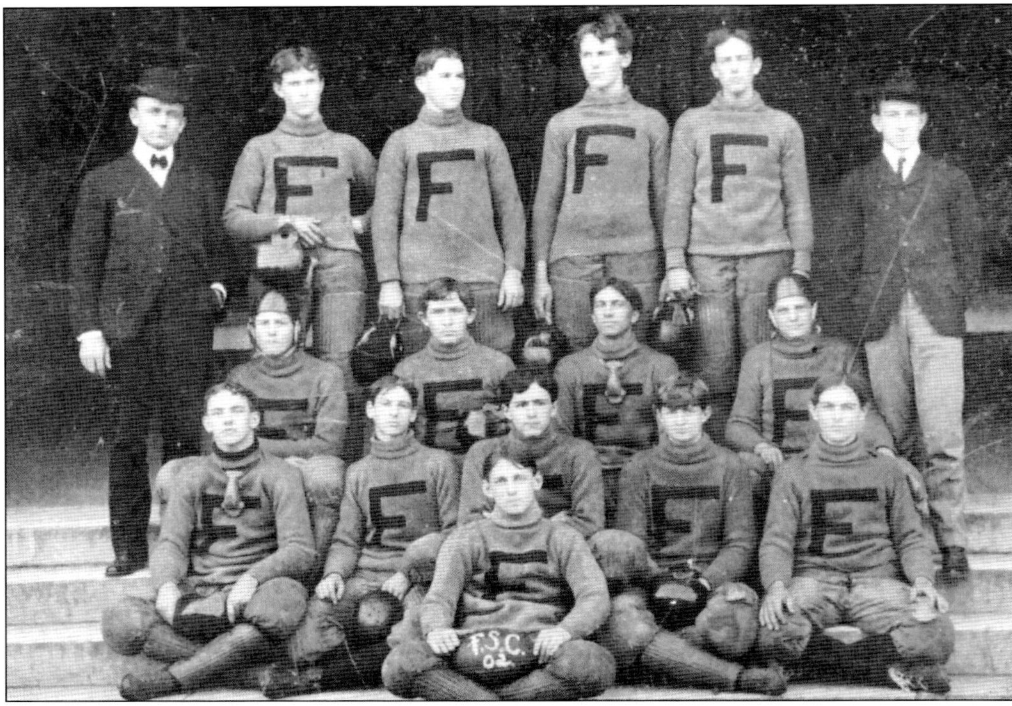

The newly minted Florida State College football team spent the fall of 1901 practicing. The following season, on November 21, 1902, they played their first game, defeating the Bainbridge Giants in Tallahassee by a score of 5-0. Coached by Latin professor and former Vanderbilt University football player W.W. Hughes, the team posted a record of two wins and one loss.

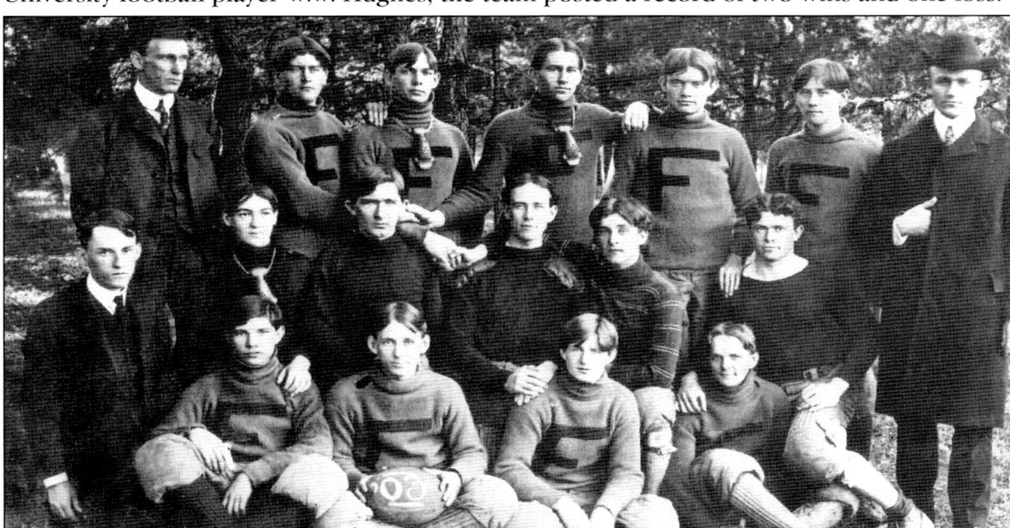

In their second season, the Florida State College football team opened with two victories in a series against their Bainbridge rivals. After that, they went on to beat the University of Florida (UF) but lost to East Florida Seminary (EFS) and Georgia Tech. Because both teams had beaten UF, the final game of the season against Stetson College was for the state title. As a result of a 5-5 tie, the crown went to Stetson because they had defeated EFS.

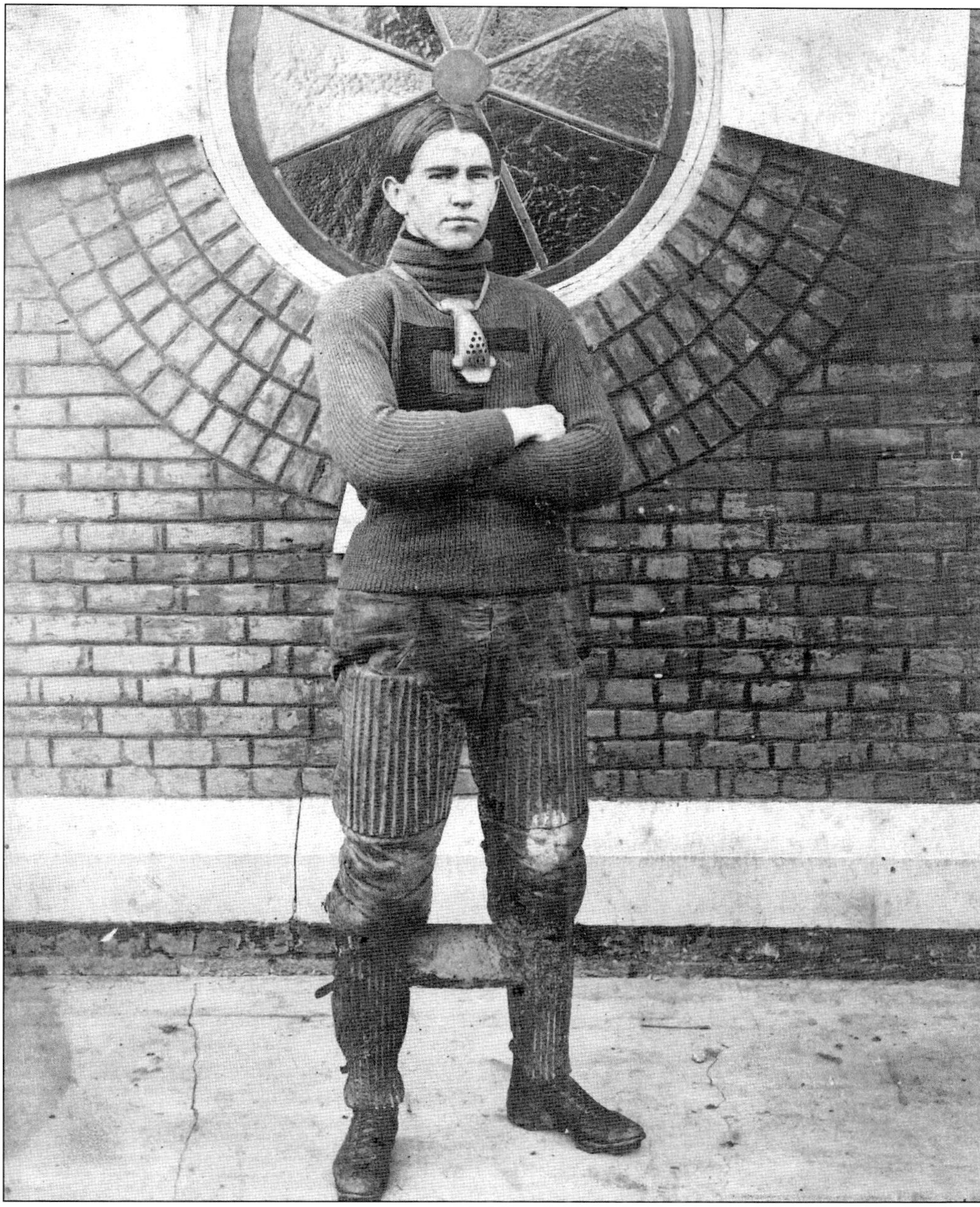

During Guyte P. McCord's years at Florida State College, he participated in numerous extracurricular activities, including the Anaxagorean Literary Society (where he served as president), the baseball team (where he played first base), and most notably, on the football team. At six feet, four inches and more than 220 pounds, McCord played guard or tackle and kicker on all three of the FSC football teams. When FSC transitioned to Florida Female College in 1905, he moved on to Washington and Lee, where he also played and lettered in football, and earned his degree in law in 1909. Returning to Tallahassee, he had a long career in law and public service, including stints as clerk of the state supreme court and mayor. (Guyte P. McCord III.)

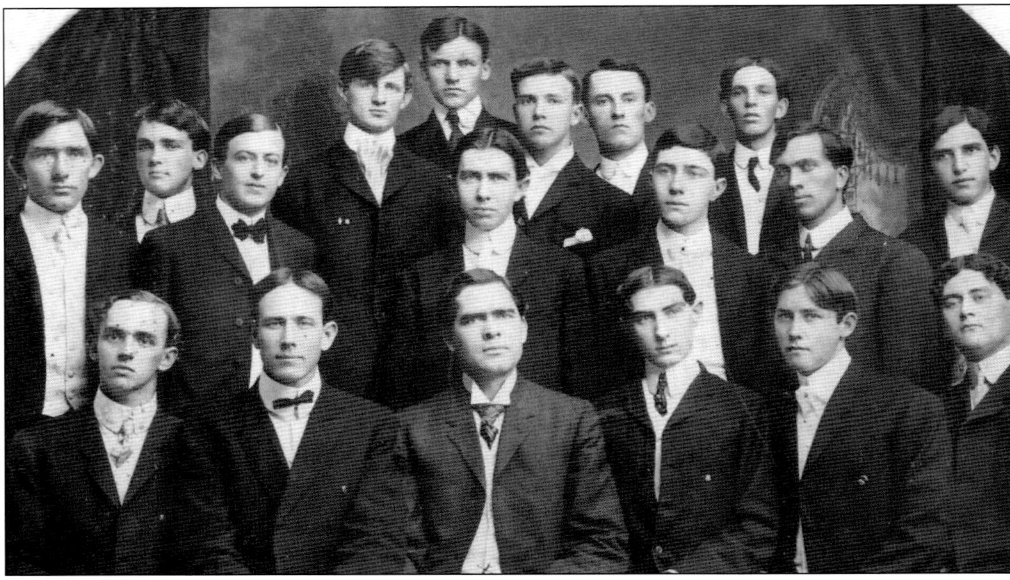

When the Alpha Psi chapter of the Kappa Alpha fraternity was chartered at Florida State College in January 1903, it was the first Greek-letter fraternity at any college or university in the state of Florida. FSC president Albert A. Murphree was instrumental in the installation of the new chapter, and he was initiated as a charter member as a result. Murphree is in the center of the first row.

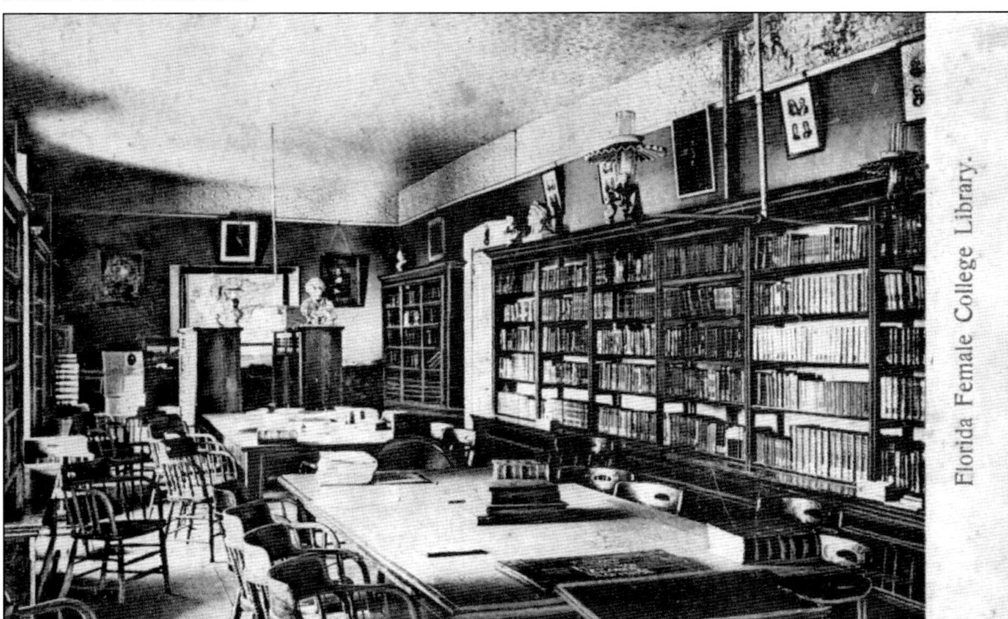

The establishment of a true library in the summer of 1903 was considered a landmark in the development of the institution. That year, with an allocation of $3,500, President Murphree was able to increase the collection to more than 5,000 volumes. Located in College Hall, the library was in actuality a classroom and not specifically designed for this use, and when the seats along the tables were occupied, it was difficult to remove books from the shelves.

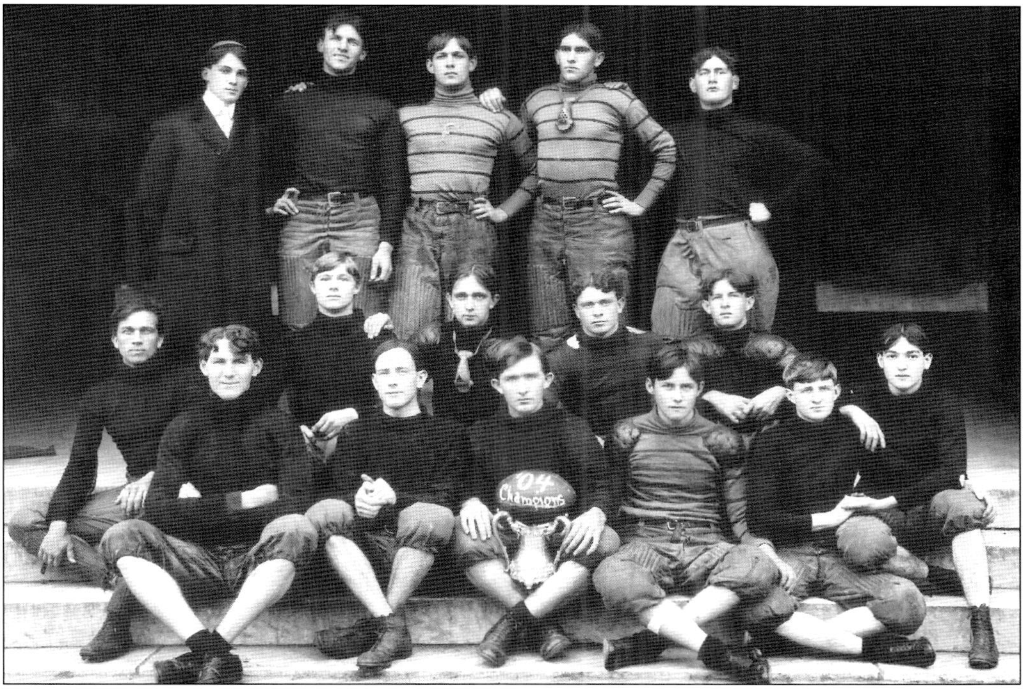

Going into the final game of the 1904 season, the Florida State College football team had posted a record of one win (against the University of Florida) and three loses. With that victory over UF, the squad was again eligible to compete for the state title against Stetson College. On November 24, 1904, FSC beat Stetson 18-6 and was crowned state champion. (Guyte P. McCord III.)

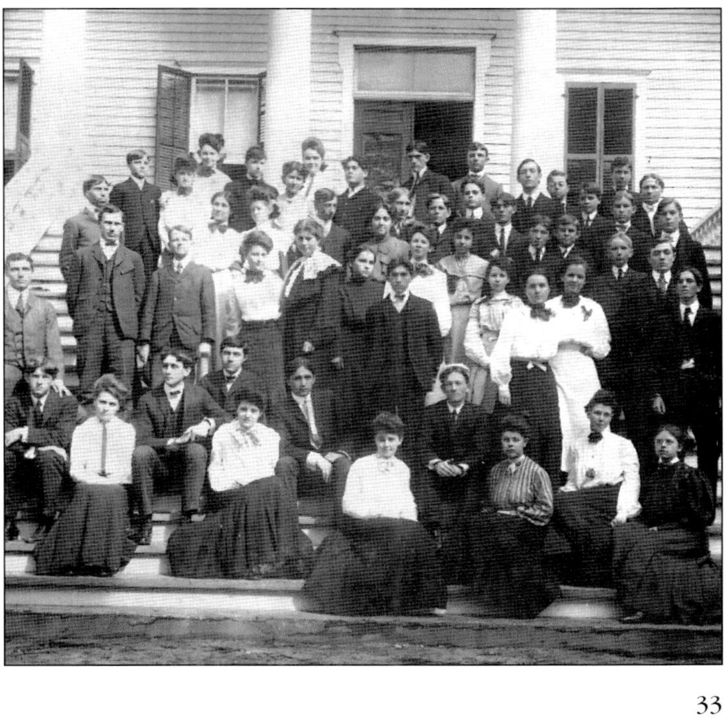

Florida State College began the 1904–1905 academic year with more than 300 students representing 35 Florida counties and two foreign countries, more than doubling the number when Murphree assumed the presidency in 1897. This growth represented the positive impact of construction of dormitories. The photograph at right is of students and faculty on the steps of either the East or West Hall dormitory. (State Archives of Florida.)

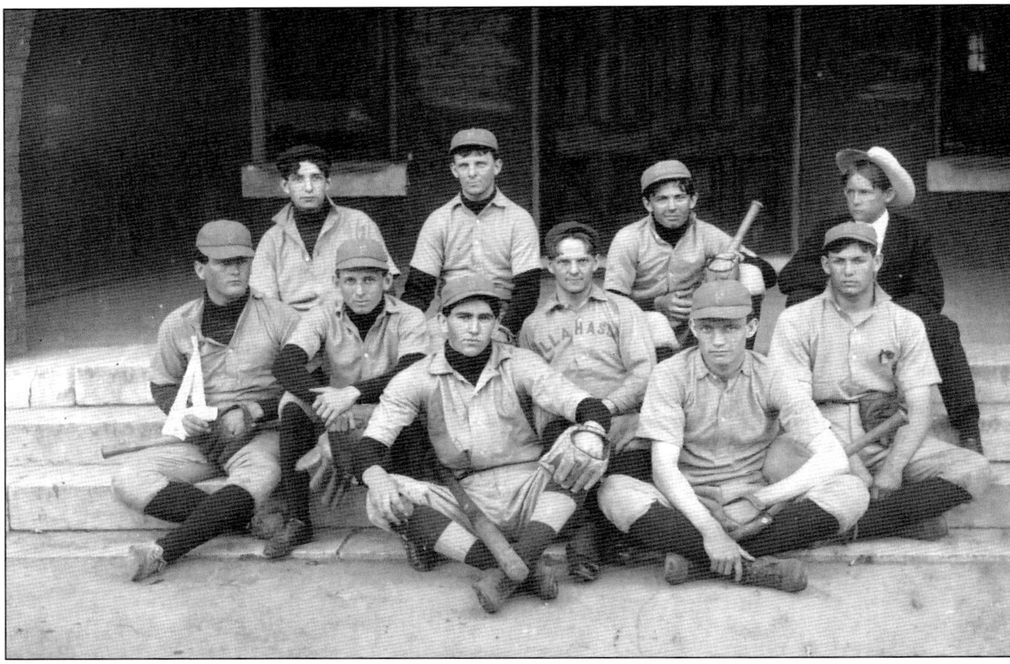

The Florida State College baseball team played such schools as the University of Florida and Alabama Polytechnic Institute (later Auburn University); however, the team played local pickup clubs for the most part. The photograph above is reproduced in the 1903–1904 FSC College Catalog. (Guyte P. McCord III.)

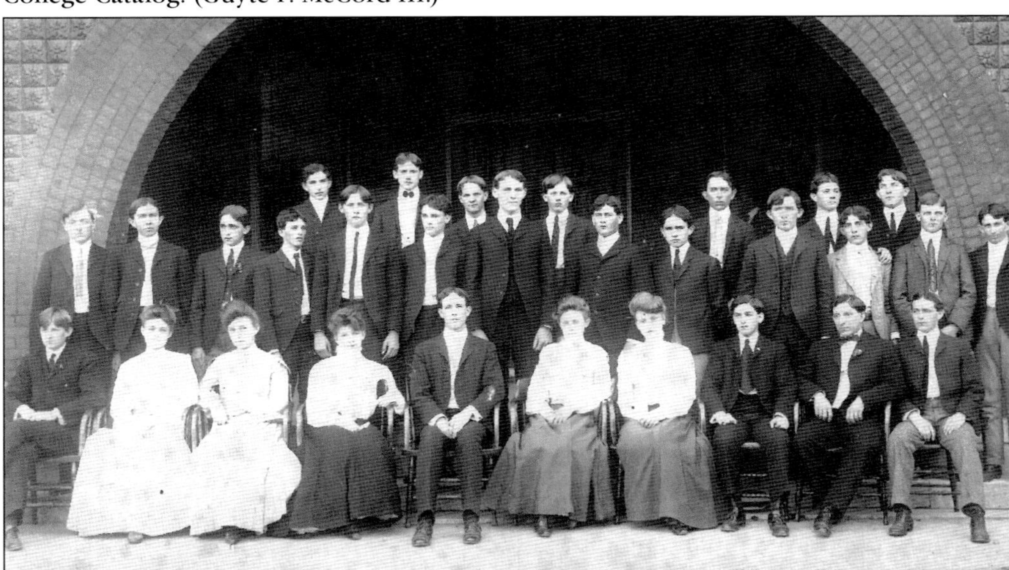

Founded at West Florida Seminary in 1897, the Platonic Debating Society was the first and the oldest debate club at Florida State College. The group participated not only in the commencement debates with the Anaxagorean Literary Society, but also in intercollegiate debates with other schools, such as Florida Agricultural College (later the University of Florida). The photograph above is the 1903–1904 club. (University of Florida Photograph Collections.)

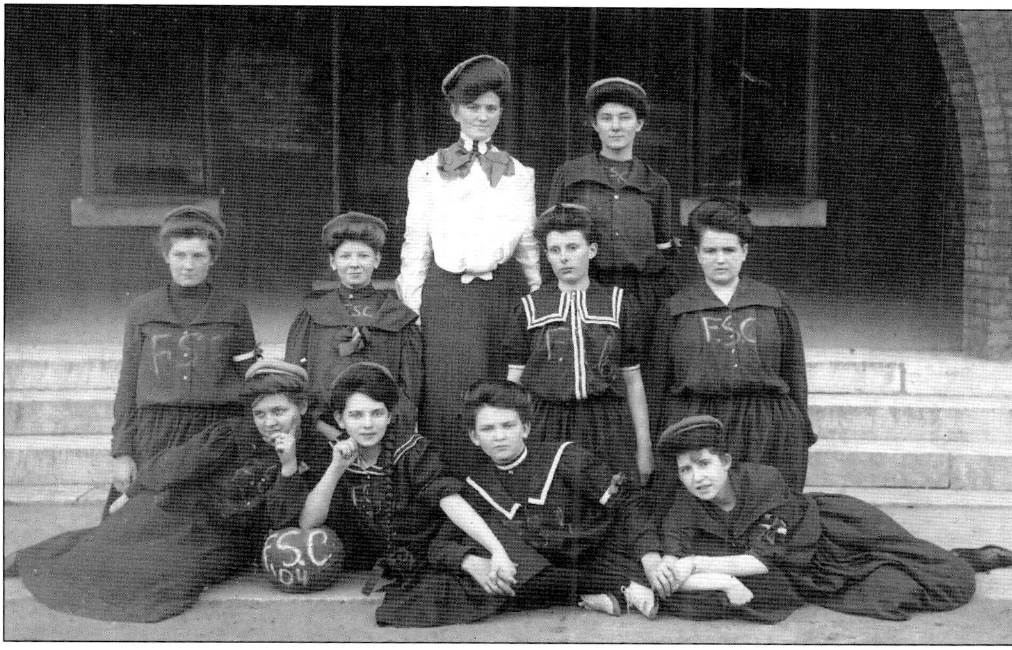

In addition to football and baseball, Florida State College students also participated in tennis, golf, men's track, and women's basketball. The photograph above is of the 1904 FSC Women's "Basket Ball" Club. Outside of football and an occasional intercollegiate baseball game, it is presumed that the rest of the sporting activities were intramural events. (University of Florida Photograph Collections.)

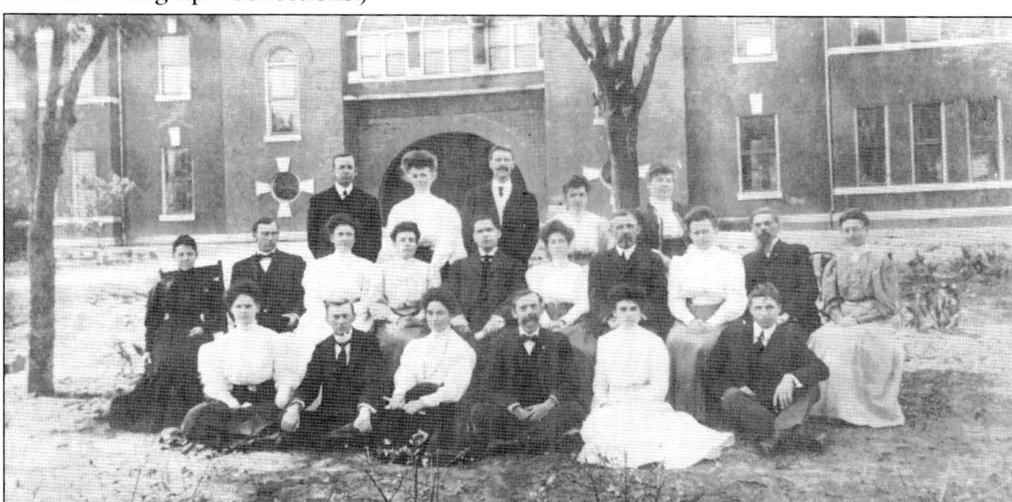

Faculty and staff at Florida State College were expected to wear many hats. H. Elmer Bierly (third row, left) taught biology, chemistry, and psychology and served as librarian. Arthur Williams (first row, fourth from left) taught history, political science, and sociology, while serving as secretary and treasurer of boarding halls. L.W. Buchholz (second row, ninth from left), was professor of philosophy, history, and education, served as the principal of the teachers' training school, and was preceptor of the men's hall. In this 1904 photograph, the group is in front of College Hall.

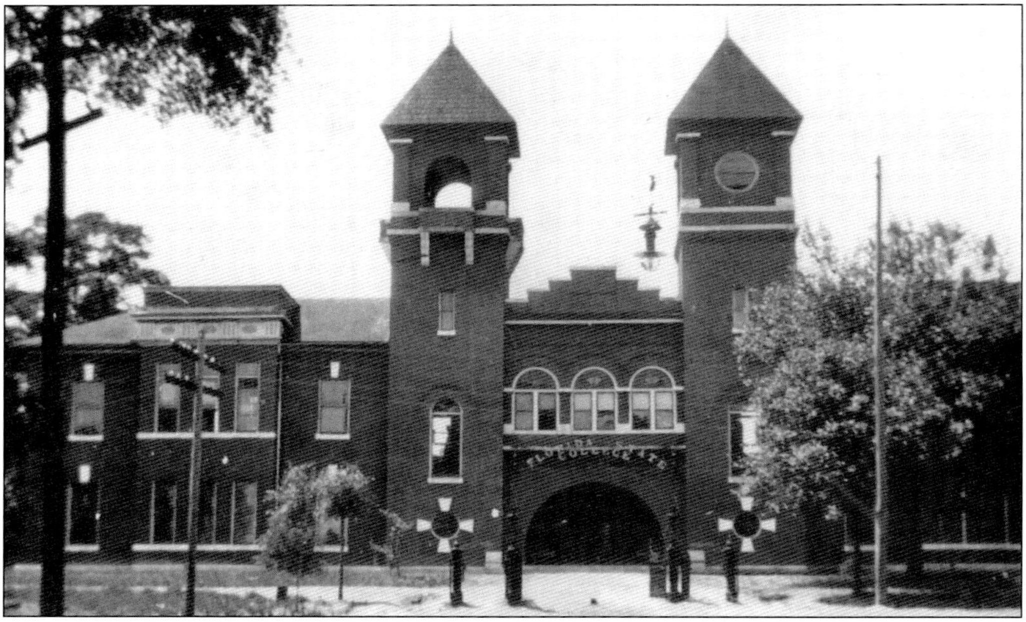

In 1898, College Hall underwent extensive repairs and remodeling, and Pres. Albert A. Murphree reported that the building with its four large study rooms and eight classrooms was put into the most-excellent condition. Unfortunately, the building was constructed on clay pipe or fuller's earth, a type of material that expanded and contracted with moisture. Because of this unstable footing, the exterior walls had many cracks, and the building was deemed dangerous. In the summer of 1909, the building was condemned, but because of the lack of classroom space, the walls were shored up and it continued to be used while a new Administration Building was constructed directly behind it. College Hall was demolished in the late summer of 1910. These two photographs are of the building during the last decade of its existence. (Below, Archives of Florida.)

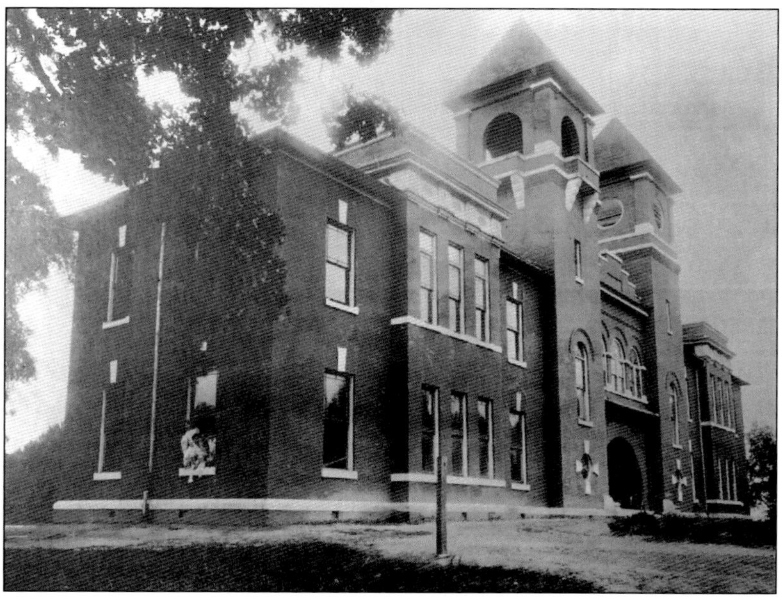

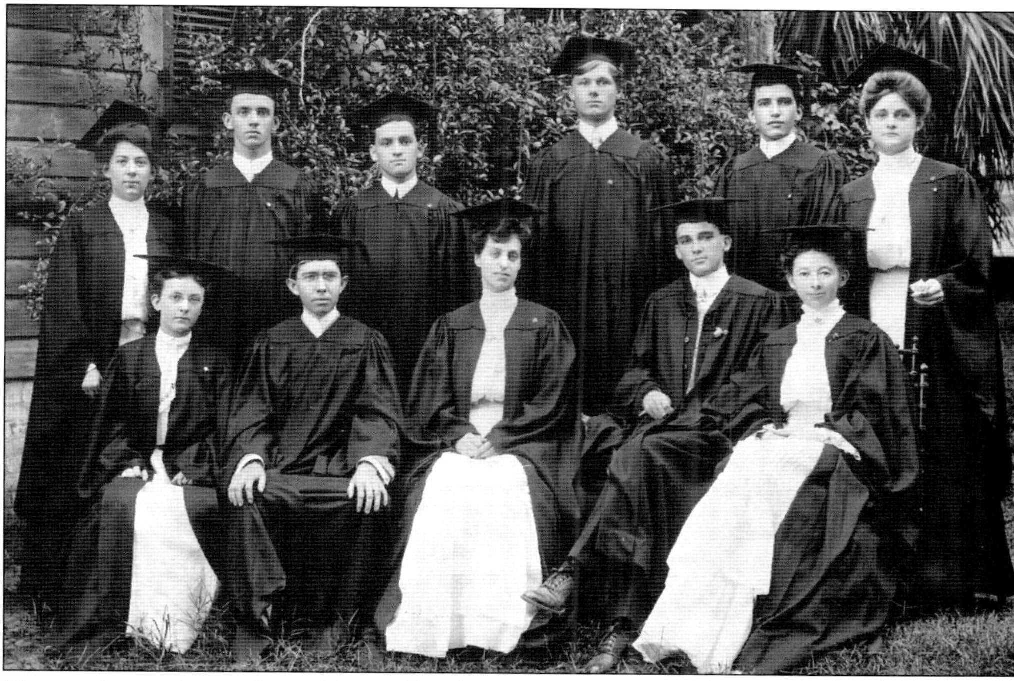

The students who graduated from Florida State College in June 1905 enjoy the distinction of being the only students who both began and ended their college careers at Florida State College. Beginning as freshmen in the fall of 1901, the very first year of FSC's existence, these students accepted their diplomas in the summer of its final year. The group is also notable because it was the first class to wear graduation caps and gowns. In the class photograph above are, from left to right, (first row) Claire Bowen, Robert Bryan McCord, Grace Cramer, S. Franklin Gammon, and Agnes Apthorp; (second row) Ruby Diamond, Burton Belcher, Arthur Joseph Shutan, David M. Cook, William Parrish Byrd, and Bershe Archer McGinniss. The FSC photograph below titled "Girls of 1905" is from the Morgan Family Collection at the University of Florida and contains some of the women in the photograph above. (Below, University of Florida Photograph Collections.)

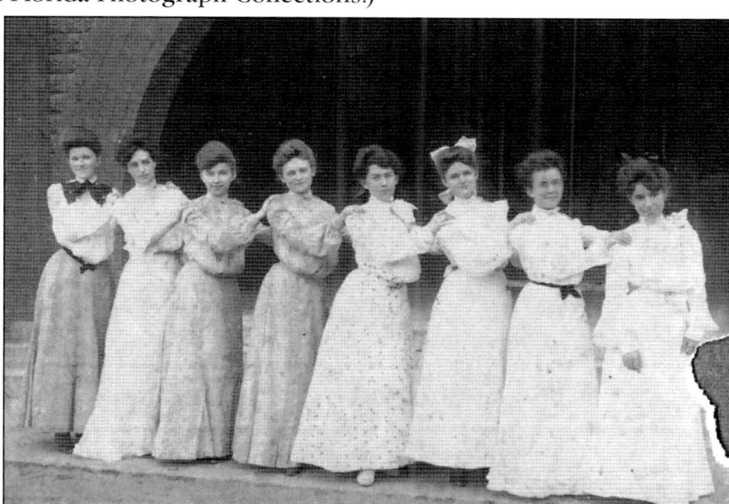

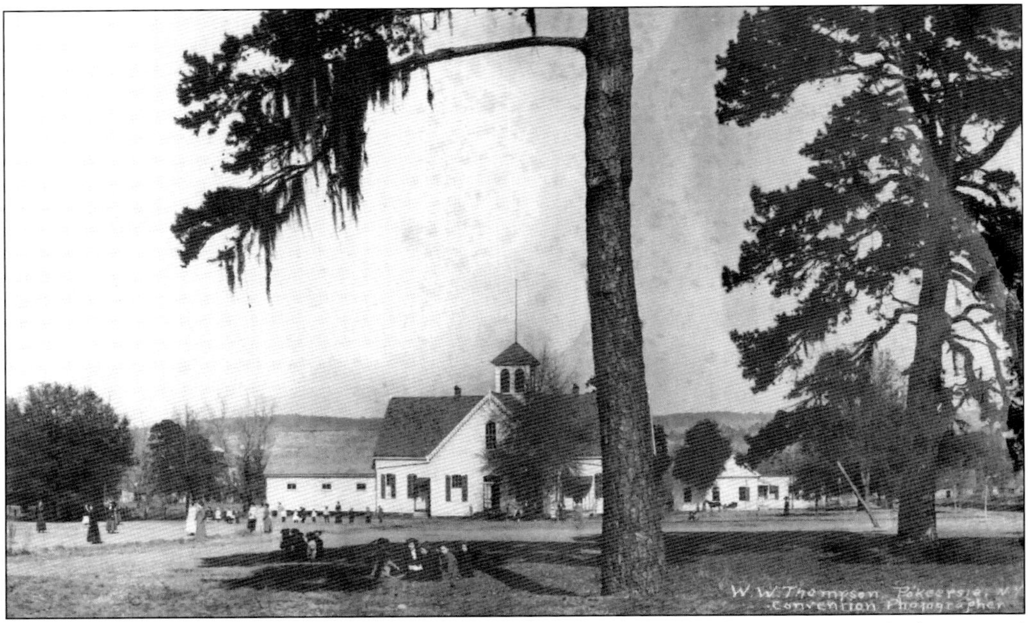

In 1905, the college purchased this small schoolhouse and the property on which it stood adjoining the northern end of the campus for use as the first gymnasium. The 1905–1906 Florida Female College catalog described the facility as "commodious," consisting of a 40-footby-70-foot main floor, and a new swimming pool. One graduate later described the swimming pool, or the "bath tub" as it was commonly referred to, as being very small and shallow.

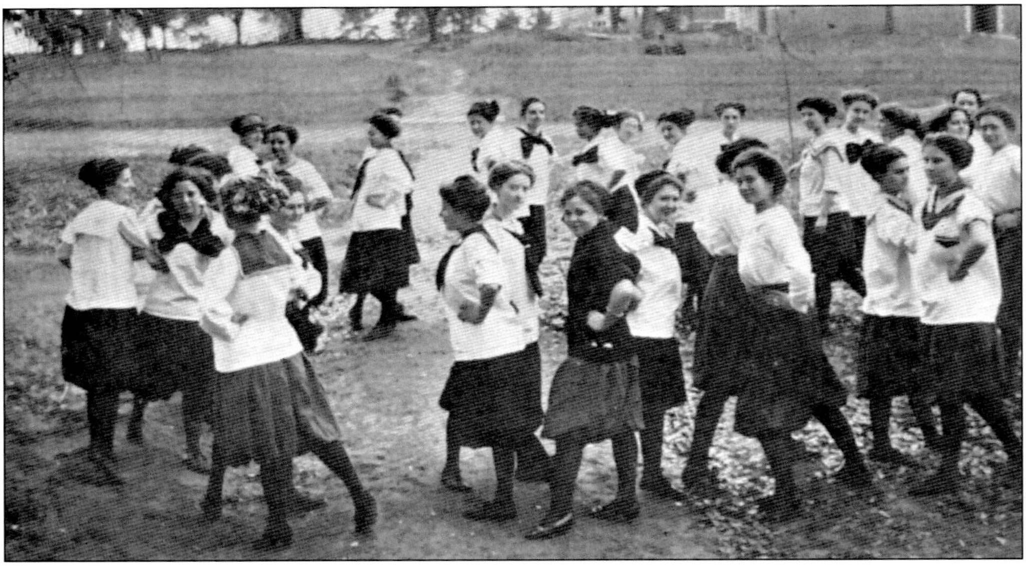

The School of Physical Culture, predecessor to the Department of Physical Education, focused on fitness and exercise and only rarely on athletics or team sports. Good health, an erect carriage, dignified bearing, elastic step, and graceful movements were the goals. Over time, the curriculum moved toward more strenuous activities, like running and jumping and indoor and outdoor games. Eventually, every student was required to take some form of physical education.

Three

Florida Female College/ Florida State College for Women 1905–1947

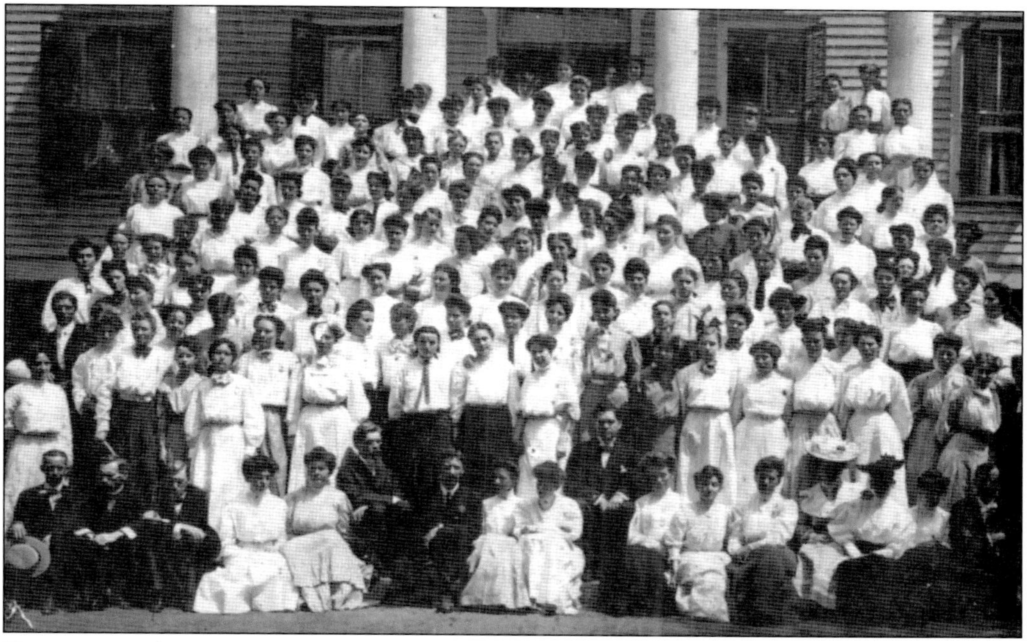

Hoping to reduce competition and duplication among the schools, the 1905 Buckman Act restructured Florida's system into four state-supported educational institutions: the Florida Normal and Industrial College for Negroes in Tallahassee; the Institute for the Blind, Deaf, and Dumb in St. Augustine; the University of the State of Florida in Gainesville; and the Florida Female College, ending coeducation in Tallahassee. The result can plainly be seen in this 1906 photograph.

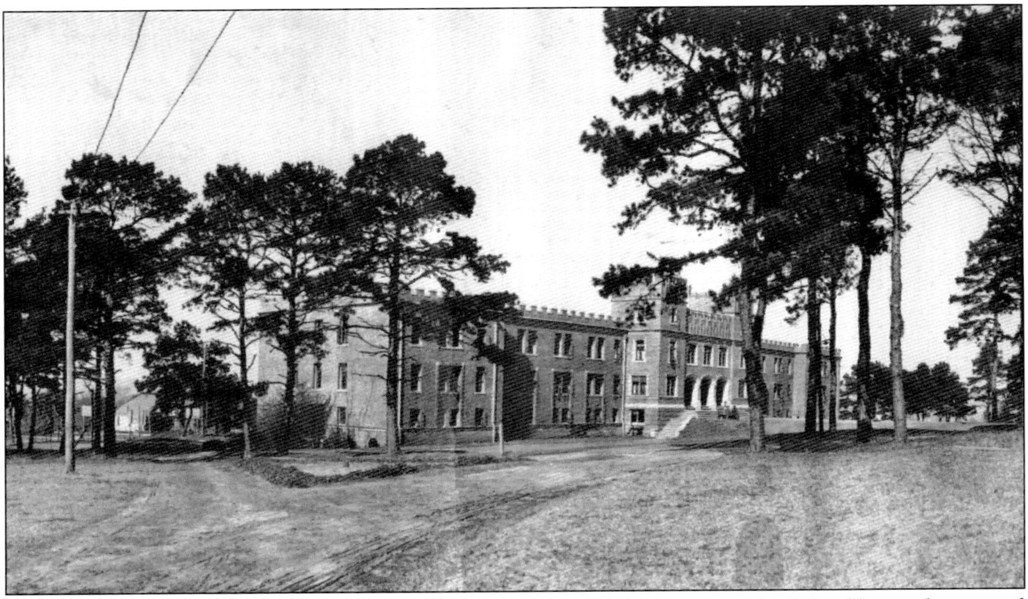

Bryan Hall was constructed in 1908 to replace West Hall dormitory, which had been destroyed by fire two years earlier. The interior consisted of 40 two-bedroom suites connected by studies and accommodating 160 students. Bryan Hall quickly became the social center of the campus, and the seniors held Class Day exercises there in 1909, inaugurating a tradition lasting many years. Today, Bryan Hall is the oldest building on campus.

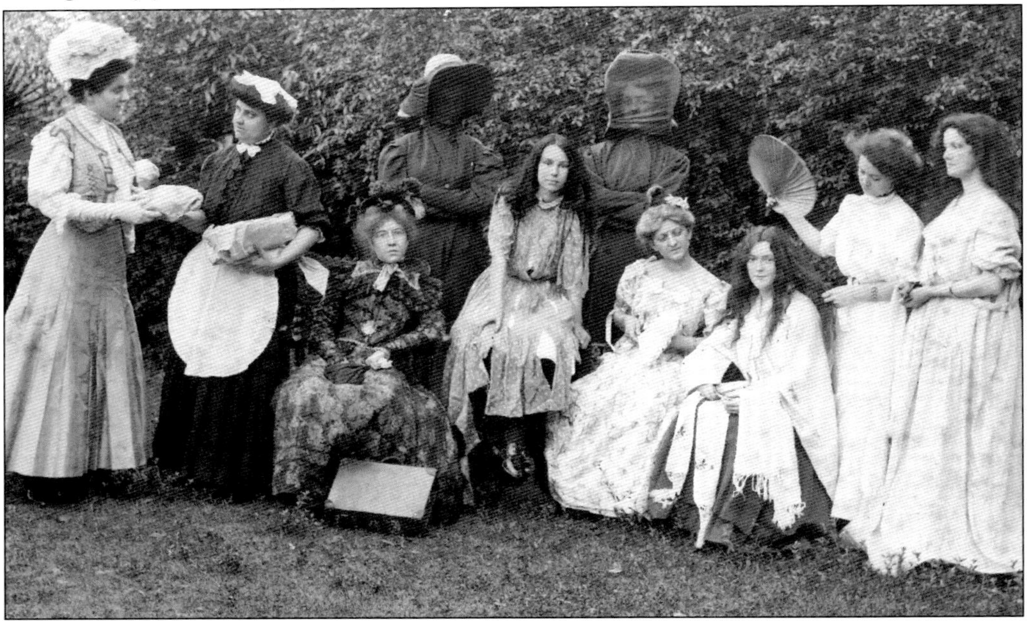

Florida Female College stage productions, such as the 1908 photograph above, might have been held in the sunken garden under the direction of the head of the School of Expression. Much of the charm of these outdoor performances was the pine-grove backdrop, which added a touch of mystery to the scenes of dramatic performances at twilight and later, as the light from the stage faded into the distance. (Archives of Florida.)

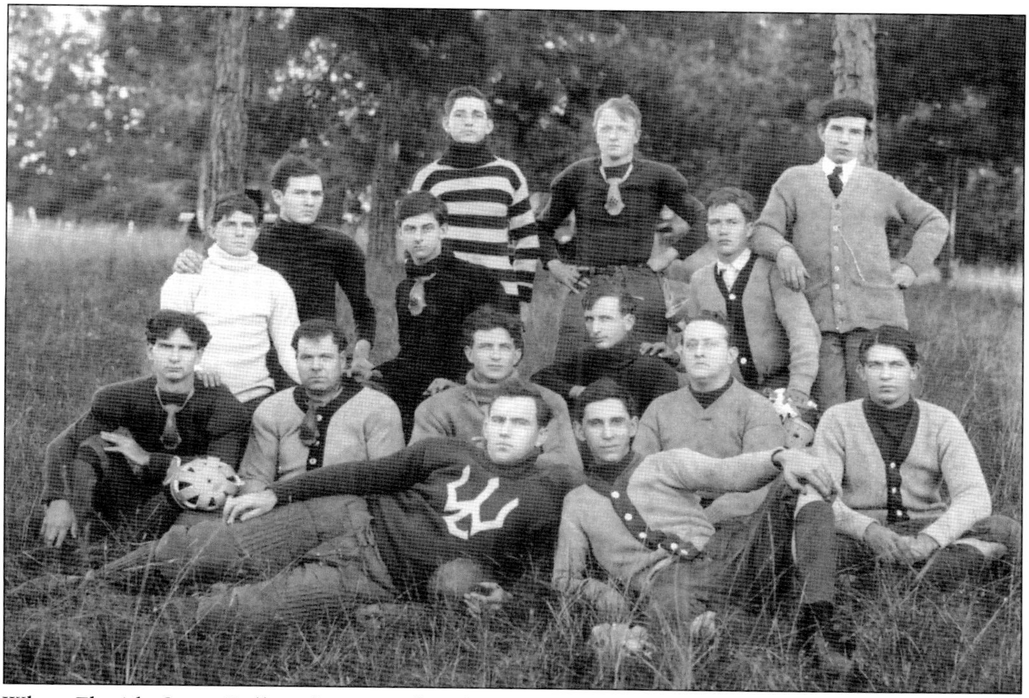

When Florida State College became the Florida Female College, male students who had not completed their education had to go elsewhere to earn their degrees. Many of the gentlemen in this 1909 photograph of the Tallahassee Athletics football team had also been on the FSC squad. Guyte P. McCord, who earned his law degree at Washington and Lee, is in the front wearing his jersey from that school, where he also played on the football team.

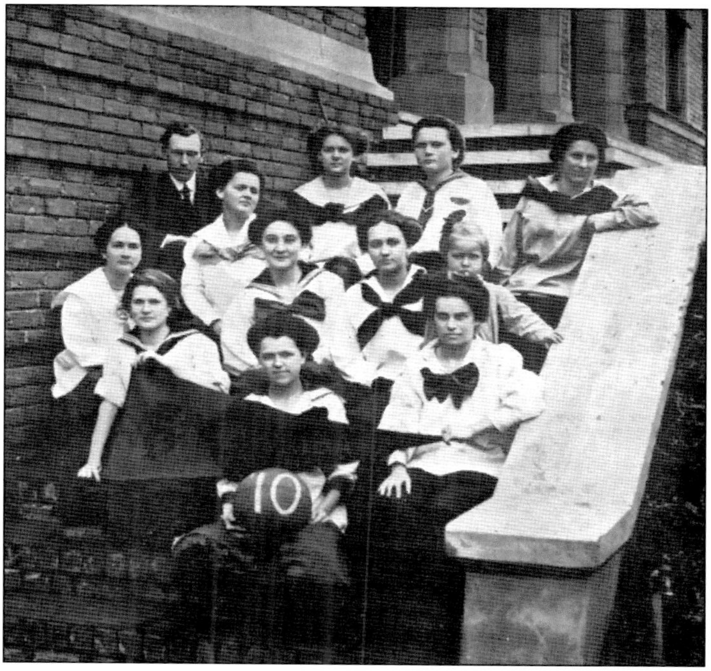

In 1905, the students at Florida Female College organized a college-wide athletic association to which all belonged. The next year, the association formed the basketball teams the Cockleburs and Prickly Pears. The victor in two out of three matches became the "college team." In 1908, the Cockleburs and Prickly Pears were supplanted by the Stars and Crescents as the main college rivalries. The photograph at right is of the 1910 Crescents.

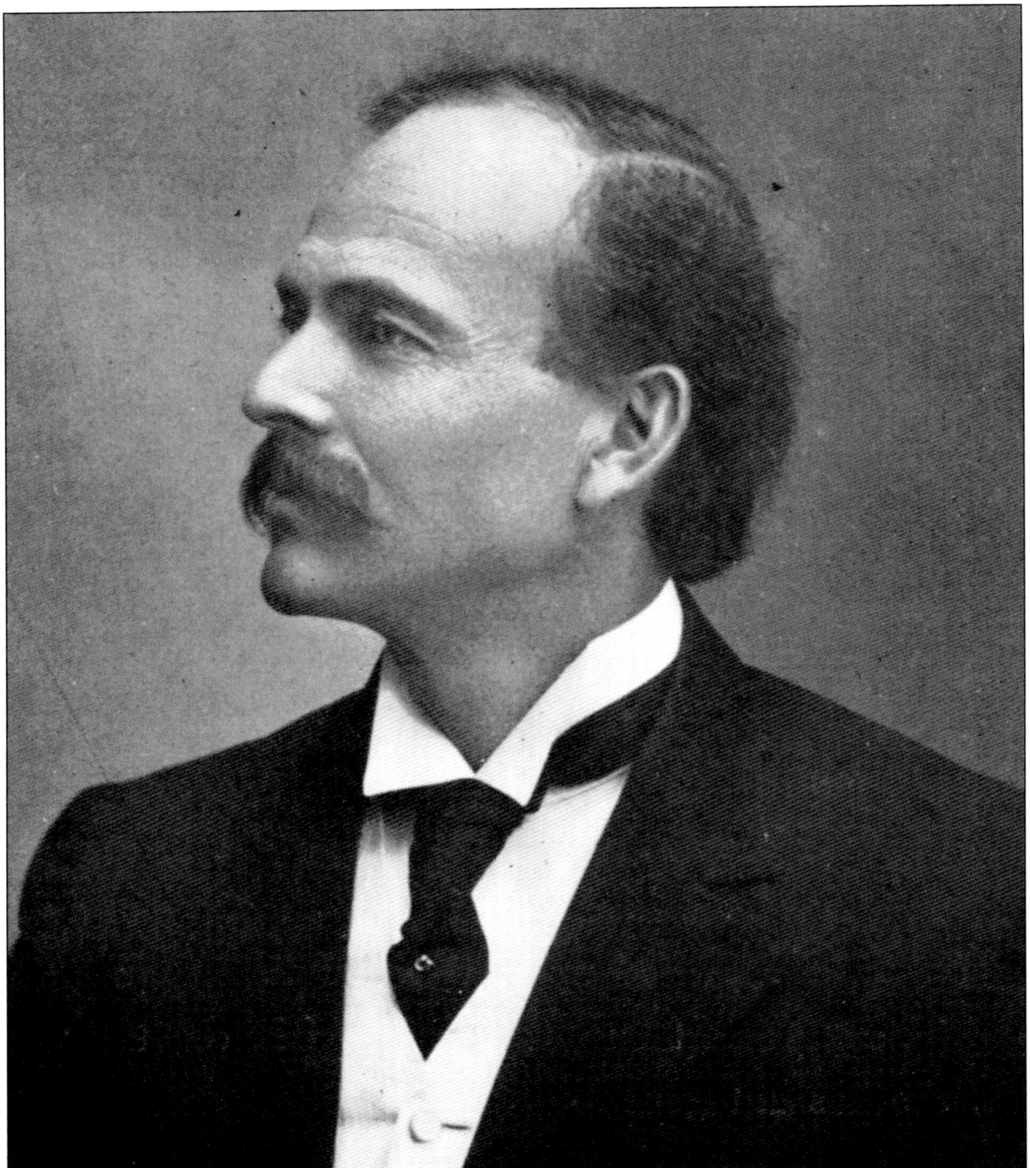

In 1908, Florida Female College president Albert A. Murphree tried to hire Edward Conradi, then principal of the Normal and Industrial Schools of St. Petersburg. Already committed to another year at that institution, Conradi declined the offer. The following year, the position was still vacant, and when Murphree again offered him the post, Conradi accepted. Before he took the position, however, Murphree accepted the presidency of the University of Florida. Conradi, who had earned his doctorate in psychology from Clark University, was then selected by the board of control as the new president at Florida State College for Women, to begin the 1909–1910 academic year. Conradi accepted the offer only after he was assured by the board that the all-female school would always receive facilities and financial support equivalent to that of the all-male University of Florida. With that assurance, he accepted the position, which he held for 32 years.

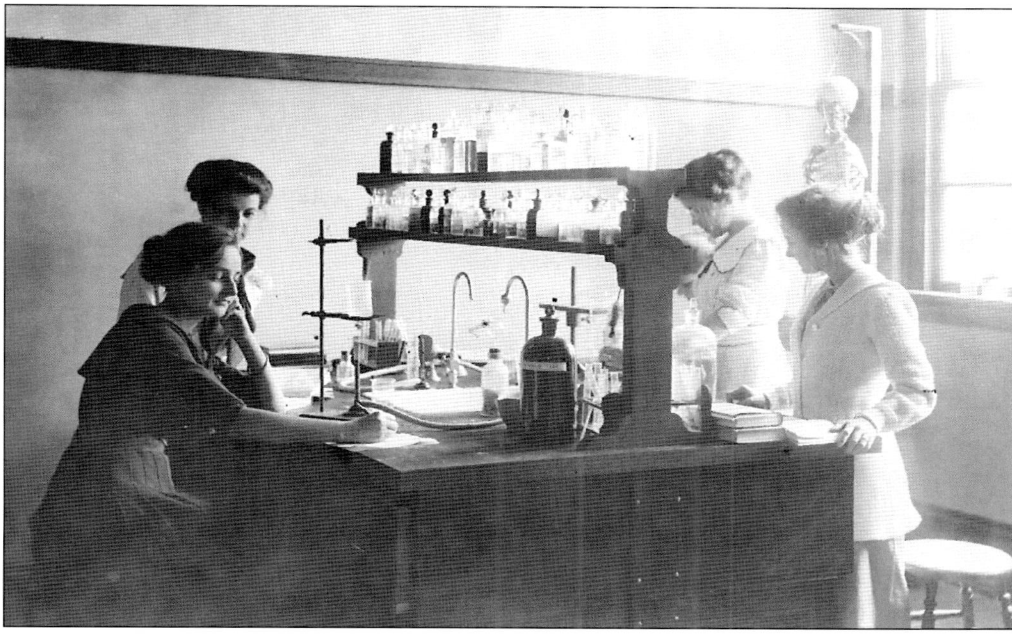

In maintaining the established curriculum through the transition from coeducation, the Florida Female College administration was determined that the school would be more than a woman's normal school for teacher training. What ultimately separated Florida State College for Women from its counterparts was its conscious effort to educate women for nontraditional professions, such as in journalism, business, and the natural sciences. The biology lab class photograph above is from 1910.

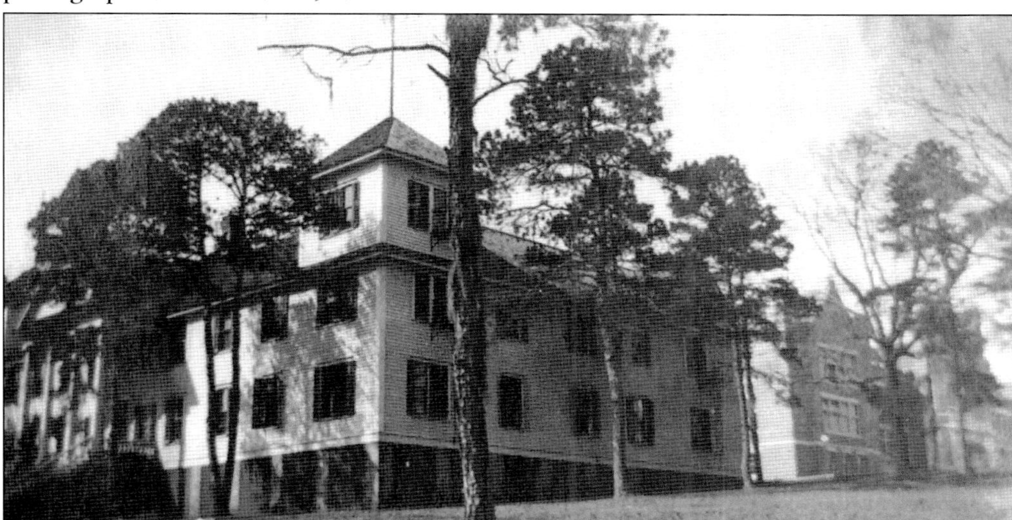

East Hall lost much of its significance as a social center at the Florida State College for Women after the construction of Bryan Hall in 1908, the new Administration Building in 1910, and the new dining hall in 1913. This collective shift freed up space that was soon renovated into more dormitory rooms for students. In the photograph above, the new Administration Building can be seen to the right.

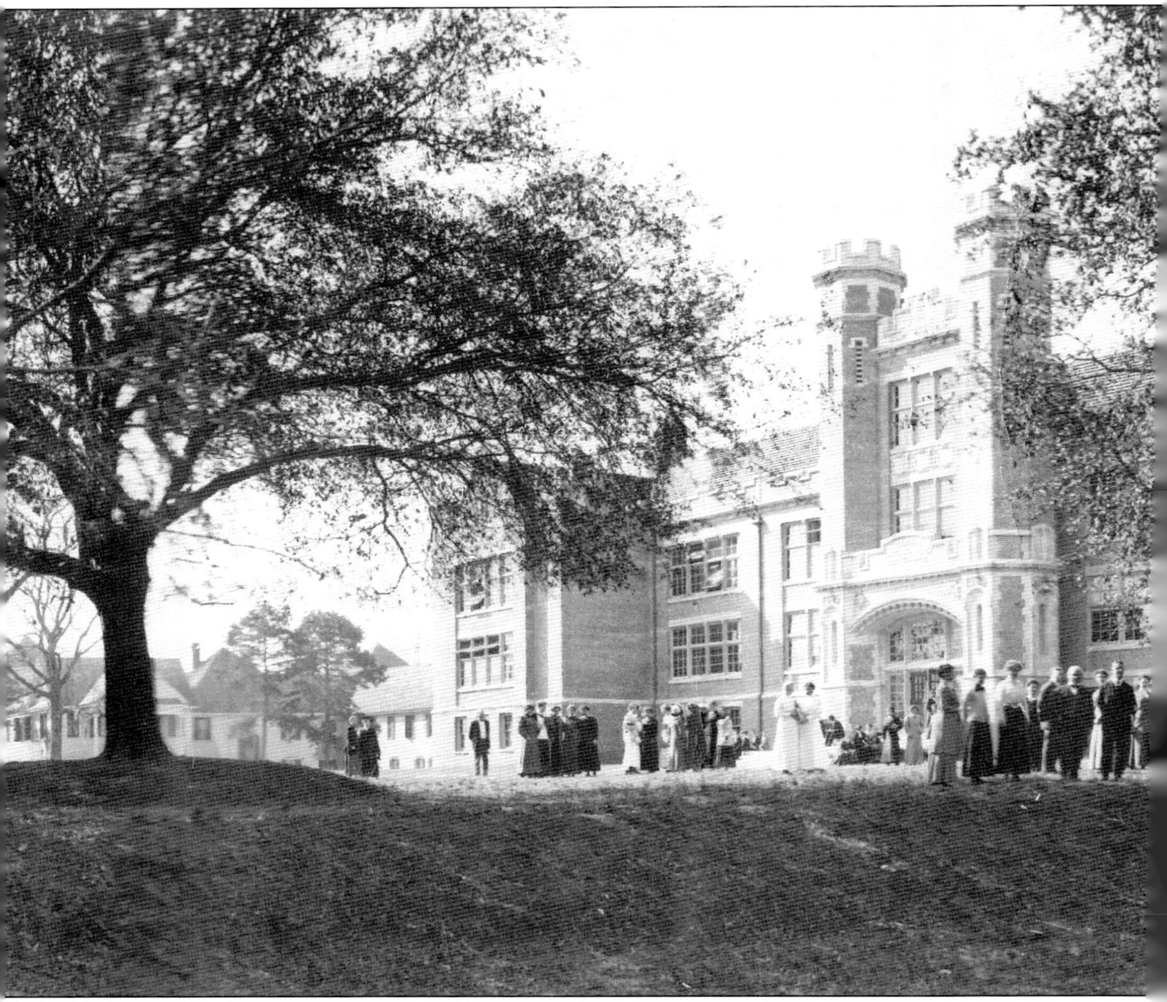

After College Hall was determined to be structurally unsound and beyond repair, it was replaced in February 1911 by a new Administration Building. Constructed directly behind College Hall, the three-story redbrick building was designed with a symmetrical front facade, including two five-story octagonal towers on either side of its main entrance. The T-shape design also contained an auditorium that accommodated 1,000 people, nearly four times the capacity of the former assembly room. In addition to administration offices, the building also

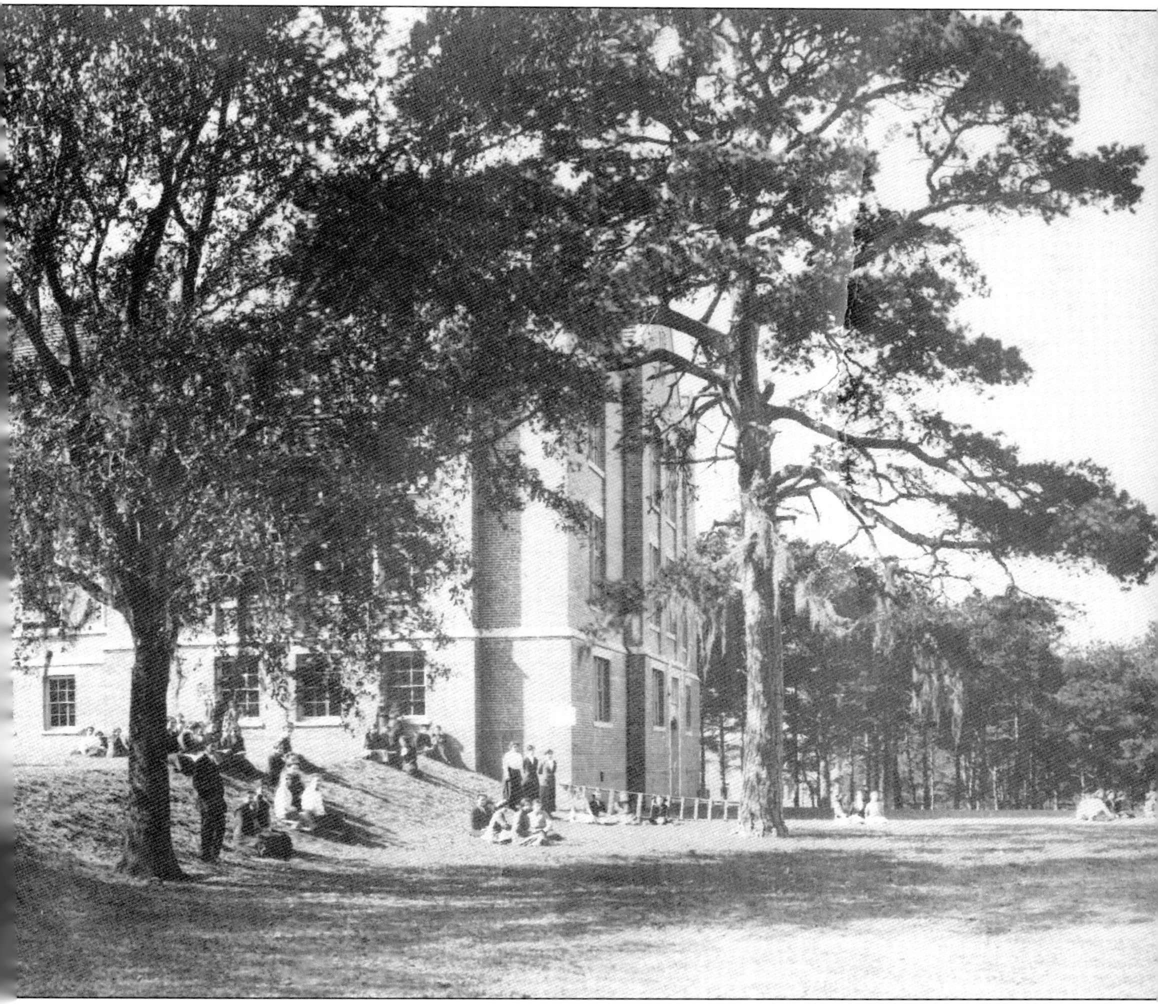

housed the Department of Home Economics, the music department, the School of Art, and the School of Expression. After College Hall was demolished, the ground was graded around the new building, and grass was planted, inaugurating a campus beautification program. In 1937, the building was named the Westcott Building, honoring alumnus and benefactor James D. Westcott Jr. East Hall, destroyed by fire in 1920, can be seen at the far left.

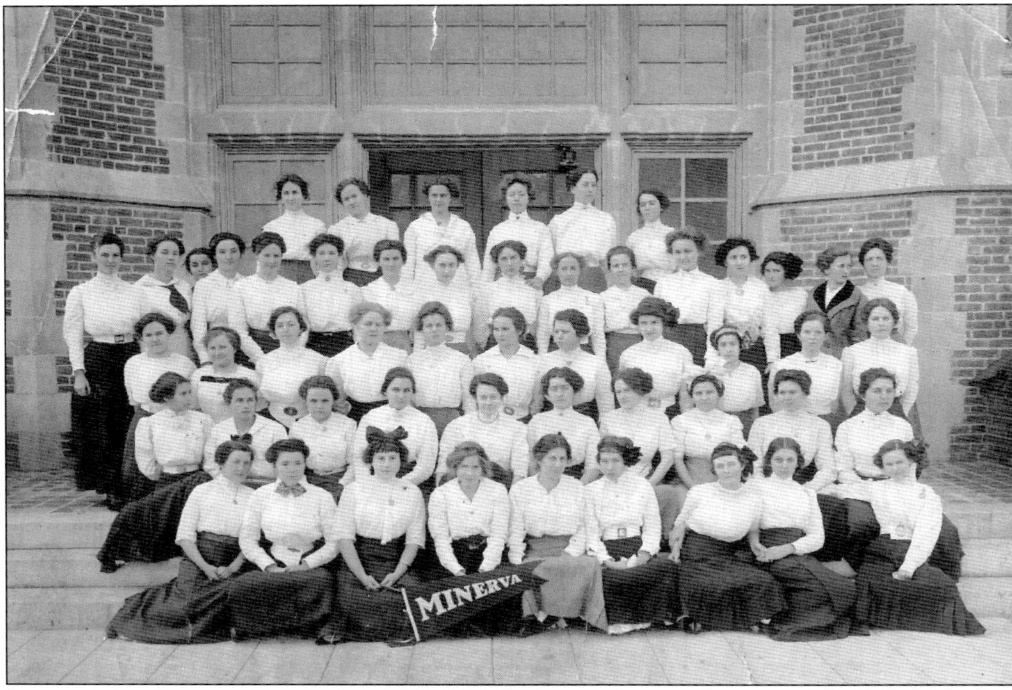

The Minerva Club and the Thalian Literary Society were both founded at the Florida Female College in 1905. The Minerva Club (above) was a literary society with the motto: "Self-knowledge, Self-reverence, Self-control." Meetings of the club offered programs that included piano and vocal performances, as well as readings on various topics related to the classics and the arts. The motto of the Thalian Literary Society (below) was "Knowledge is power," and their "yell" was "Thalian, Thalian girls are we, Full of joy and poetry. There are others but none like us, We are the girls that make a fuss!" The Minerva Club and the Thalian Literary Society participated each year in the Inter-Society Debate, and the two organizations also produced the campus literary magazine, the *Talisman*.

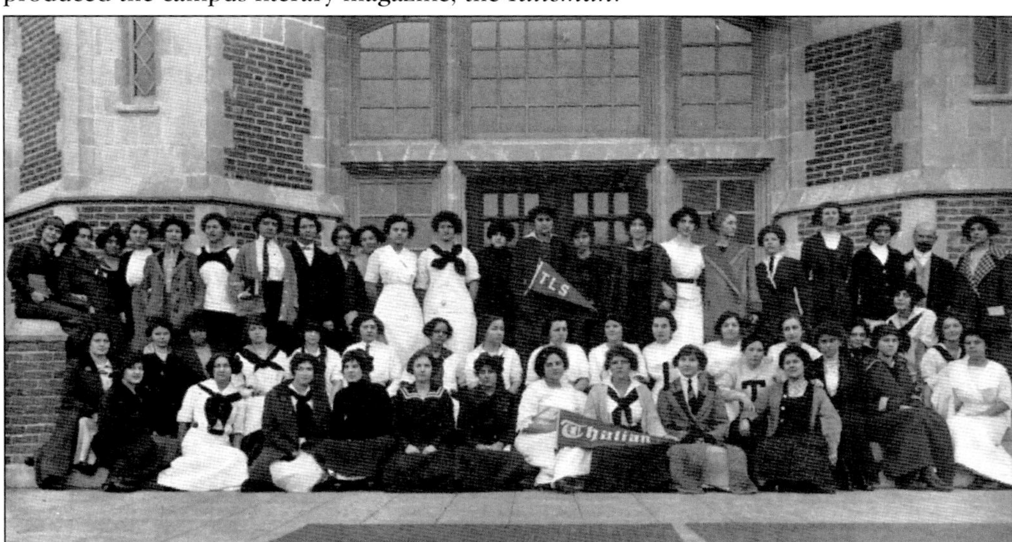

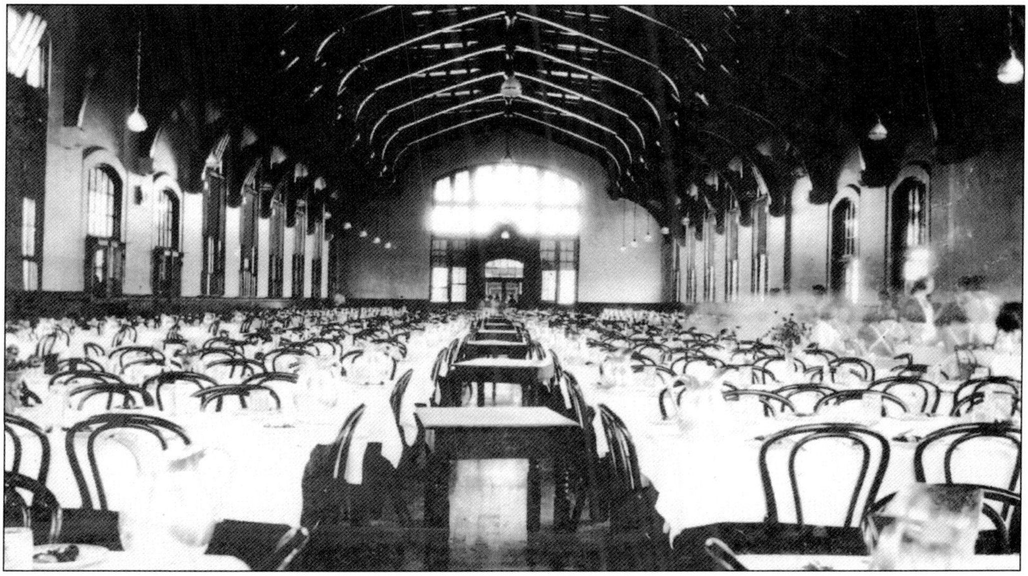

In 1913, construction began on the single-story dining hall that could accommodate 550 people. Located behind Bryan and Reynolds Halls, the facility included a two-story wing that housed the kitchen, bakeshop, dish-washing room, refrigeration rooms, and storerooms. The interior was unique to campus with high, exposed-beam ribbings in the ceiling, creating an impression of grandeur. This interior design was taken from the dining hall at Winthrop College in Rock Hill, South Carolina, which emulated that at Christ College in Oxford, England.

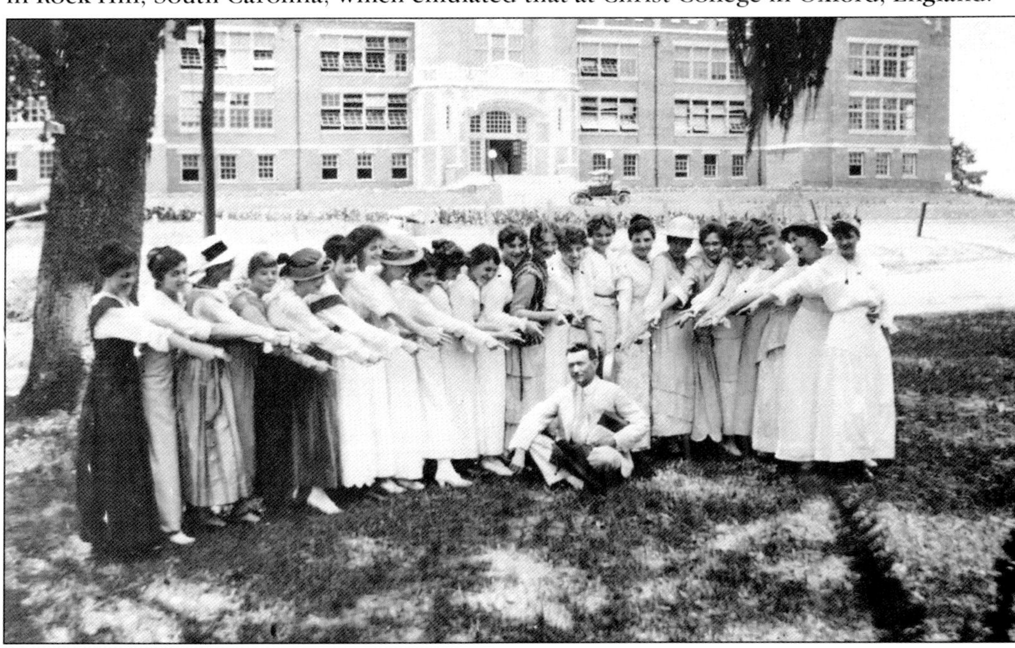

John G. Kellum, business manager for the Florida Female College and then Florida State College for Women from 1907 to 1945, was the custodian of the buildings and grounds and other material resources of the college, as well as the manager of its financial affairs. In the 1915 photograph above, he is being singled out by a group of students. (Archives of Florida.)

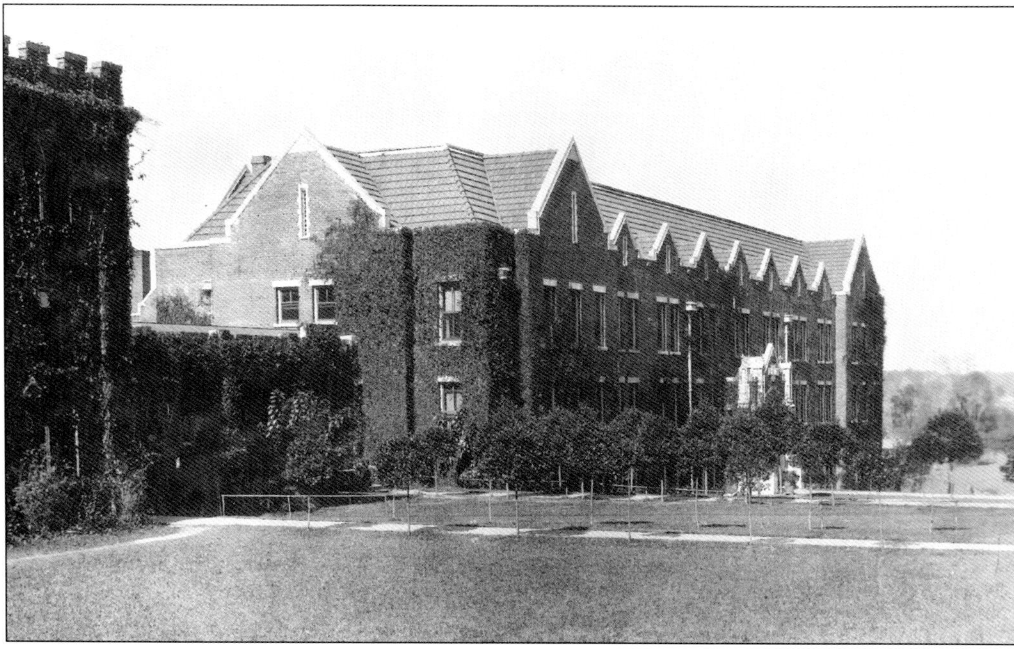

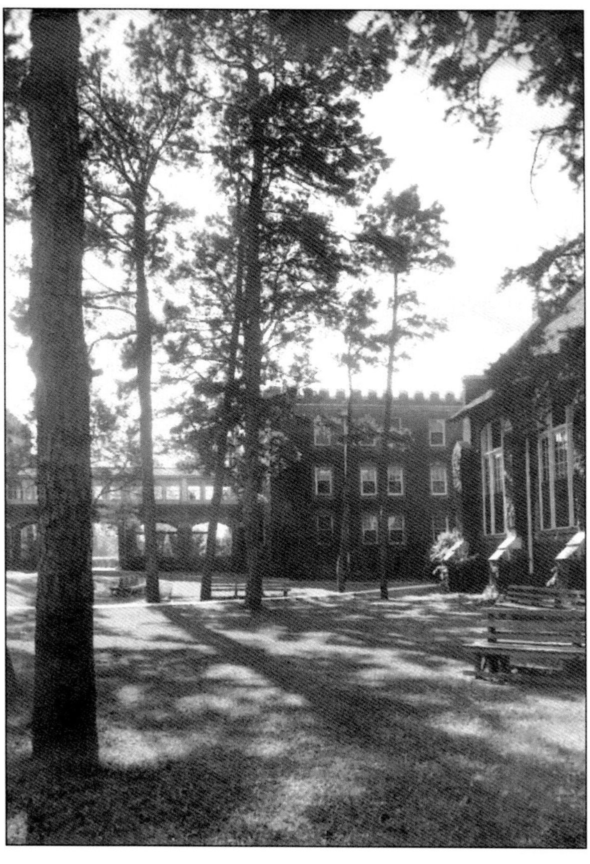

As Florida State College for Women became successful, enrollment increased. In 1911, the state legislature approved the construction of an *L*-shaped dormitory to supplement Bryan and East Halls. Named after Mary Reynolds, the first lady principal who had died in 1909, Reynolds Hall was ready for occupancy on February 3, 1913. A few years later, a 25-room annex was added, and the attic space was converted into living quarters in 1926.

With the construction of Reynolds Hall and the dining hall in 1913, a series of arcades were developed connecting all of the dormitory and dining facilities on the east side of campus. With these connectors, students were able to traverse the campus without setting foot outside. Eventually, the arcades would stretch from Jennie Murphree on the far north, down to Bryan, and across to Landis Hall. This photograph shows the arcade between Bryan and Broward Halls.

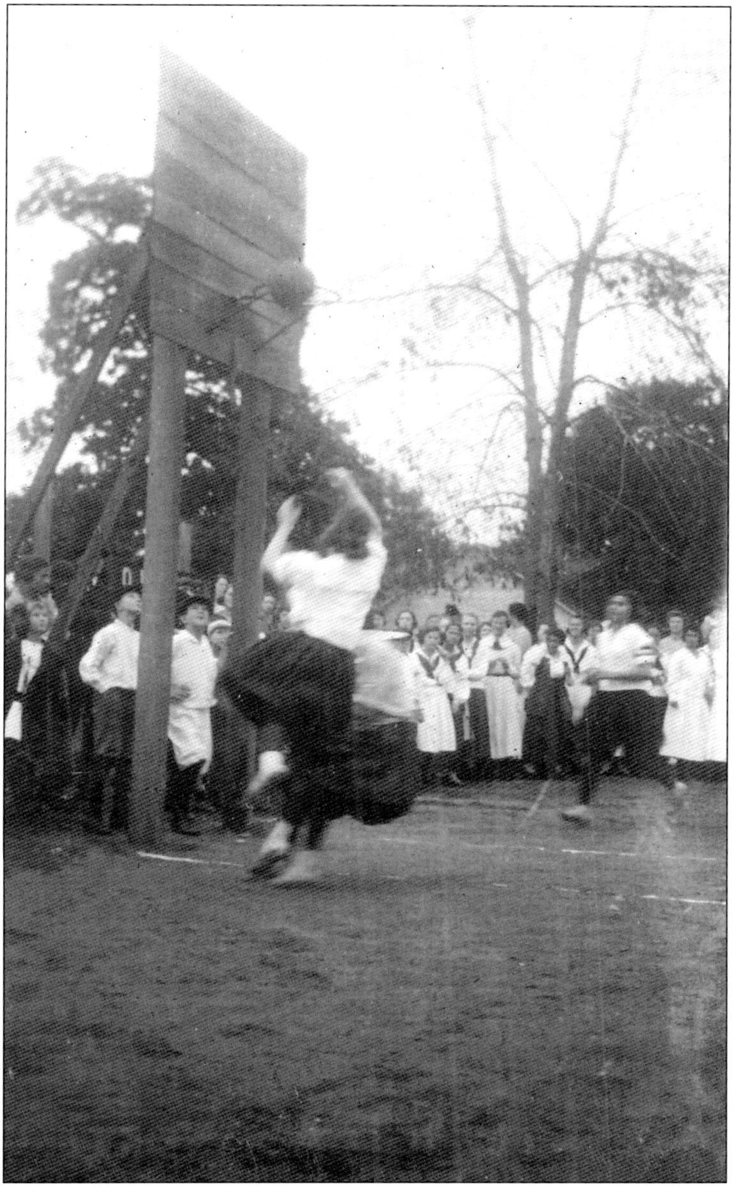

Possibly because the Star and Crescent teams were seniors-only or more likely to make the games more inclusive, during the 1912–1913 academic year, class teams were organized with the sub-freshmen and sophomores (graduating in the odd years) against the freshmen and juniors (graduating in the even years). Two years later, each side had developed team colors, songs, and cheers. The "Even" team took the junior and freshmen class colors of green and yellow, while the "Odd" team chose the senior, sophomore and sub-freshmen colors of red, white, and purple. In 1915, the *Florida Flambeau* campus newspaper formally named the teams "Odds" and "Evens" and declared them successors to the Stars and Crescents. Those early Thanksgiving Day basketball games inaugurated an annual event at the Florida State College for Women that surpassed all others, except possibly graduation day. With it came a mountain of rituals and traditions.

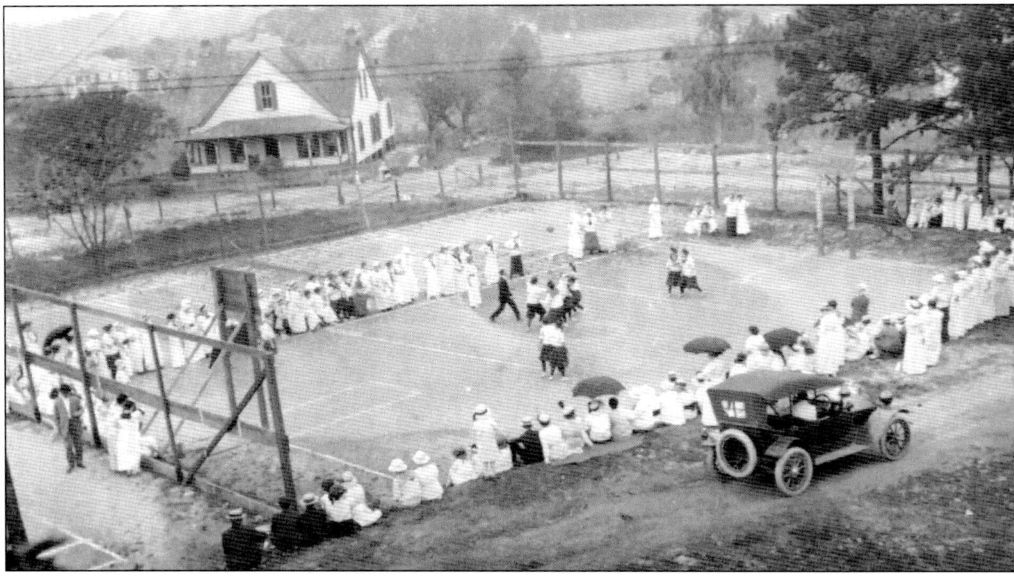

In 1913, DuBois Elder, director of the School of Physical Culture and Expression, proposed field day, a spring-term, college-wide celebration of physical fitness. The day-long competition, the first of which occurred on April 8, 1913, showcased a variety of athletic activities, including tennis, basketball, swimming, gymnastics, and track events, such as broad jump, distance throws, and relay races. All students in the college and in the State School for Teachers and all children who attended the kindergarten, or Model School, participated in field day activities. The first field day was so popular that it became an annual event, and the following year it was expanded to two days of competitions. The photograph above is from the 1914 field day basketball game, and the photograph below is from the 1918 competitions.

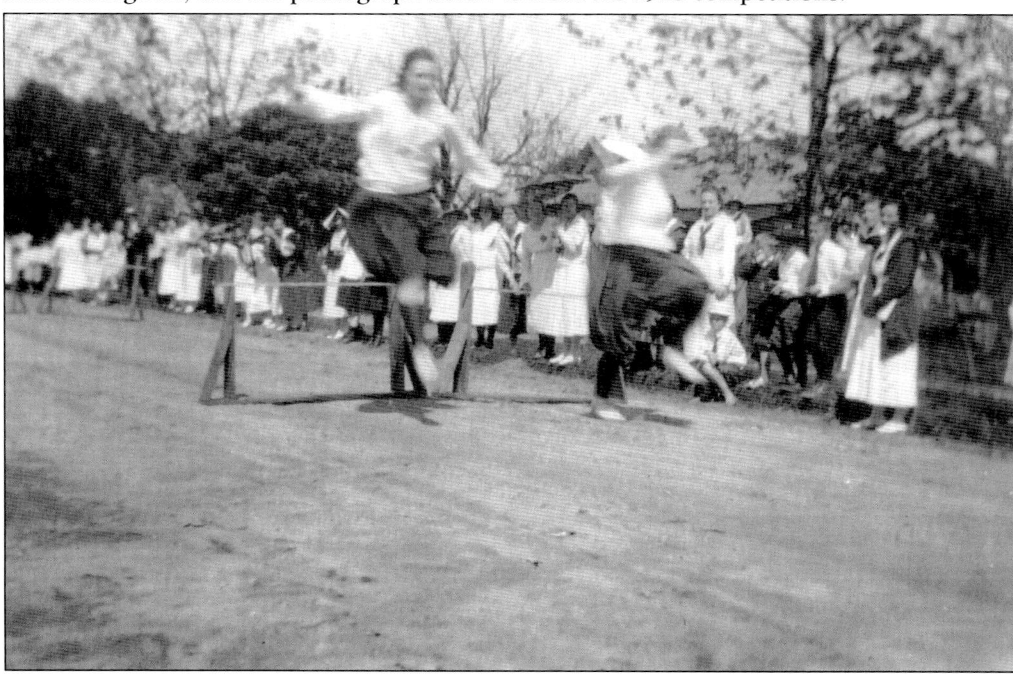

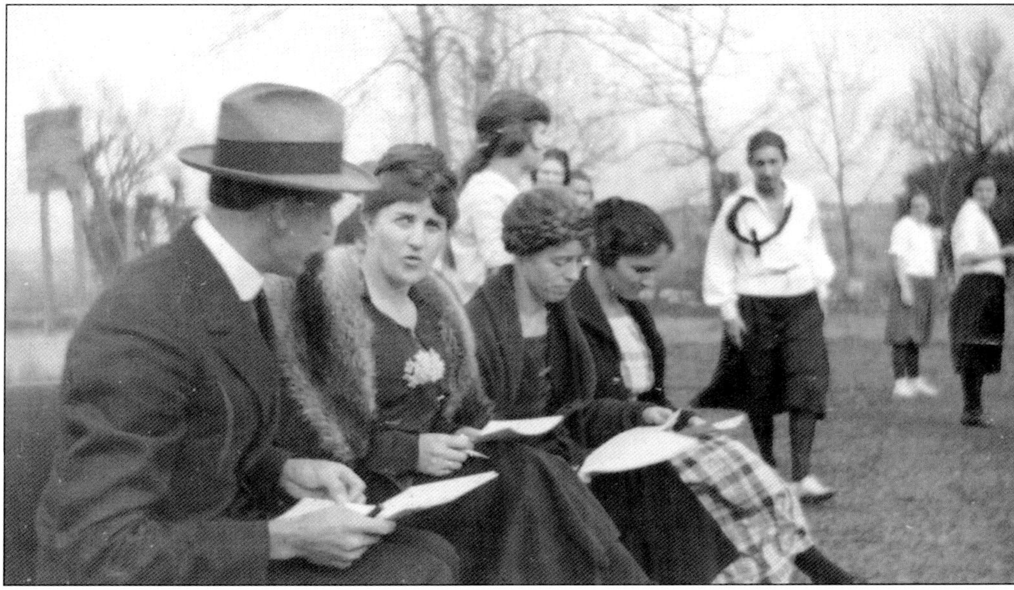

The Department of Physical Culture conducted the annual field day in accordance with accepted track and field standards, so students who excelled received nationwide—and even worldwide—recognition. Florida State College for Women faculty members served as judges. In the photograph above, probably from the 1921 field day competitions, are (from left to right) sociology professor Raymond Bellamy, voice instructor Emma Boyd, business instructor Luella Richey, and physical education instructor Katherine Montgomery.

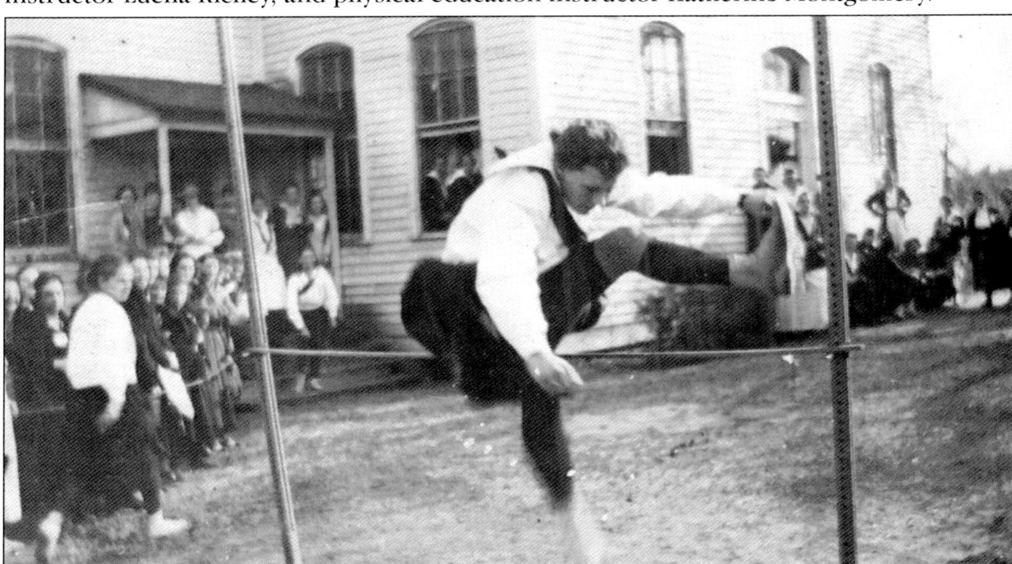

Beginning with the 1920 field day, the school expanded its track and field events. The standing high jump, one of the new competitions, was won by Helen Harris (class of 1922). The popular Harris, an education major, was senior class president and May Queen. After graduating, she returned to FSCW, spending a year or two as an instructor in physical education. The gymnasium can be seen in the background.

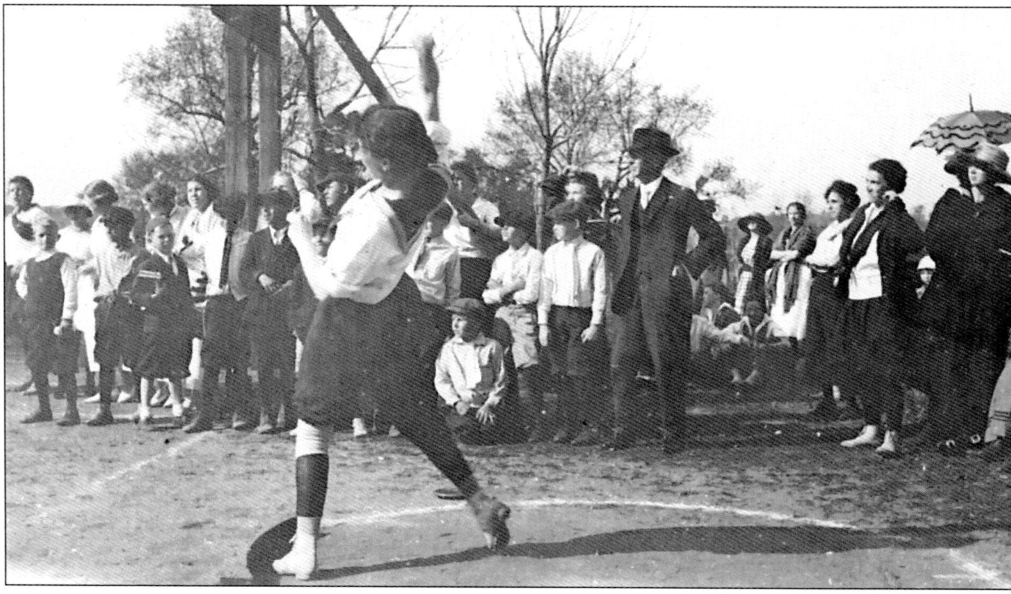

During the 1920 field day competitions, freshman Nell Carroll broke national records in the discus throw and the hurl ball. The records, however, were not officially accepted because of a three-foot grade in the athletic field. The college regraded the field, and the next year, Carroll set a world discus mark at 98 feet, two inches and threw the hurl ball 112 feet, seven inches. The photograph above is thought to be of her record-breaking throw.

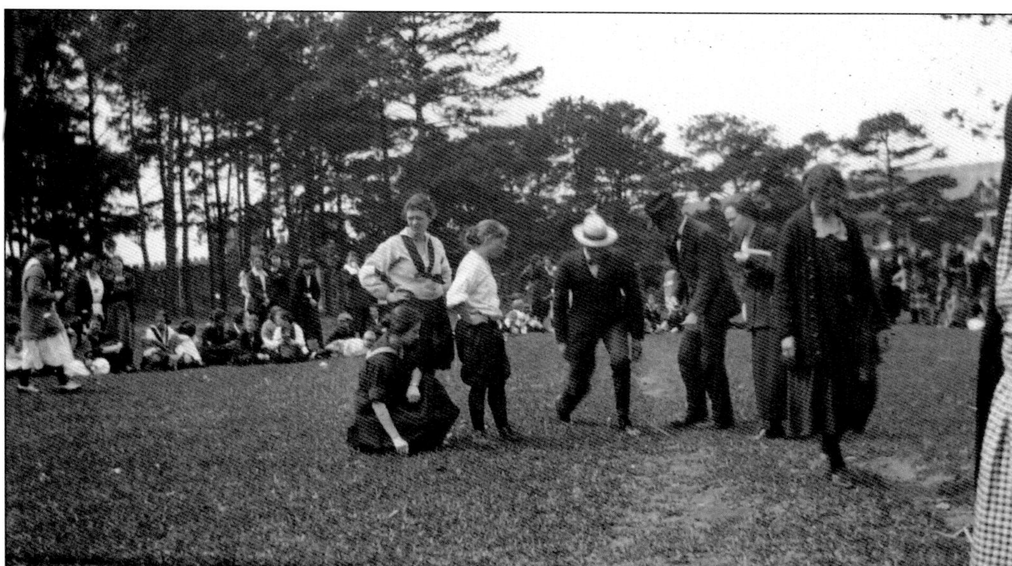

The photograph above is of field day judges taking the measurement in a throwing event. Included in the photograph are Helen Harris (class of 1922) standing at left, Leota Carruthers (class of 1922) standing second from left, and physical education instructor Katherine Montgomery (class of 1918) walking to the right. Bryan Hall and the rooftop of Reynolds Hall can be seen in the background.

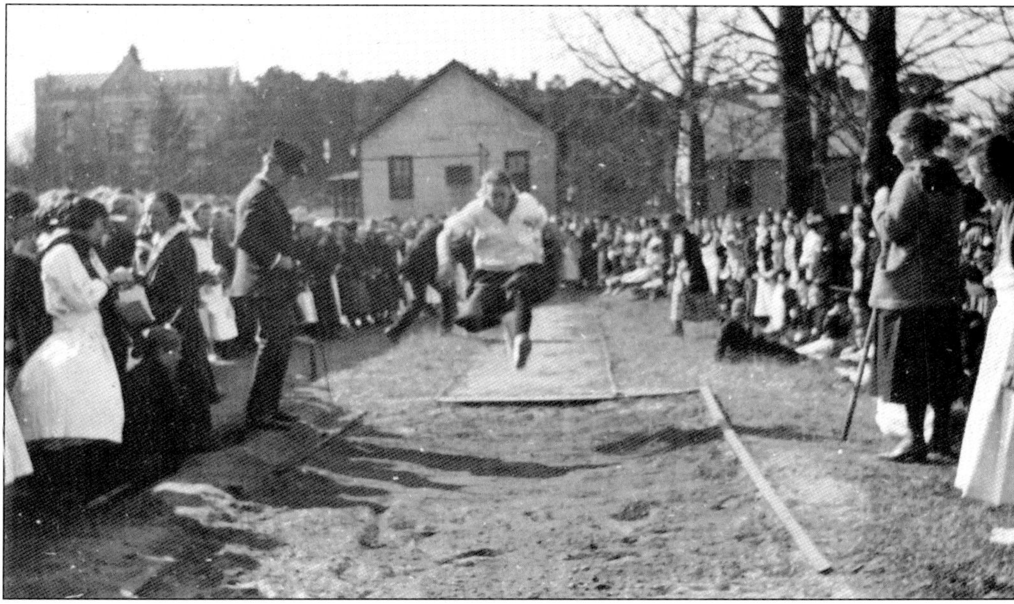

Over the years, the popularity of field day waxed and waned with the enthusiasm of each class. In 1922, the athletic association awarded a banner to the class that exhibited the most spirit rather than to a single student in an effort to encourage greater participation. Possibly because the students began to channel their enthusiasm more toward the Odd and Even team competitions, by the end of the 1920s, enthusiasm began to lag with the last FSCW field day held in 1932. The photograph above shows Dorothy Dodd's (class of 1923) effort in the running hop, step, and jump. Dodd would go on to become the first state archivist in 1941 and served as the state librarian from 1952 to 1965. The photograph below is an interesting angle on the high jump competition.

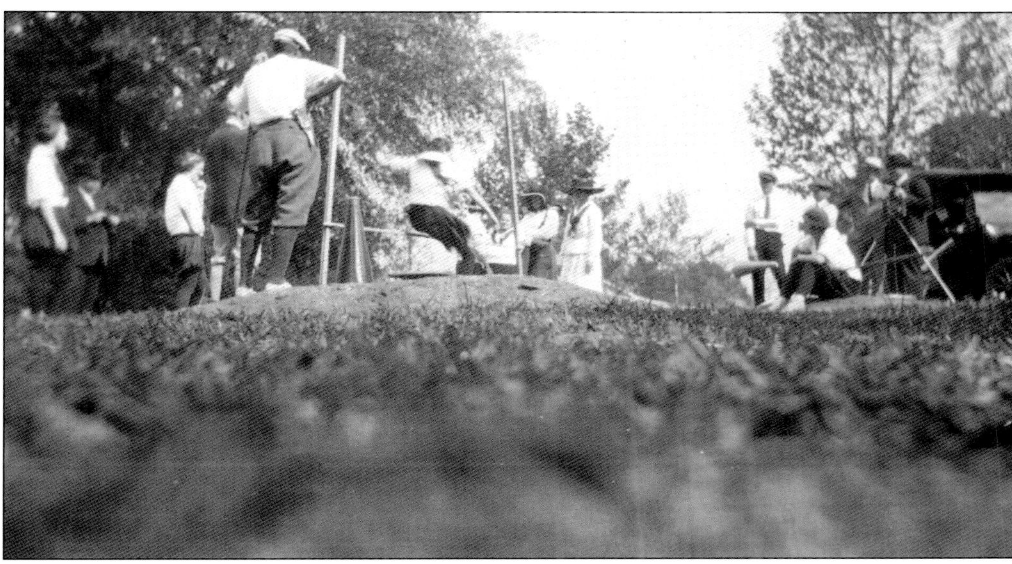

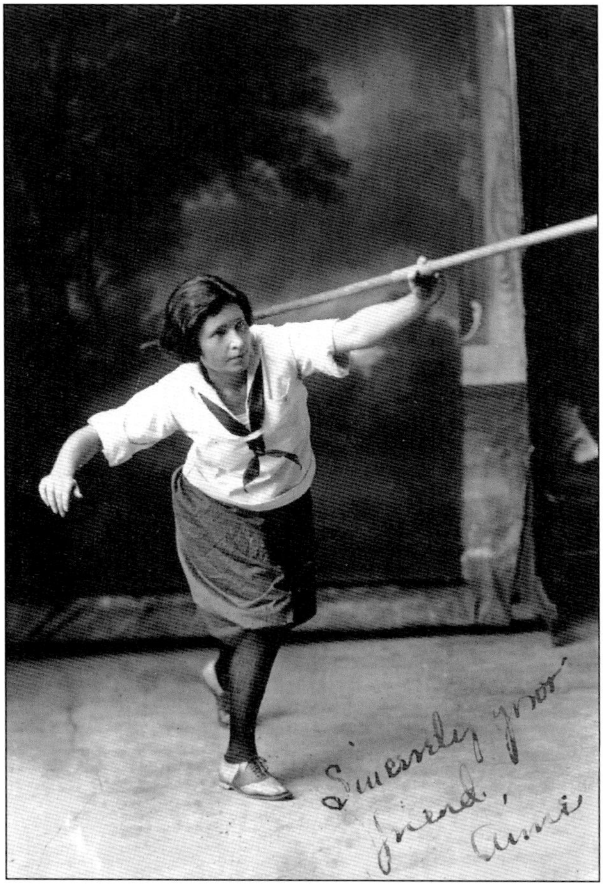

Florida State College for Women student Anne Harwick (class of 1922) gained worldwide fame as a track star and represented the college at a national track meet in New York where she took first place in the javelin throw. The accomplishment qualified her to represent the United States at the first Women's International Track and Field Meet in Paris in August 1922 (held in association with the 1922 Olympic Games).

In early years, Florida State College for Women celebrated spring with a lavish pageant. During World War I, however, the elaborate spectacle was replaced with an old-fashioned and less expensive May Day celebration. The event was an elaborate program that included a May Pole dance and the crowning the May queen. The festivities took place among the pines behind the Administration Building, and the audience sat in the sunken gardens in front of Bryan Hall.

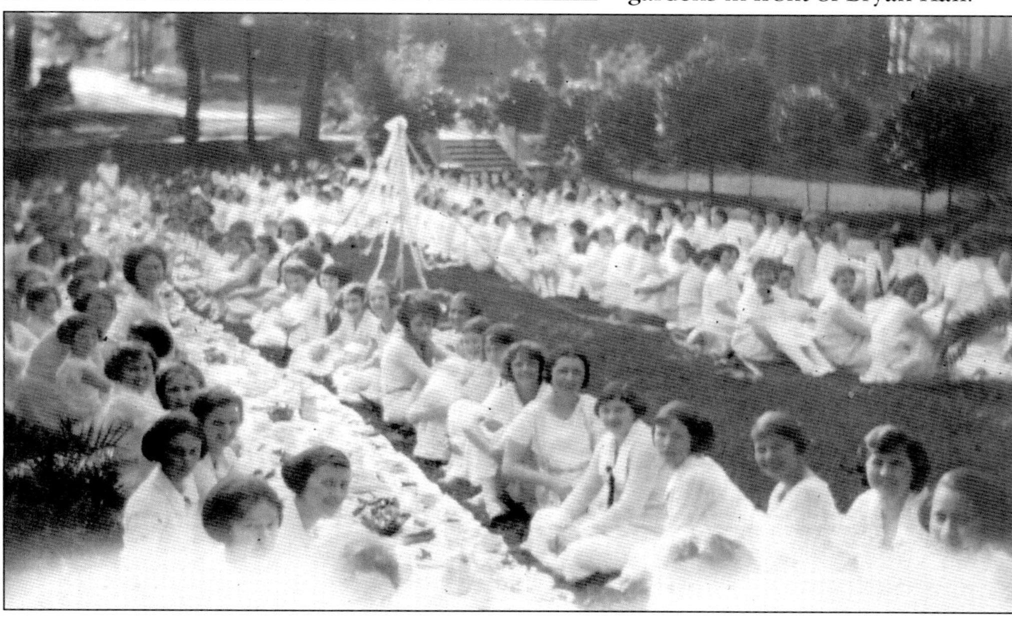

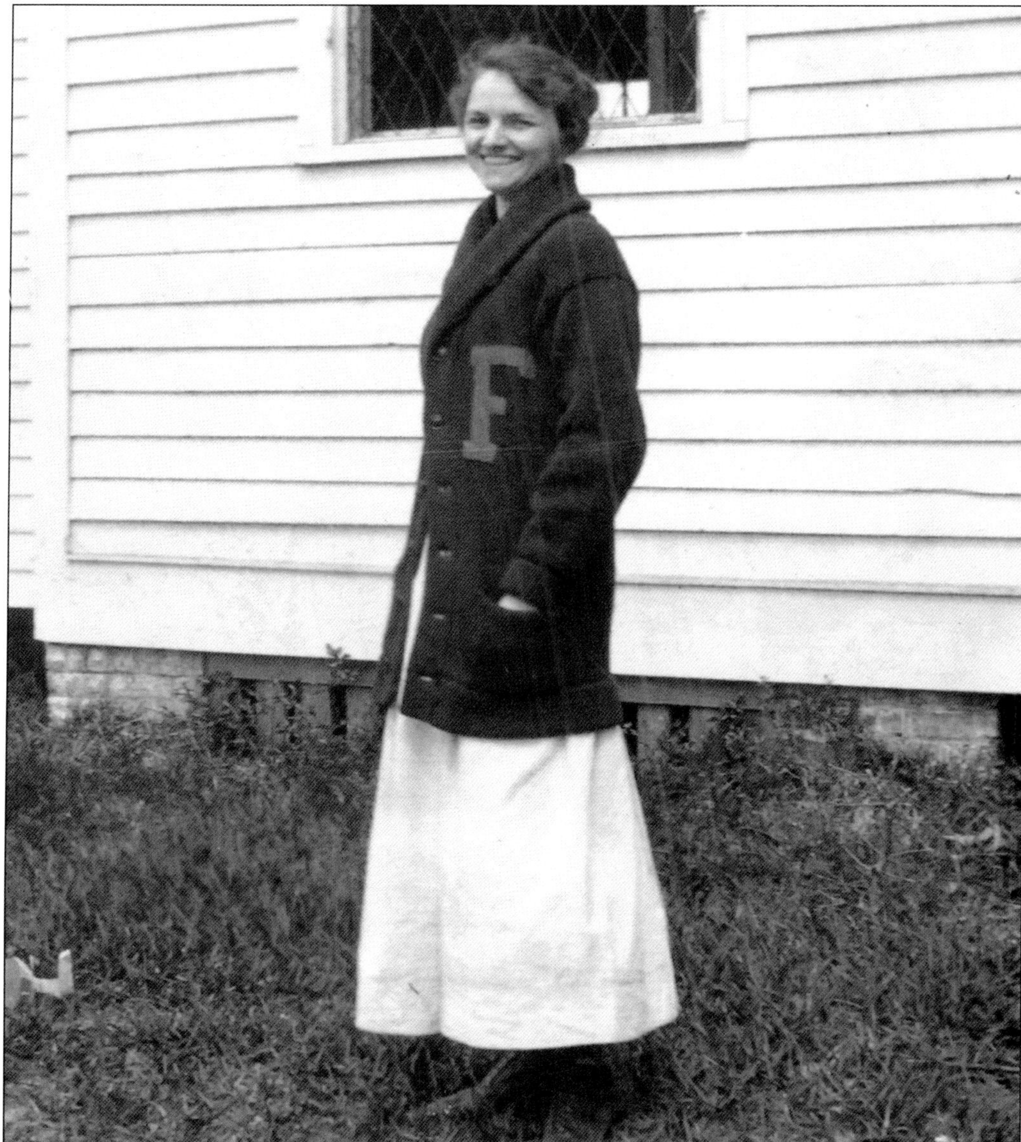

Born in Texas, Katherine W. Montgomery moved to Florida with her family after the turn of the 19th century. She taught public school to save money, and at age 20 in 1914, she entered Florida State College for Women. She was active in sports, student government, and the YWCA, and served as sports editor on the *Florida Flambeau*. She was hired as an instructor in physical education two years after graduating in 1918, and she was appointed the first director of physical education in 1923. She helped design the new gymnasium that opened in 1929. "Miss Katie," as she was affectionately known, developed one of the best physical education programs in the country, along with a well-regarded professional program that turned out highly qualified physical education instructors and professors. She continued through the transition to FSU and on October 1, 1958, the exact date that her resignation became effective, she died at the age of 64. The photograph above is from her senior year at FSCW.

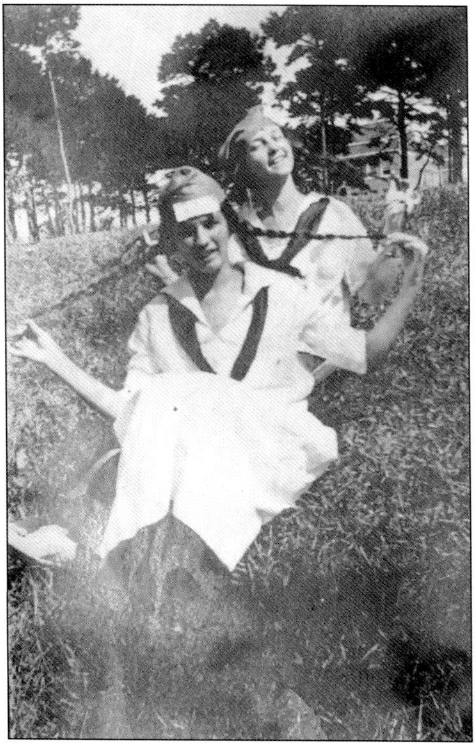

Introduced during the first week of class in the fall of 1917, Sophomore Week was intended to initiate freshmen to the duties and responsibilities of college life. The practice, however, quickly turned into an opportunity for the sophomores to harass and haze their younger classmates. When the faculty began to fear that the custom could get out of hand, the sophomores agreed to limit the "hazing" portion of the ritual to a single-day activity ("Sophomore Day"). The harassment was generally nothing more than wearing costumes, odd hair and makeup designs, and unusual rituals when freshmen met sophomores. Throughout the week, the freshmen were required to wear special "rat caps." The final day of the weeklong ceremony featured a bonfire, skits, and a dance in the dining room. By 1926, the ritual had been essentially eliminated.

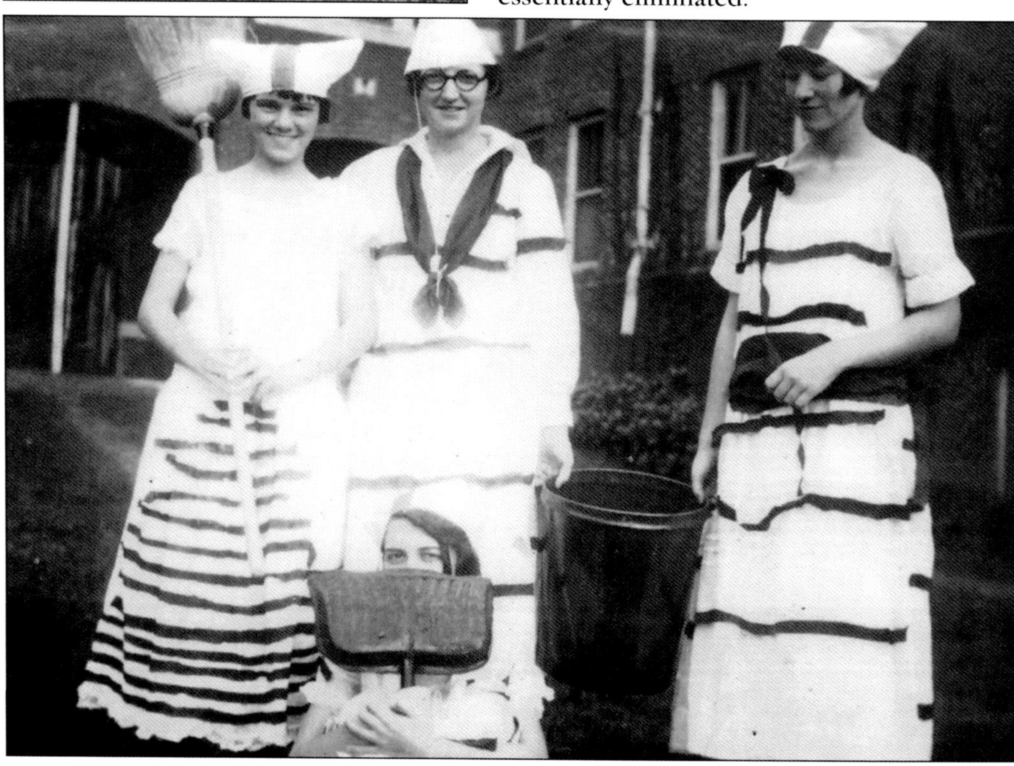

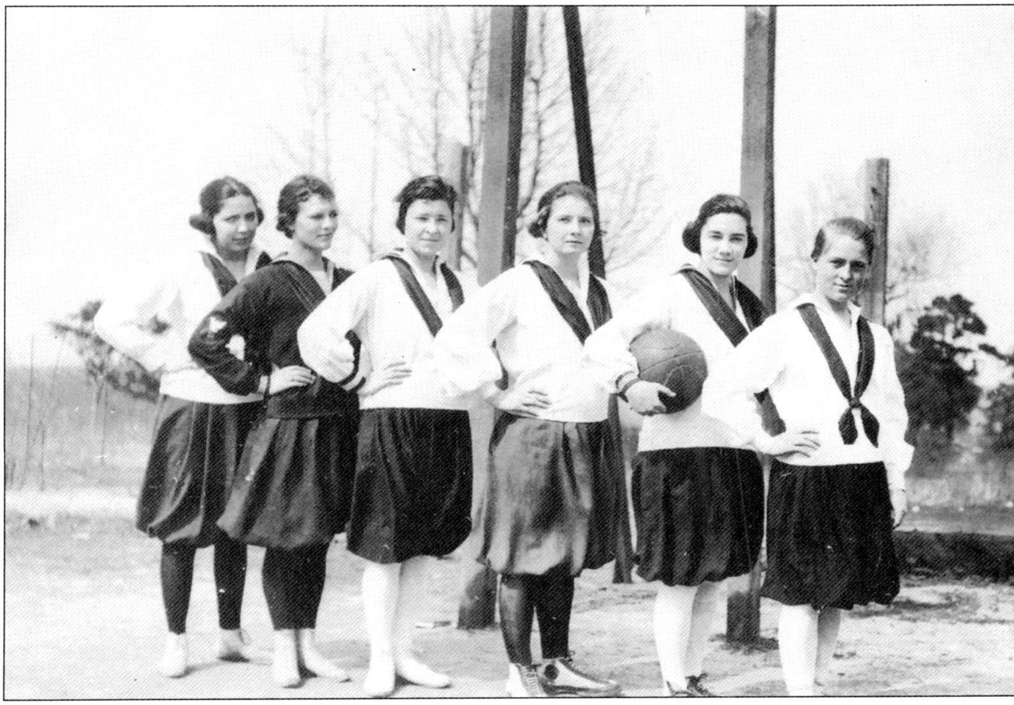

Advertised in a 1917 publication as being, "For the Out-door Girl of Good Taste," the Jack Tar Middy was the athletic apparel of the Florida State College for Women in the late 1910s and early 1920s. Typically comprised of a white middy blouse, black bloomer shorts cut off just below the knee and cotton stockings, the signature item of the ensemble was the large sailor-style tie in the front. According to Pres. Edward Conradi, every student wore the "middy-suit" most of the time during this period. It is, in fact, difficult to find photographs of students from that period where they are not wearing the apparel.

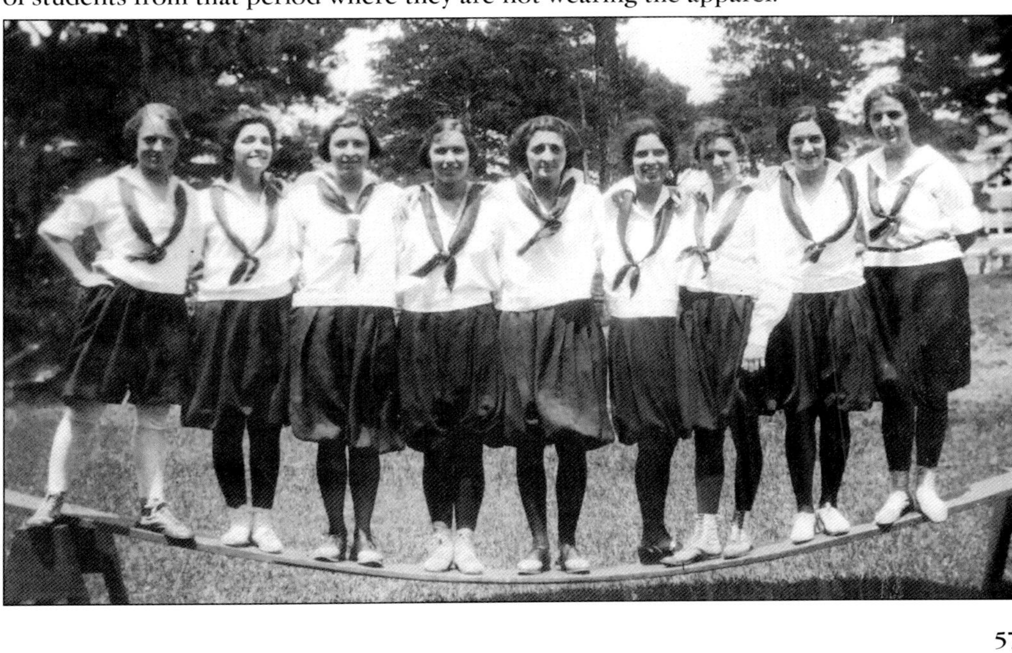

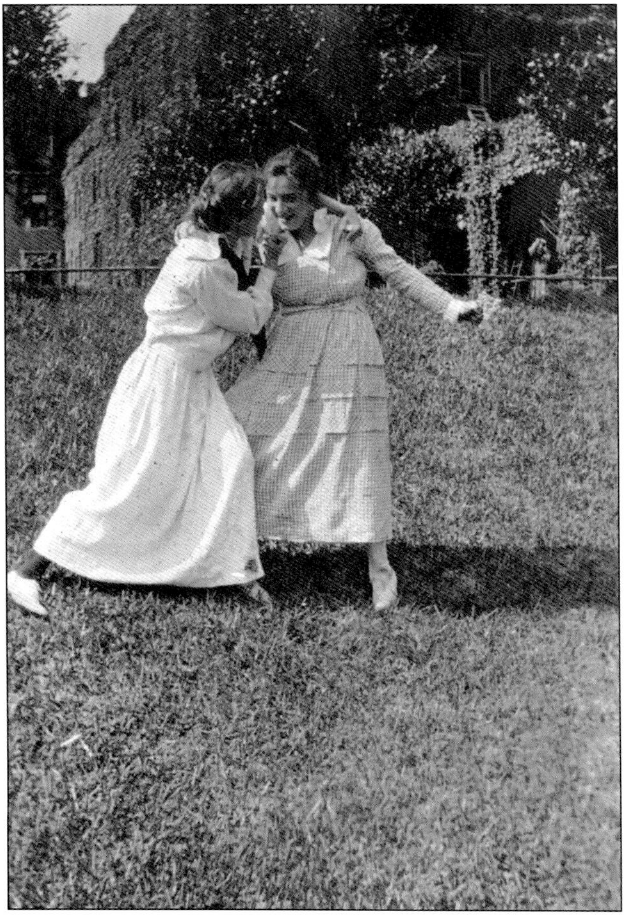

In this photograph, Florida State College for Women student Lucile Luttrell (class of 1920) and her friend and classmate Elizabeth Robinson (class of 1922) mug for the camera. During the 1910s, students with personal cameras were a rarity. Students who did not own cameras had to either obtain photographs from their friends or purchase them from campus photographers.

East Hall suffered a number of small fires between 1916 and 1920, however none involved injuries or significant loss of property. The inevitable occurred on Sunday, October 31, 1920, when the dormitory burned to the ground. There were no injuries, but very little property was saved. As a result, the college housing situation became even more dire with displaced students dispersed all over campus in makeshift sleeping quarters.

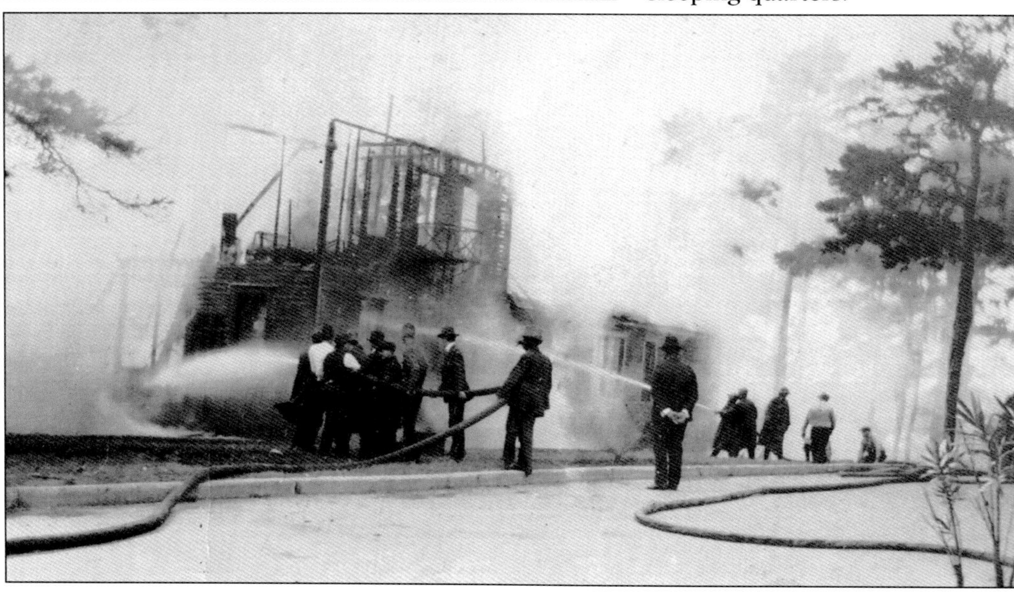

Thanksgiving Week was laden with Odd and Even rituals. Wednesday began with the early-morning ringing of the dining hall bell, marking the start of Color Rush. From the main gates, chosen runners raced to place their Odd or Even team colors on the doors of the main buildings on the campus. In earlier years, the teams tried to affix their colors to the highest points on the buildings, but this aspect of the competition was eliminated for safety reasons. The colors remained up until the games ended.

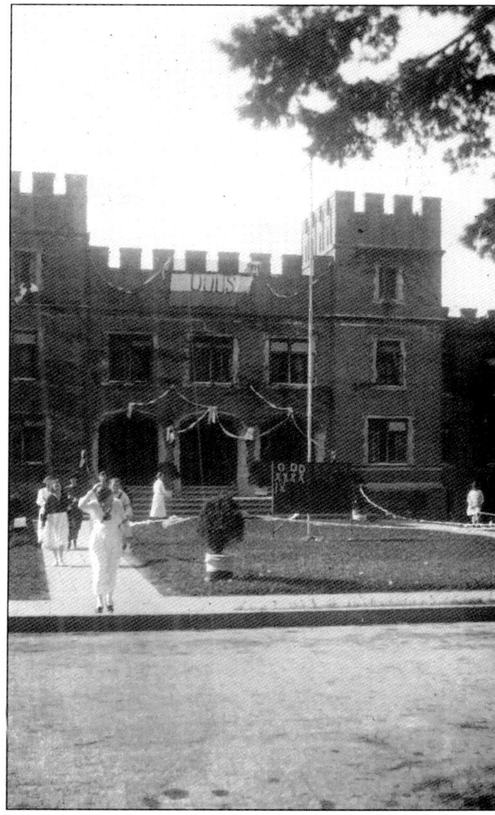

The main gates and fountain were specifically targeted for decorating each year prior to the annual Thanksgiving Day basketball games. The gates, presented by the classes of 1916 and 1918, were declared "forever Even" and decorated by that team, and the fountain, a gift of the classes of 1915 and 1917, was named "forever Odd" and decorated by that squad.

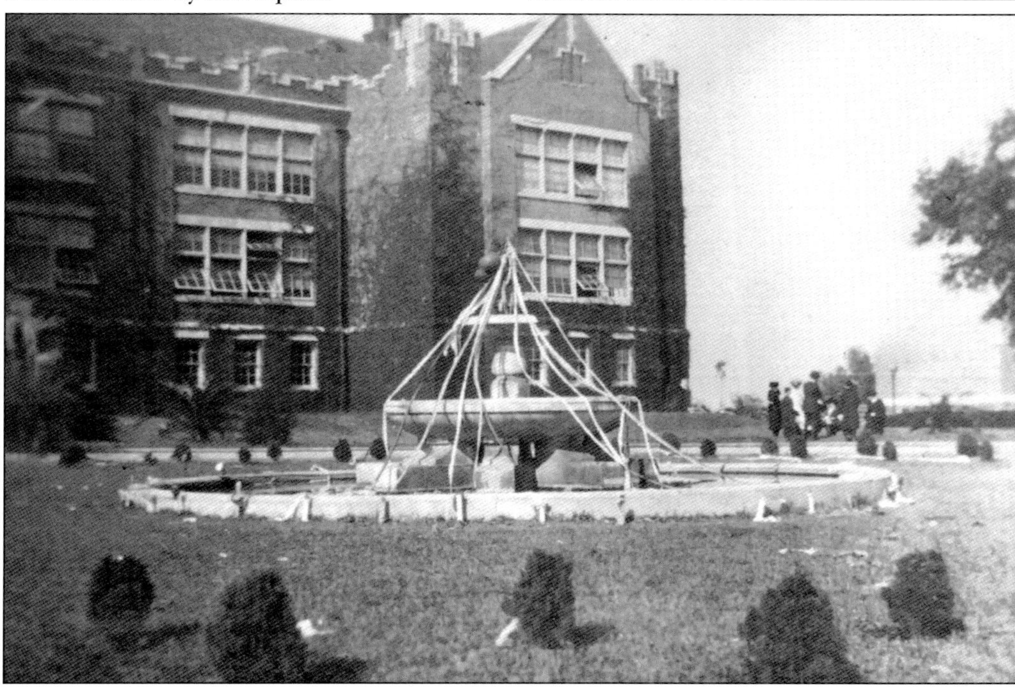

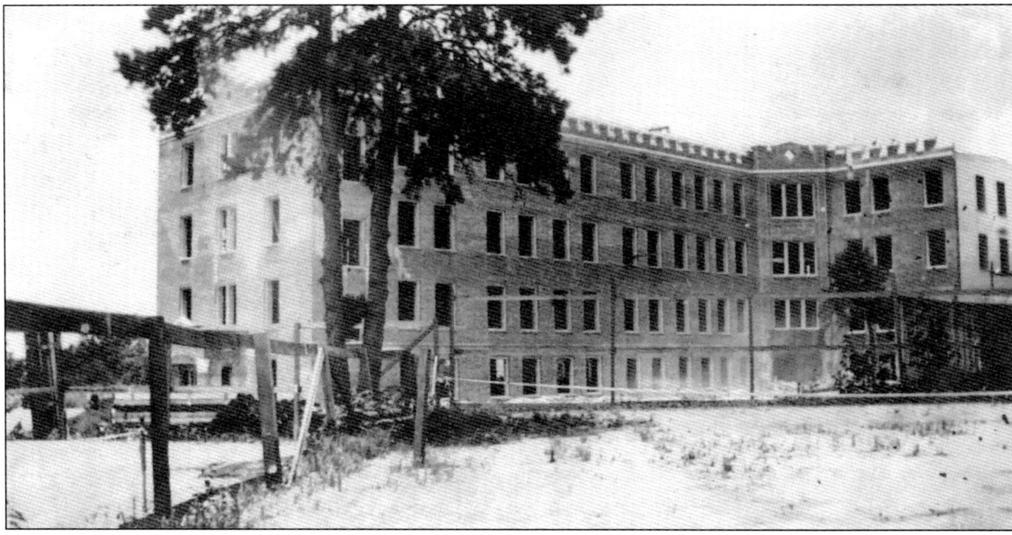

With funding appropriated, construction began on Broward Hall directly behind Bryan Hall. Because of wartime shortages, completion fell beyond the September 1918 due date. With the building far from complete but their rooms reserved, students began that fall term in rooms with no doors, lights, or beds. The four-story, *L*-shaped structure, notable for the crenellated parapet that surrounds the entire building, was named for former Florida governor Napoleon Bonaparte Broward.

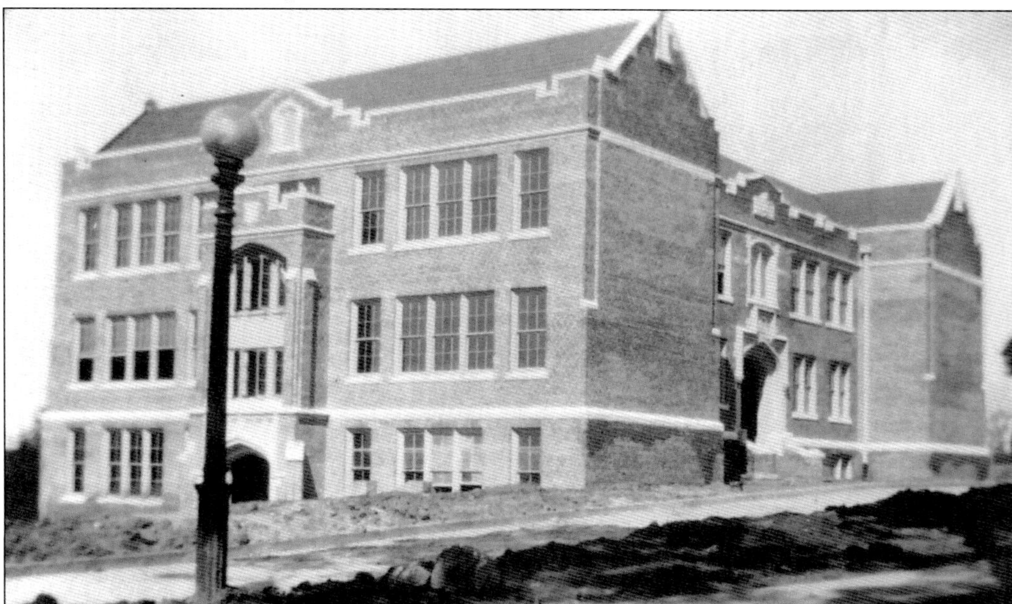

Wartime shortages delayed the opening of the Education Building, which was northeast of the Administration Building, until the summer of 1919. All four elevations of the two-story, rectangular structure are symmetrical. The main entrance on the south side is ornamented with distinctive, whimsical, cast-stone frogs and an owl. The oldest continuously used classroom building on the campus, it was renamed the Psychology Building in the 1950s and Francis Eppes Hall in 1997.

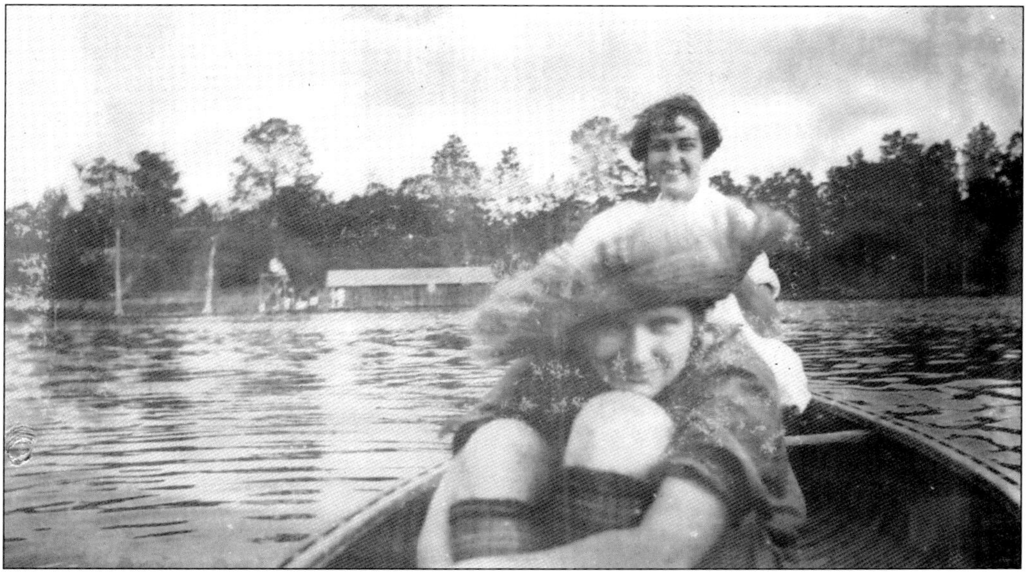

In 1915, the Florida State College for Women administration secretly purchased approximately six acres with 200 feet of waterfront property on Lake Bradford, southwest of Tallahassee, as a recreational area for the students. The administration continued to enlarge the compound, and in time, Camp Flastacowo was established. The lake soon became a favorite destination for students, who enthusiastically made the five-mile hike to participate in cookouts, boating, and swimming.

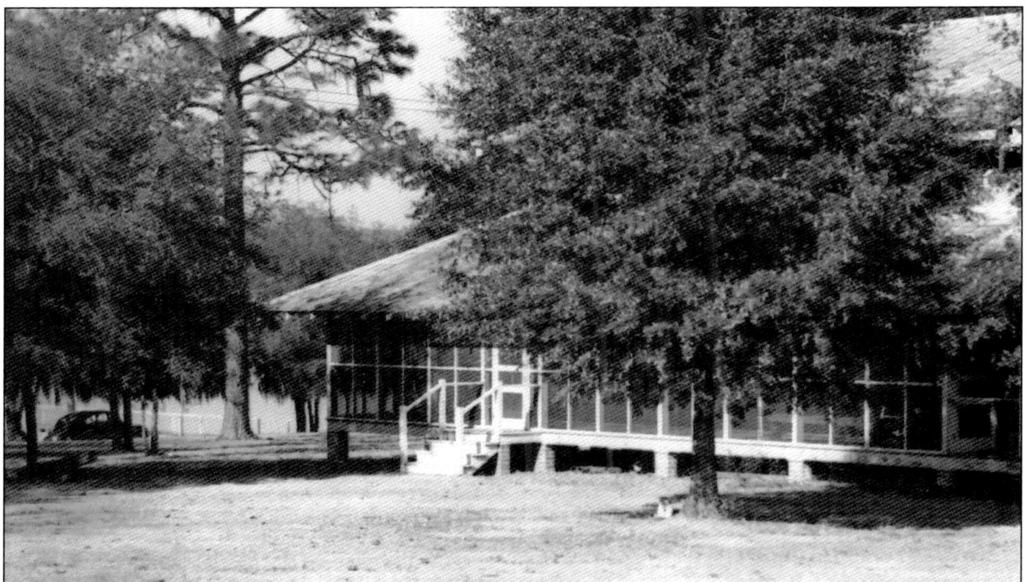

In 1920, the board of control inspected Camp Flastacowo and approved its further development. In 1922, the students organized a camp fund to solicit donations for camp improvements, and the next year, construction began on a camp house, which included sleeping porches and kitchen facilities. The college then constructed a wharf and boathouse and by 1930 had fenced off the area and hired a full-time caretaker.

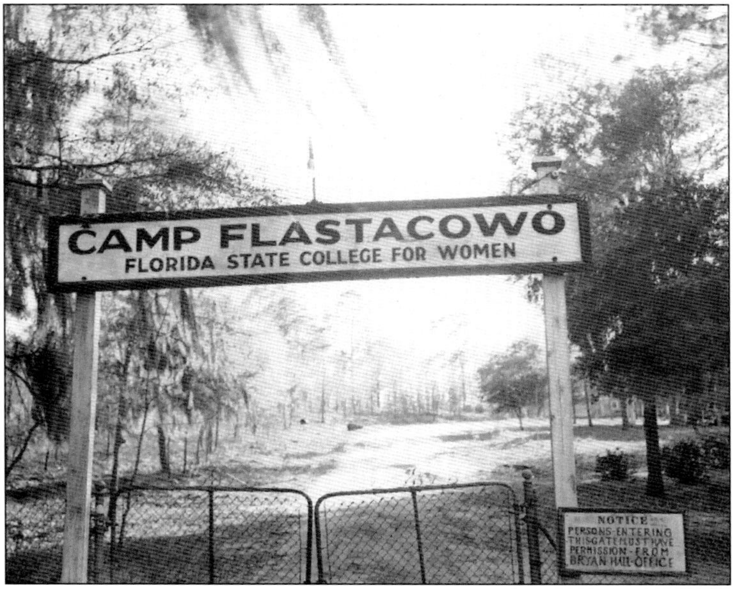

As the Florida State College for Women developed over the years, Camp Flastacowo became an integral part of student life. Pres. Edward Conradi actually used the camp as a major selling point for prospective students. The president believed that, "the college should cultivate this phase of recreation since Florida is known the country over for its unusual facilities in water sports and outdoor life."

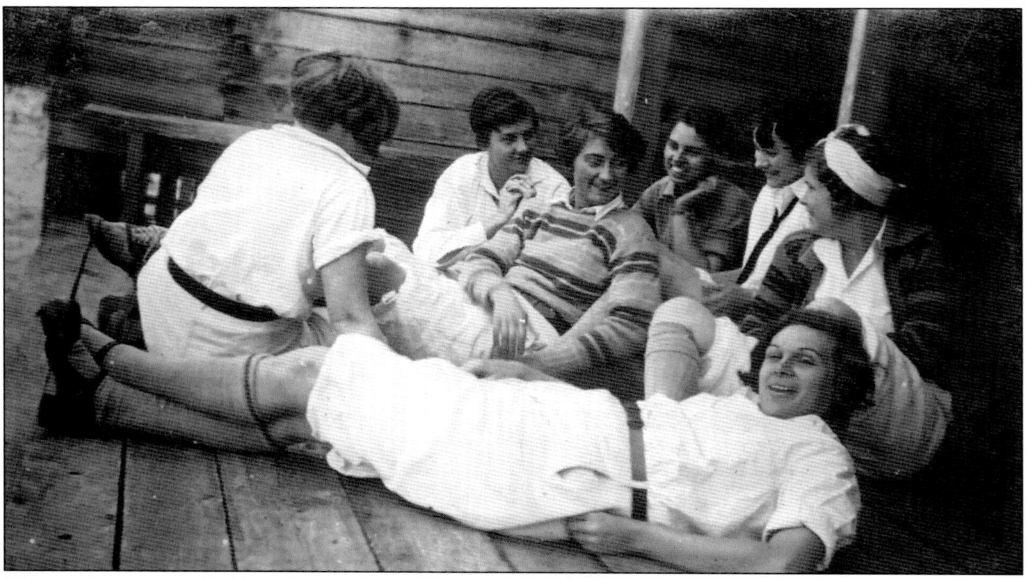

Throughout the 1930s, Camp Flastacowo's popularity as a weekend retreat for students and faculty increased in proportion to the severity of the Depression. By then, three large rustic cabins provided sleeping quarters for students and chaperones. Students slept on cots on sleeping porches, and chaperones, often professors and their wives, slept in individual rooms.

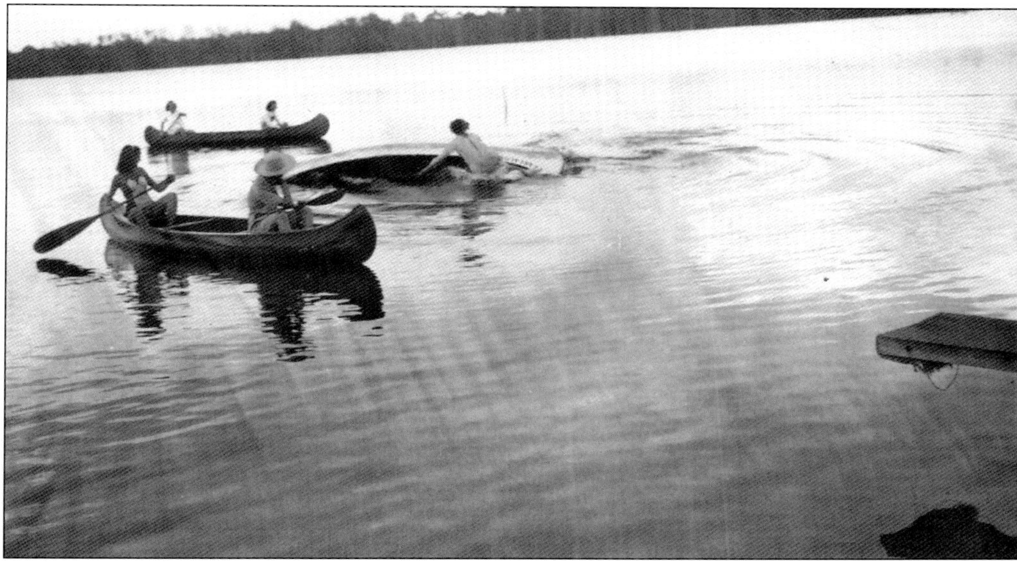

The wooden dock with lifeguard towers facilitated diving and swimming and other recreational water activities at the camp. Canoeing, either in small traditional three- or four-person crafts, or in large "war" canoes that held up to 10, was one of the most popular activities with the Florida State College for Women students. In time, Camp Flastacowo added rowboats, kayaks, and even a rifle range.

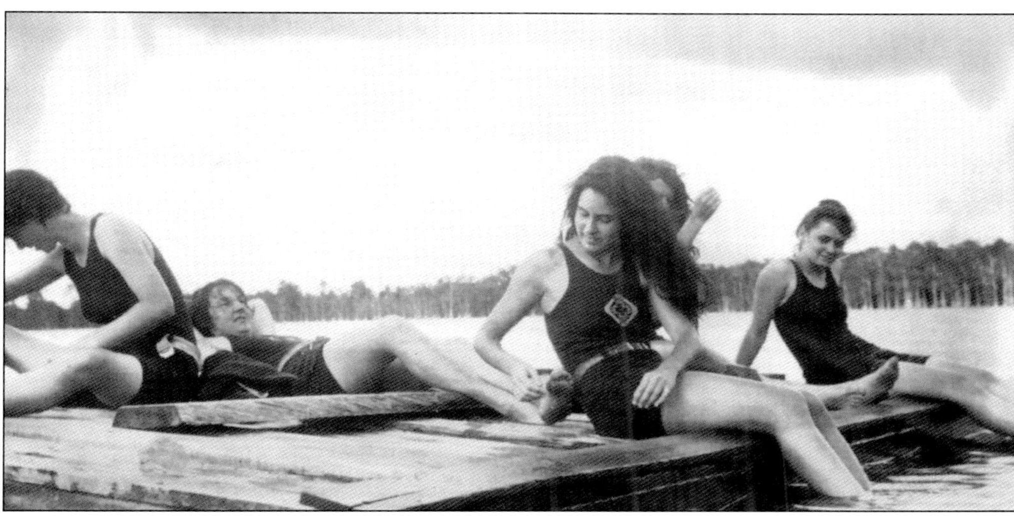

At one time, the Florida State College for Women's Life Saving Corps was said to be the largest college corps in the country. Courses were taught under the direction of American Red Cross lifesaving field representatives. Members of the corps worked towards their Senior Life Saving Certificate and were always on duty to supervise swimmers in the pools and at Camp Flastacowo. (Archives of Florida.)

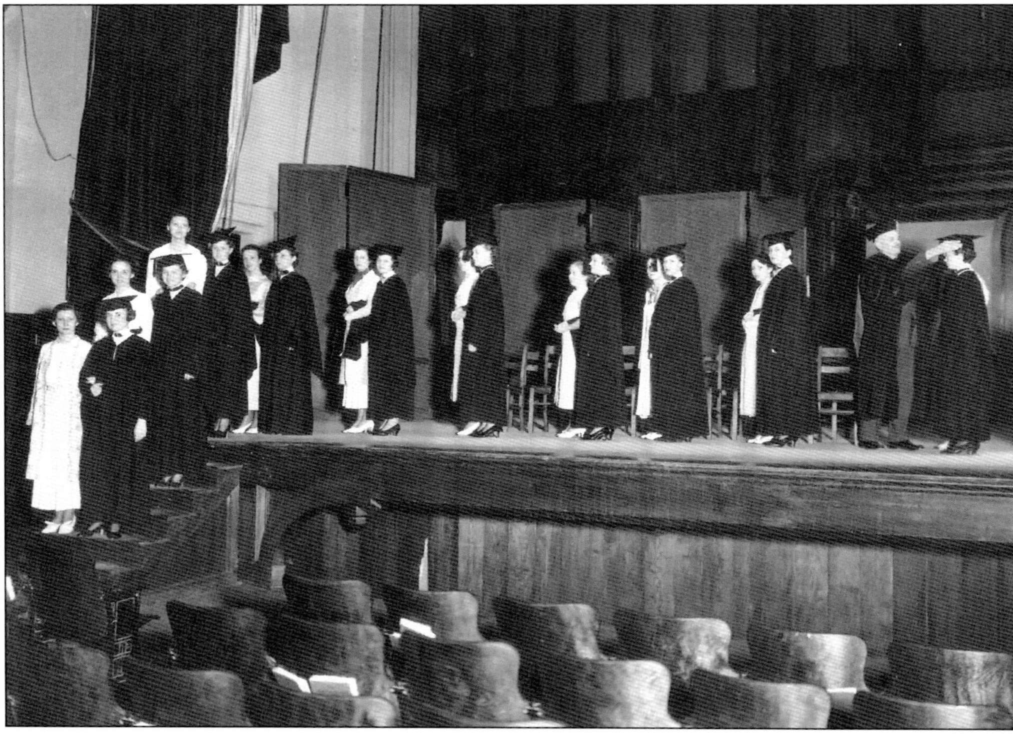

Held in the auditorium, investiture provided an opportunity to build relationships between classes. Dressed in their academic robes, the seniors were called forward and ascended the stage side by side with their sophomore sisters carrying their mortarboards. After the two crossed the stage, the senior knelt (or stood) in front of the president, and the sophomore handed the president the cap, which was placed on the senior's head.

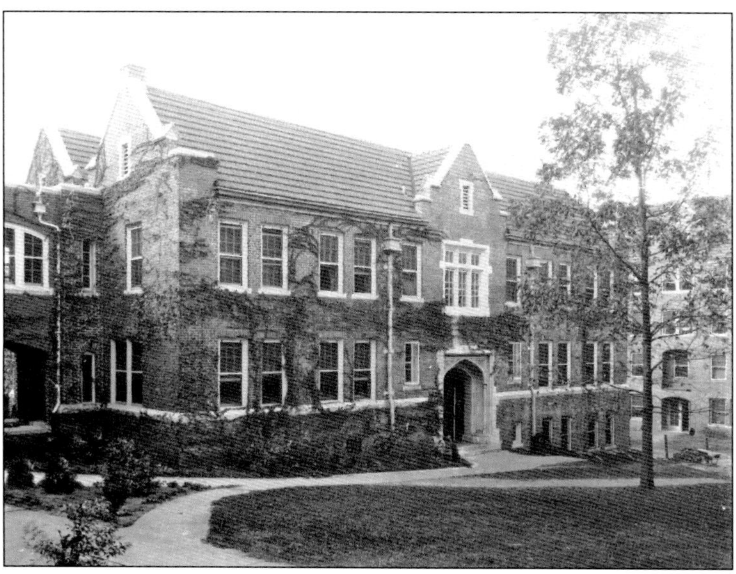

In September 1921, the college completed construction of its first freestanding infirmary, located north of the Reynolds Hall west wing behind Jennie Murphree Hall. The new building included a modern operating room with an adjoining two-bed recovery room, as well as two sleeping porches with 24 beds. In this 1929 photograph, the west wing of Jennie Murphree Hall can be seen on the right.

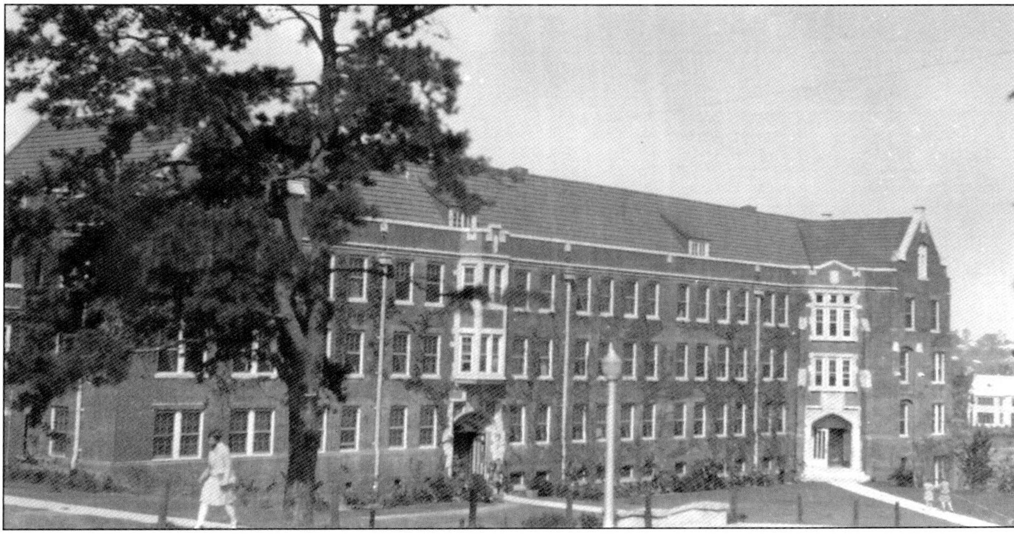

In 1921, the legislature authorized the construction of a dormitory to replace East Hall, which had been destroyed by fire the previous year. Located just beyond Reynolds Hall, the first part of the *L*-shaped, three-story, redbrick building was completed in May 1922. The west wing was added in 1924, and the attic space was converted into living quarters in 1926. The building was named Jennie Murphree Hall, after the wife of former president Albert A. Murphree, who had graduated from Florida State College and had died the year before this structure was complete.

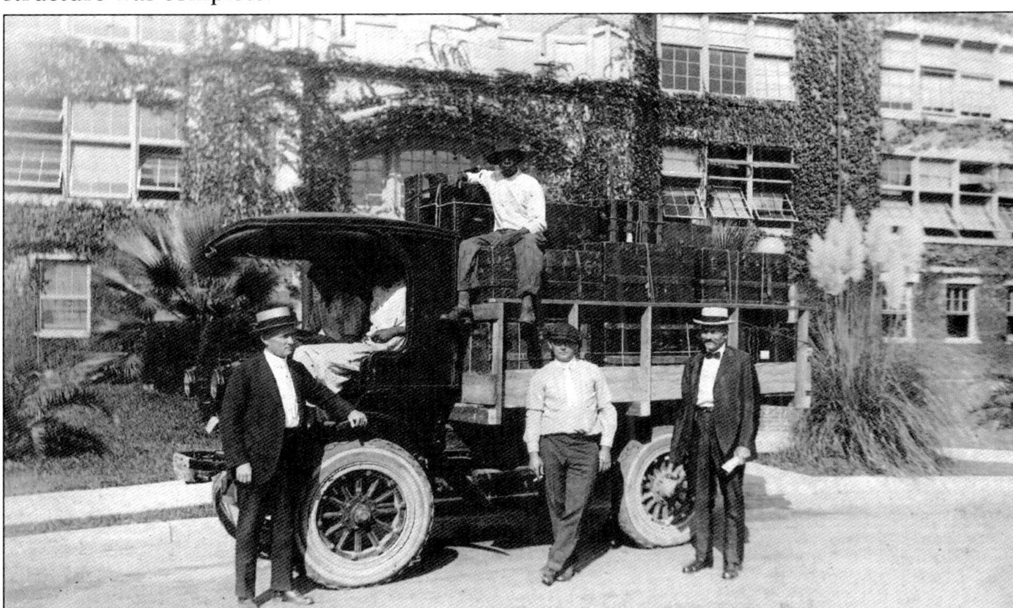

In the early years, nearly all Florida State College for Women students journeyed to and from Tallahassee by train. Regardless of the time of day or night, one or more of the men on the faculty met students at the station. In the photograph above, business manager John G. Kellum stands to the far left, and Pres. Albert A. Murphree stands to the far right of a truck laden with luggage.

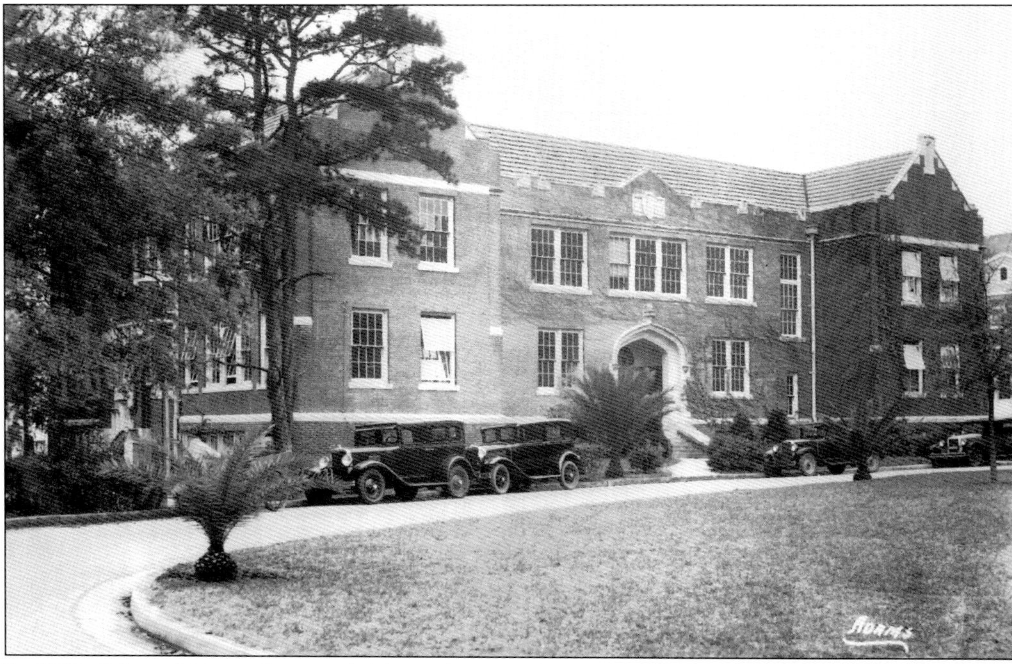

In 1920, Edward Conradi again lobbied the state for more classrooms and laboratory facilities. The next year, the legislature approved the funding, and construction began on the former site of East Hall. When the facility was completed in 1923, the chemistry and home economics and extensions departments moved in. The new Science Hall complemented the Education Building and was located on the site of what is now the Diffenbaugh Building.

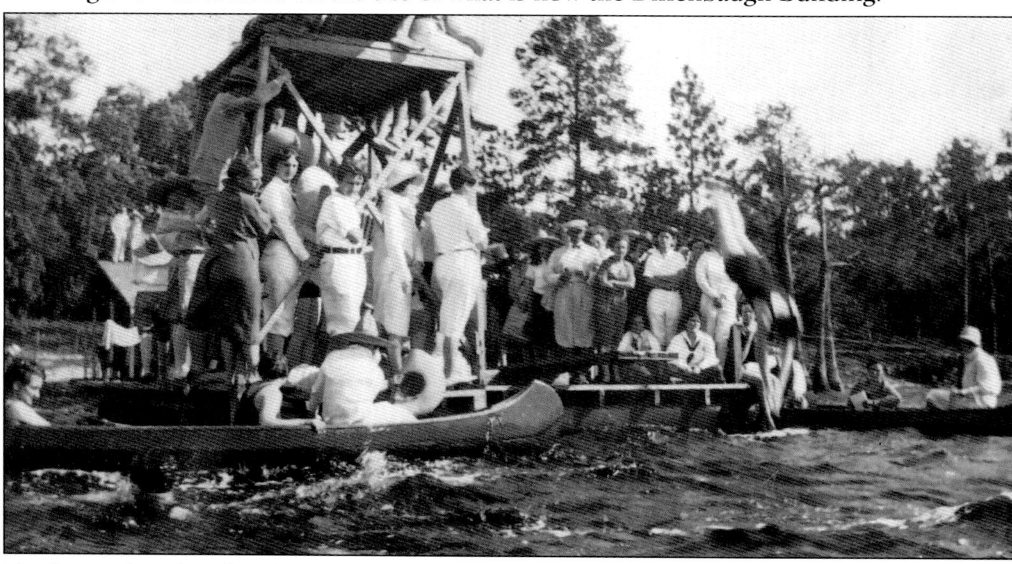

Not long after the Florida State College for Women acquired recreational property at Lake Bradford, the college held its first annual Water Sports Day on May 13, 1918. The competition had three categories: diving, swimming, and Odd and Even team sports. By the early 1930s, organized swimming competitions and activities moved to the indoor swimming pool in the new Physical Education Building. The photograph above is from the 1926 competitions.

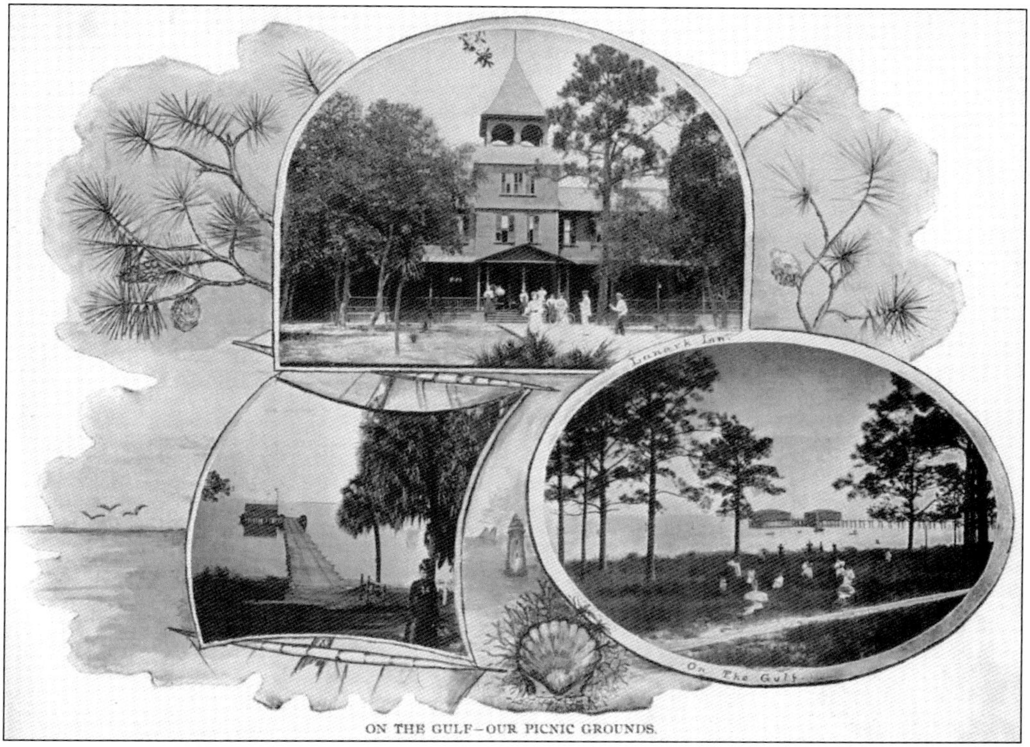

Students at West Florida Seminary, Florida State College, Florida Female College, and Florida State College for Women led active lifestyles, and because of their proximity to the water, whether rivers, lakes or the Gulf of Mexico, they took advantage of these nearby resources for recreation and relaxation. The image above is from the West Florida Seminary 1901 yearbook, the *Argo*.

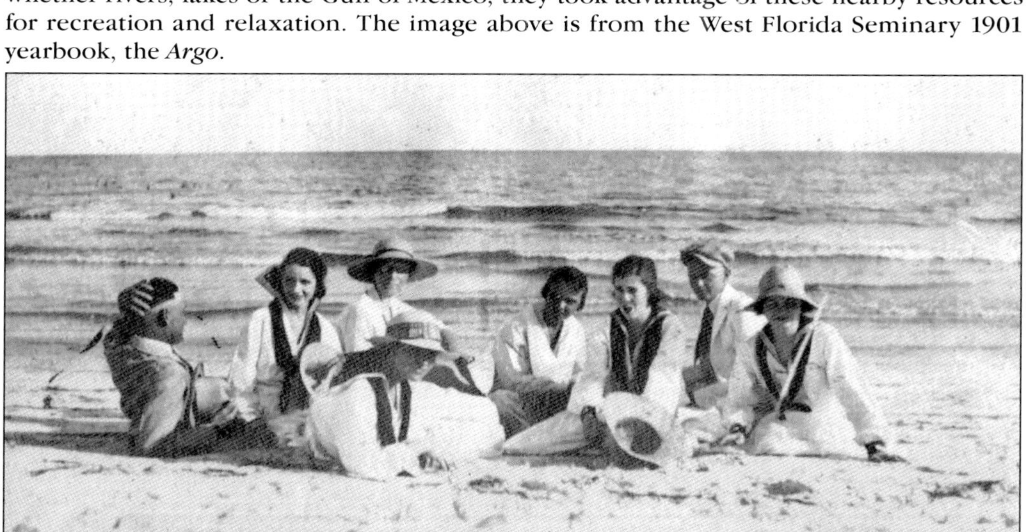

Florida State College for Women student Lucile Luttrell (class of 1920) was involved in numerous social activities with her Kappa Delta sorority sisters. The photograph above is from a June 1919 "house party" at the coastal resort known as Lanark on the Gulf of Mexico. On this occasion, they ventured across the bay to Dog Island, where this photograph was taken.

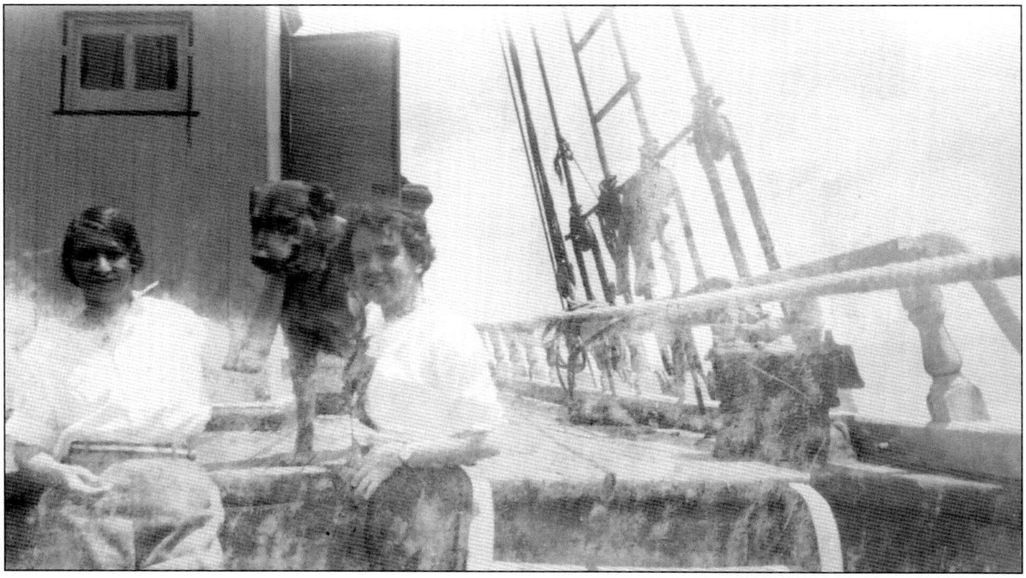

On their excursion to a house party at Lanark Bay during Easter 1926, Florida State College for Women student Carolyn Doyle (class of 1926) and her friends came upon the *Anna M. Hudson*, a ship that had been blown ashore during a storm. Doyle and her friends appear to have befriended Captain Cooper and his crew, who held a birthday dance on the open deck of the ship.

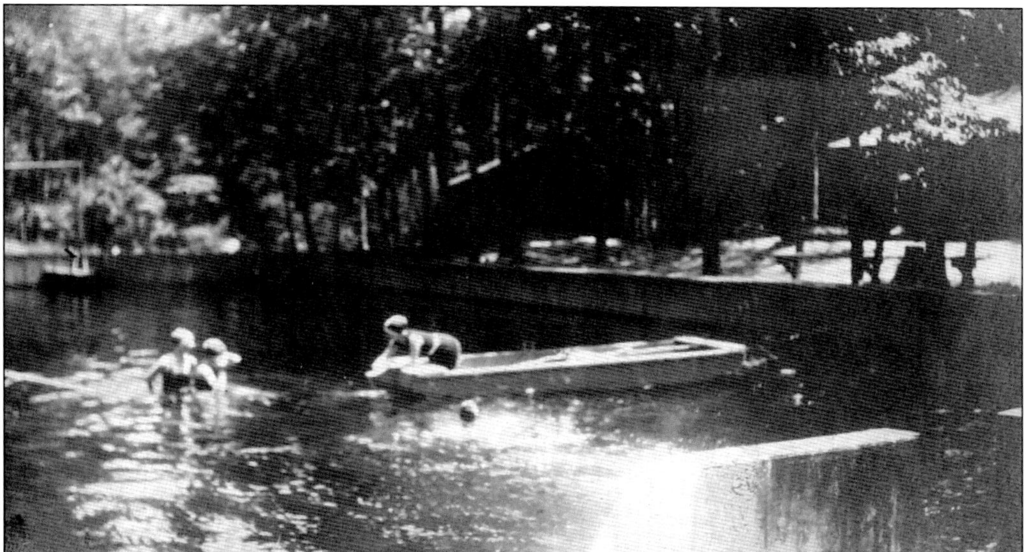

Another popular site for Florida State College for Women students' water recreation was the natural springs and swimming pool south of campus at Newport, on the St. Marks River in Wakulla County. This photograph is from another Kappa Delta sorority house party at Newport in May 1920.

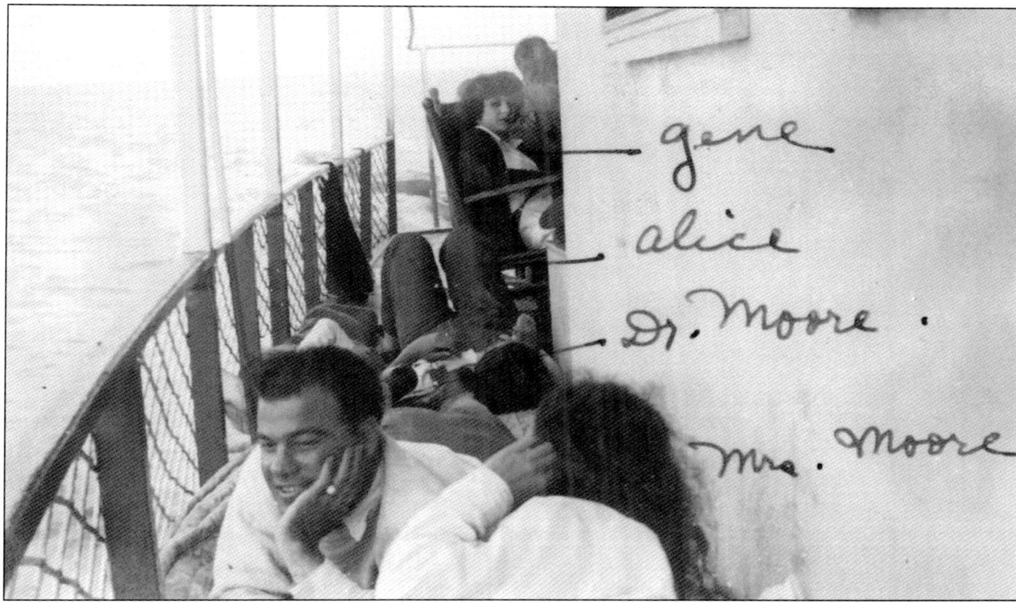

On one occasion around 1928–1929, Florida State College for Women student Helen Smoyer (class of 1930) journeyed to the Gulf of Mexico with the faculty and her classmates for what she labeled their "Famous Week-end Boat Trip." In her photographs, she identifies many of the guests. In the photograph above, "On the big boat" are sociology professor Coyle E. Moore, his wife, and some of Smoyer's classmates. In addition to Moore and his wife, identified in the photograph below are botany professor Herman Kurz, botany and bacteriology professor Alban Stewart, and others. According to Smoyer's annotations, the smaller boats were pulled out into the open waters where they drifted and fished.

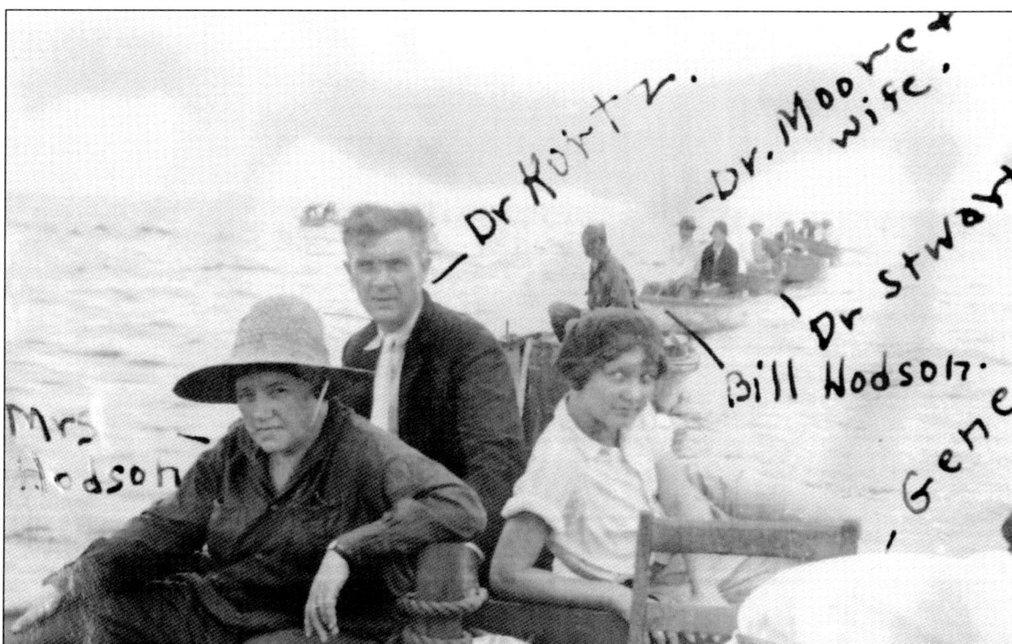

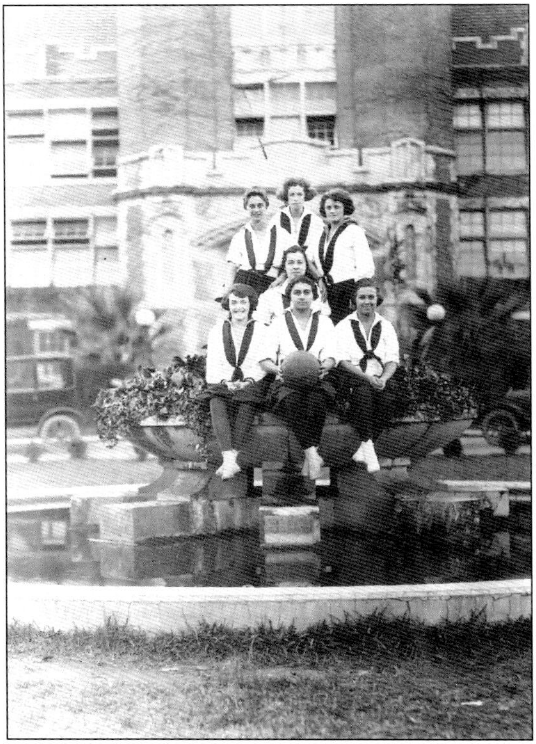

Two of the most iconic images in Florida State University history are from the 1922 *Flastacowo* yearbook and depict the Odd and Even basketball teams. The photograph at left is of the Odd team on the Administration Fountain, which had been a gift of the Florida State College for Women classes of 1915 and 1917. Pictured, in no particular order, are Annie Bruce (class of 1923), Mariam Olsen, Gladys Vaughn (class of 1925), Elizabeth Ray (class of 1926), Ruth Whittier, Ida Merriwether (class of 1923), and Lucille Reese (class of 1925).

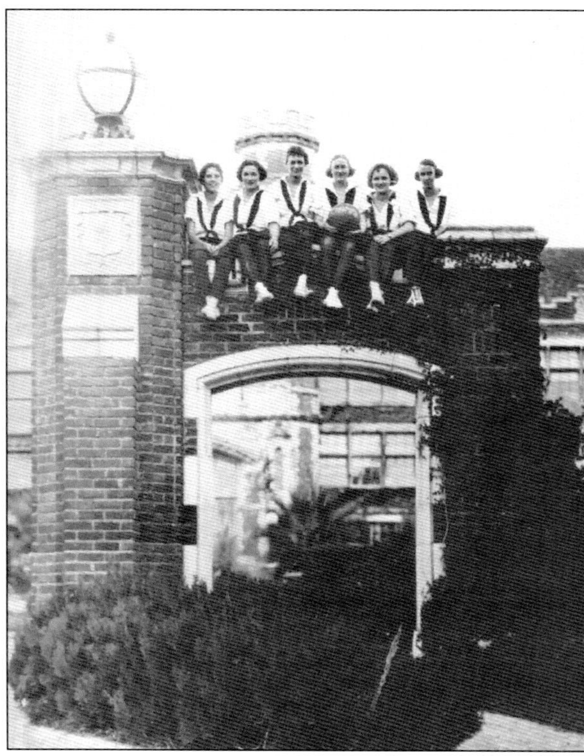

The companion photograph depicts the 1922 Even basketball team on the main gates, a gift of the Florida State College for Women classes of 1916 and 1918. As indicated by the basketball, the Even team was the 1922 basketball champions. Pictured, in no particular order, are senior class president Helen Harris (class of 1922), Ethel Henry (class of 1924), Ina Simmons (class of 1924), Elizabeth Robinson (class of 1922), Ella Williams (class of 1924), and Elsie Jones (class of 1924).

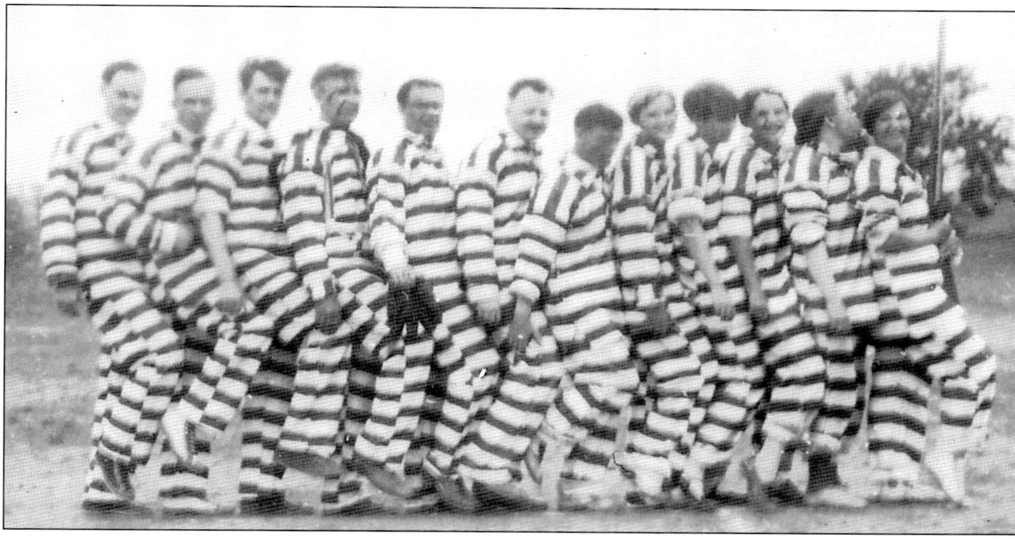

The Florida State College for Women faculty-senior baseball game was an annual event "long looked forward to by the seniors, who take what revenge they can for long-term papers, tests and other nuisances." The game was also an opportunity for faculty members to let their hair down, and it was not uncommon for the faculty to dress up in outrageous costumes. In 1929 and possibly throughout the late 1920s, the faculty chose to dress in convict uniforms. According to one source, the faculty marched out in lockstep to the baseball diamond, followed by the "guard," J.G. Kellum, "with a gun across his shoulder." According to the student newspaper, "Many of the faculty looked at home in their stripes. It was hard to visualize them in any other garb."

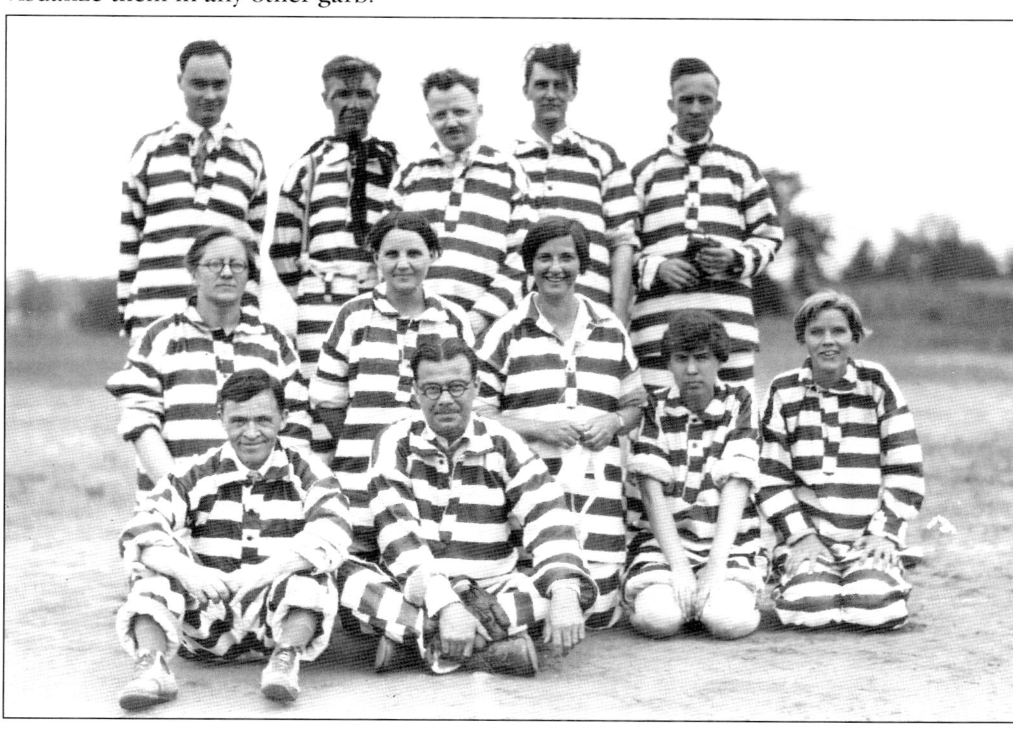

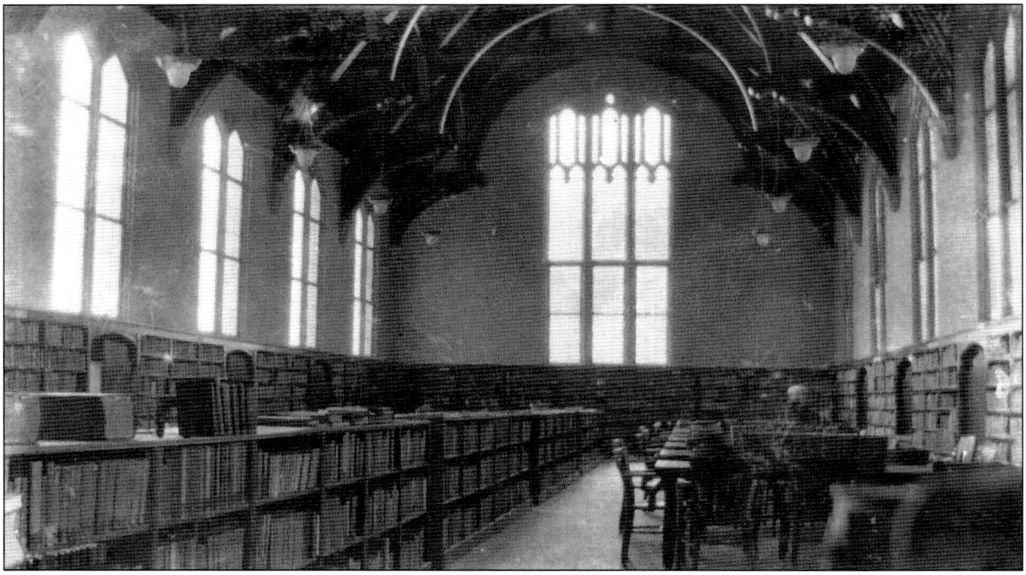

In 1923, the legislature approved funding for a freestanding library to replace the crowded space used as a library in the Administration Building. The building, a two-story, single wing structure located south of Bryan Hall and west of the Science Building, housed a reading room and a few smaller side rooms used for classrooms.

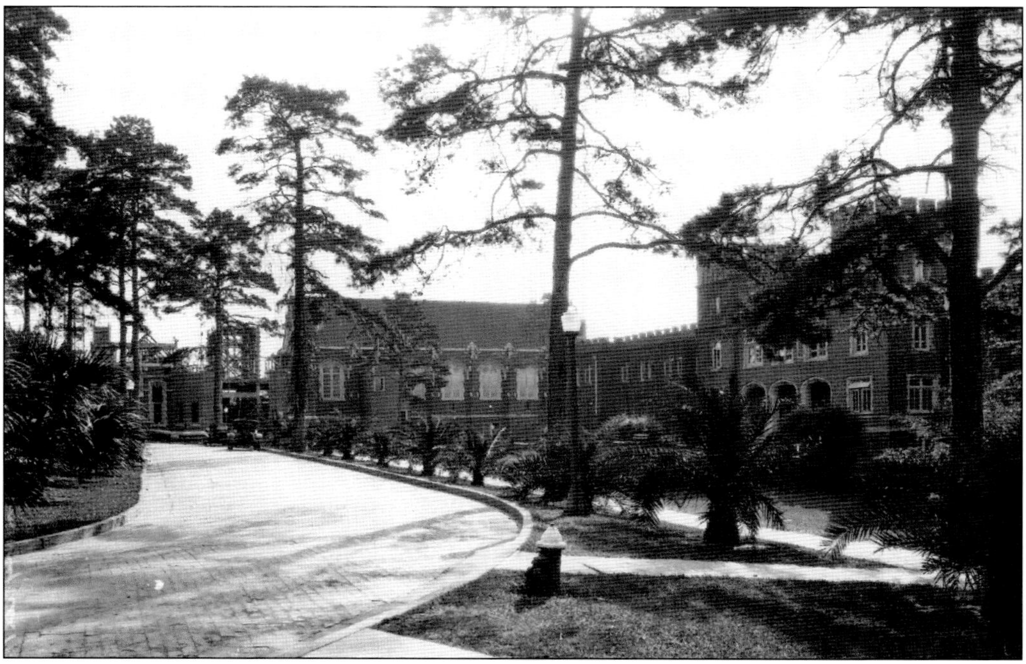

The collection of 25,500 volumes, 250 magazines, assorted newspapers, and journals combined with the students filling all available seats meant the new library was outgrown almost before it opened. Edward Conradi quickly requested the construction of a central entrance and east wing to alleviate the overcrowding. The 1929 additions can be seen under construction in the photograph above.

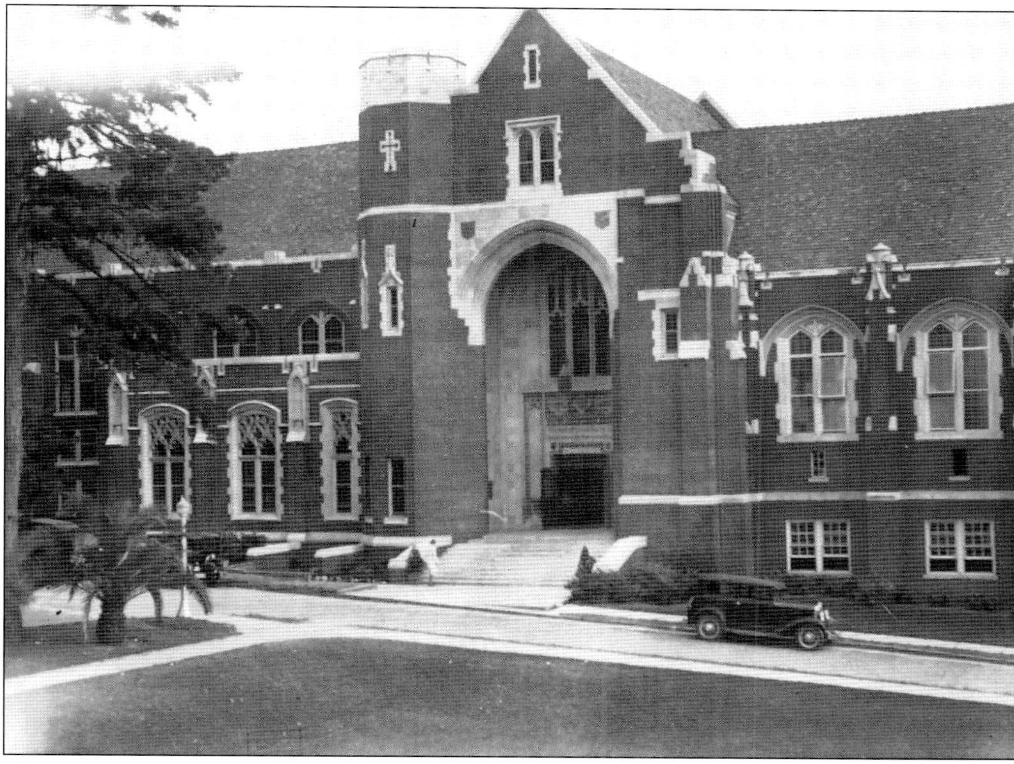

The new additions complimented the existing section and entailed the most elaborate exterior architectural elements and ornamentation of any building on campus. When completed, the library could accommodate 130,000 volumes and offered meeting rooms, seminar rooms, offices and work rooms for library-related activities, such as technical services and shipping and receiving. The structure utilizes pier buttresses, stone tracery, and paired lancet windows beneath pointed arches.

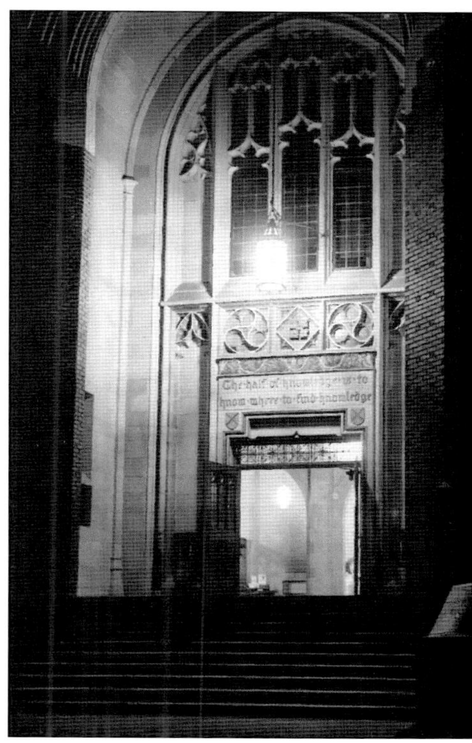

Within the Gothic archway above the recessed door is displayed the anonymous maxim, "The half of knowledge is to know where to find knowledge," in gold leaf. In 1956, the library moved to a new building on Landis Green, and in 1961, the old library was renamed Dodd Hall in honor of the former dean of arts and sciences William G. Dodd.

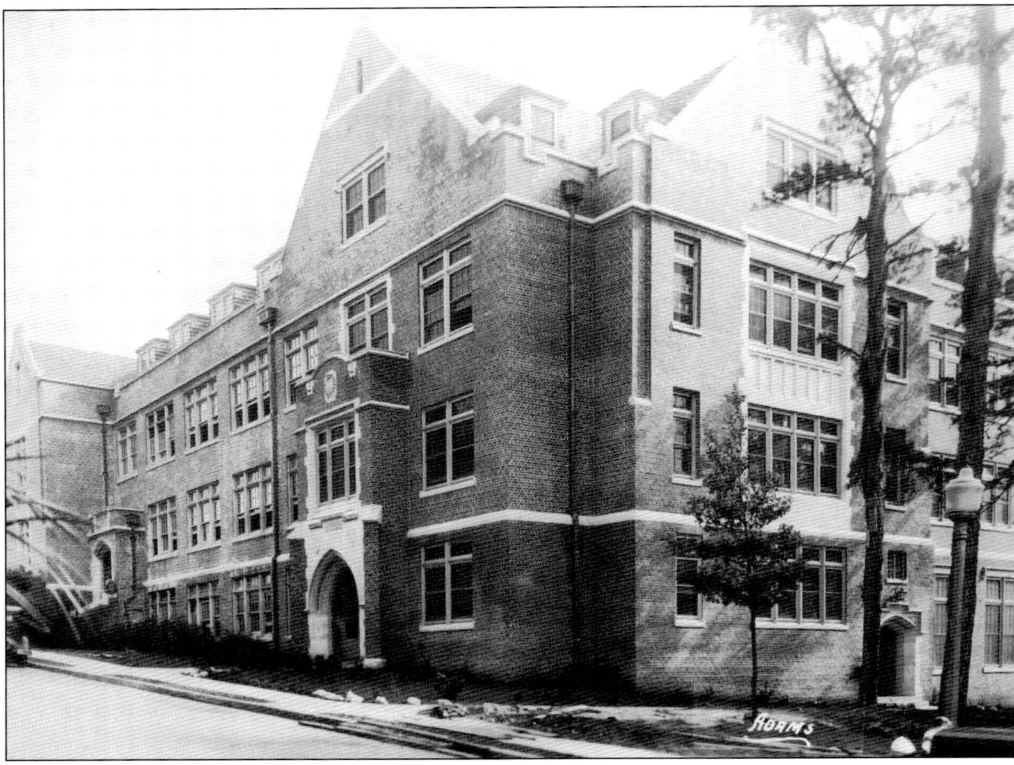

In 1927, a third classroom building was constructed to house the home economics and commerce departments. The new structure was on the south side of the Administration Building, between Science Hall and the new library. Officially named the Social Sciences Hall, it was more commonly referred to as the History Building. In 1931, it was expanded and in 1963, it was renamed the Williams Building, after history professor Arthur "Pi" Williams.

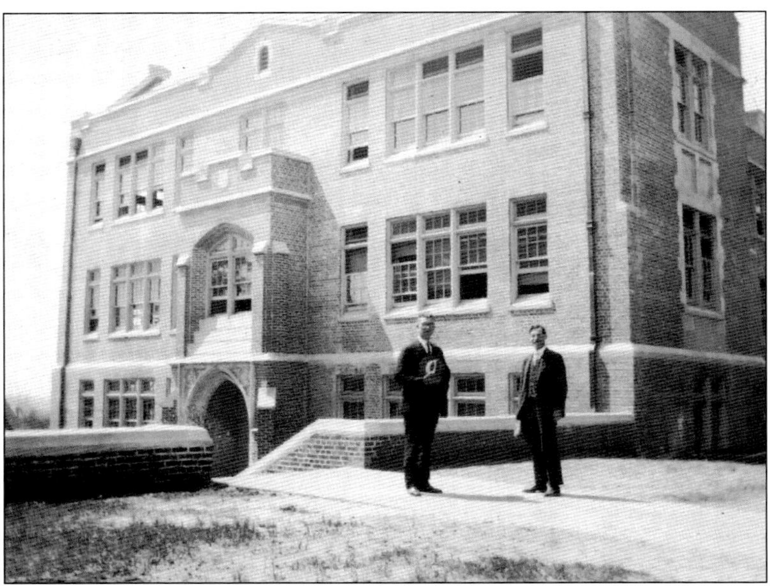

Florida State College for Women botany professor Herman Kurz and famed botanist and environmentalist Roland Harper stand outside the History Building. Harper did much of his research in Florida, and he and Kurz collaborated on papers. The third floor of the building had an experimental greenhouse for the botany department.

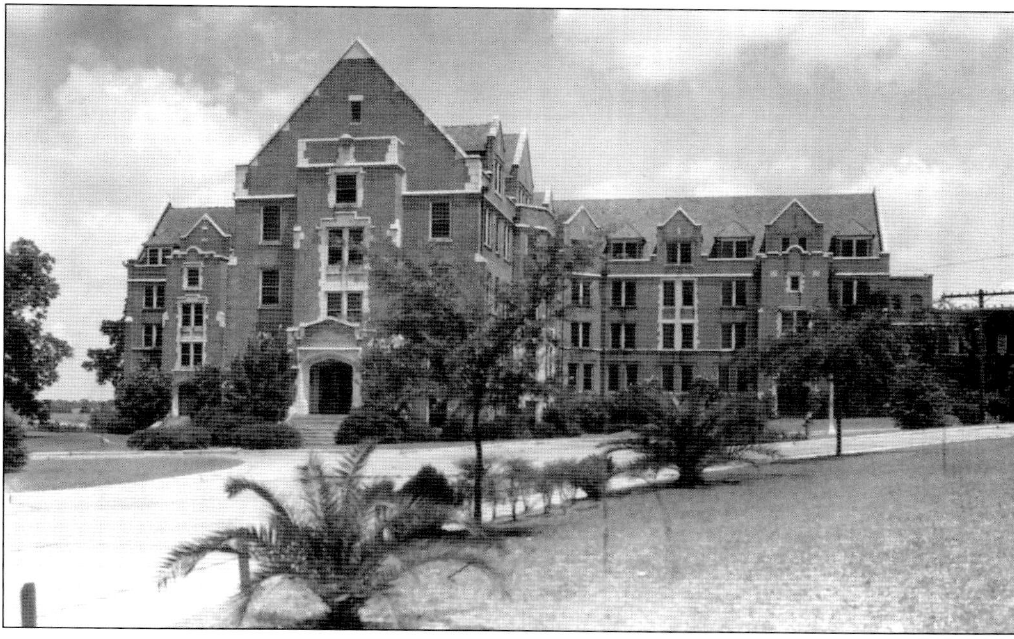

In 1925, Florida State College for Women received funding for the construction of a *T*-shaped, three-story dormitory to be located to the west of Broward Hall. Built in two sections, it was ultimately completed in 1928. Each room in Gilchrist Hall had two lights, electrical outlets, and extra-long beds. Residents had access to four small parlors and one large living room for entertaining.

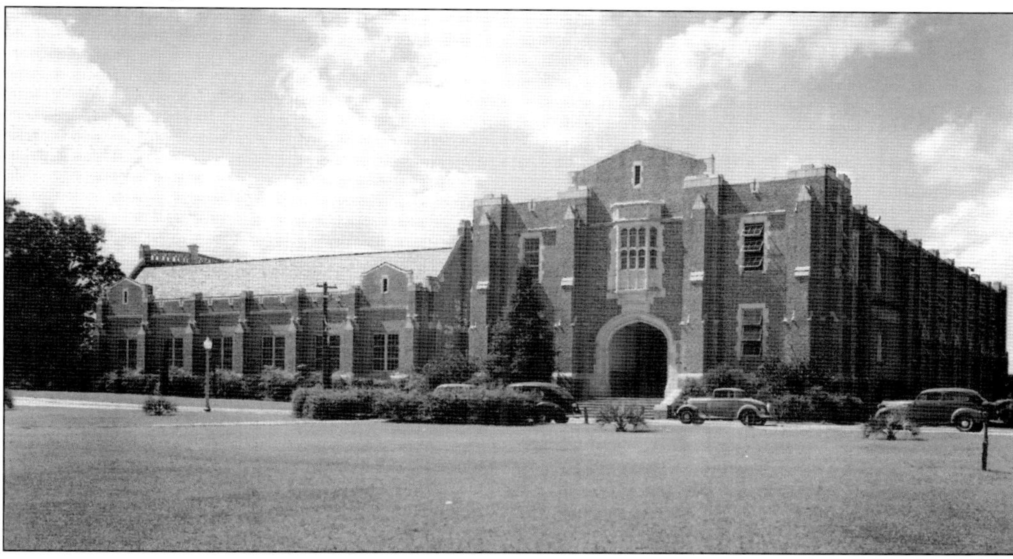

To accompany Florida State College for Women's well-appointed athletic field, tennis courts, basketball courts, and track, President Conradi believed that the school needed a dedicated indoor athletic facility. In 1929, the new Physical Education Building opened on the far western edge of campus as the largest and most state-of-the-art college structure to that point. The *T*-shaped building was constructed in three stages, beginning with the west and south wings, as seen above.

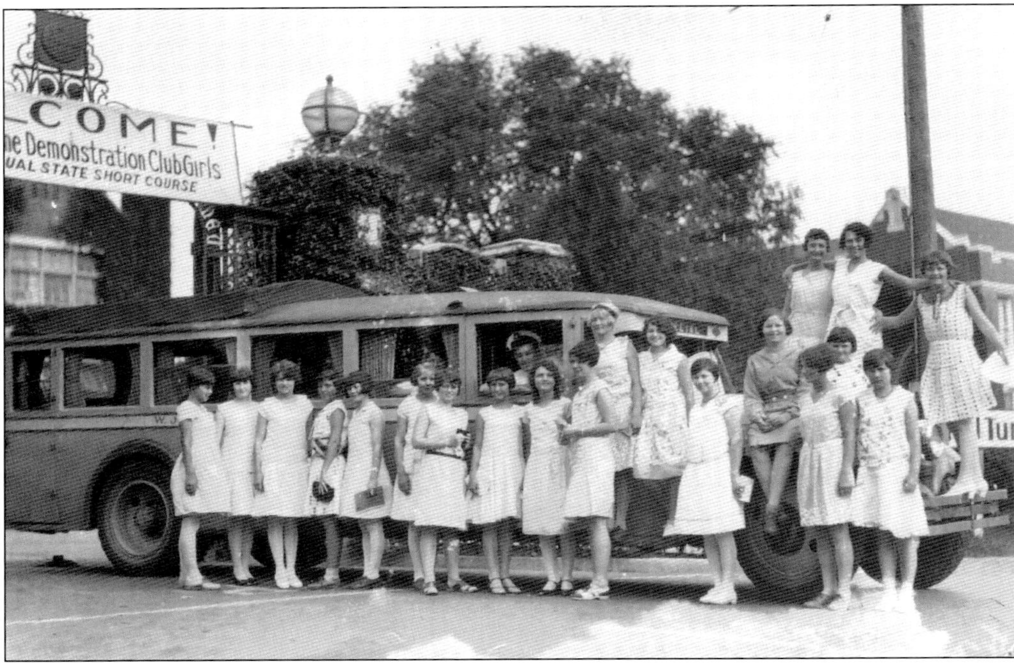

Beginning in the 1910s, "tomato clubs" (or "canning clubs") were established in public schools throughout Florida. These clubs, the first 4-H programs in Florida specifically for girls, taught about the cultivation and canning of produce and were overseen by the Florida State College for Women as part of the mission of FSCW's School of Home Economics. FSCW's extension program included four major activities: free, two-week, on-campus short courses for women over 16 years old; publications of bulletins devoted to domestic practices; annual training conferences for county home-demonstration agents; and club work. The photograph above from around 1930 is of a group of young women at FSCW for a 4-H short course and includes 17-year-old Florence Smock (near the telephone pole, middle), from Eustis, Florida, who was selected the nation's healthiest girl by the US Department of Agriculture. The photograph below, probably from a few years later, is of a stepping-stone demonstration at a short course. (Archives of Florida.)

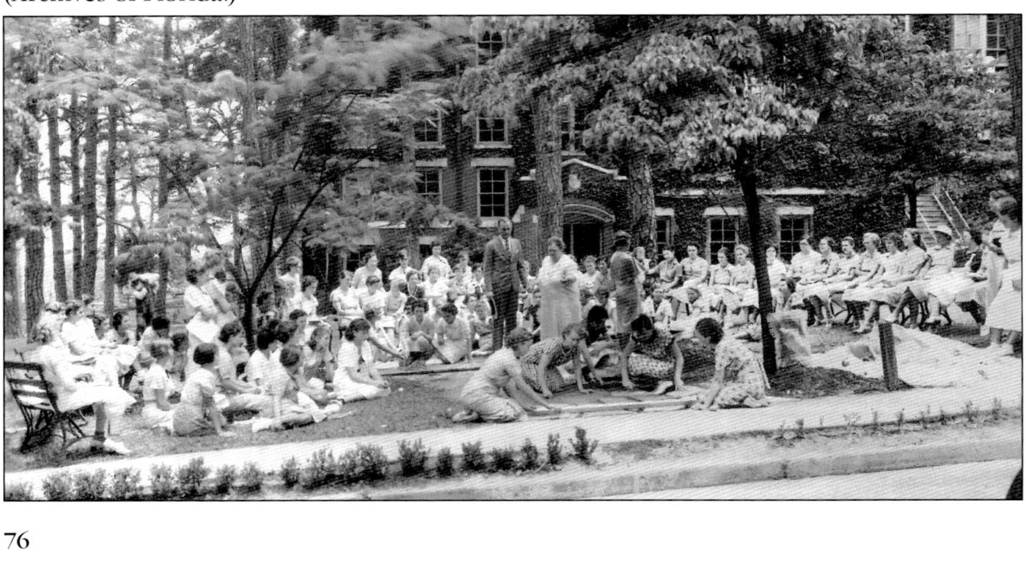

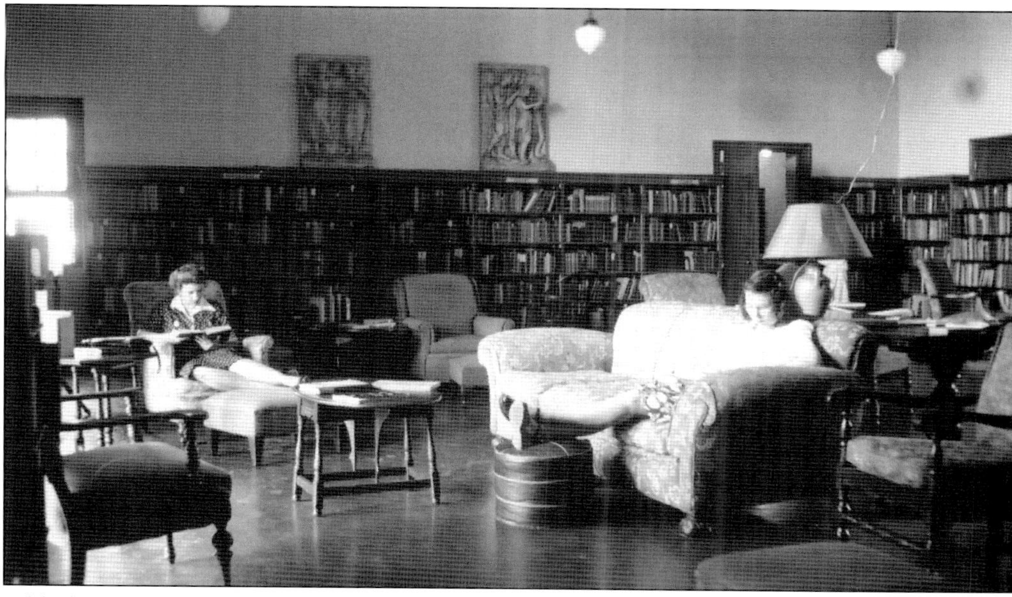

Added to the new library building in 1931, the Browsing Room was intended as a room for recreational reading in a pleasant, "home-like atmosphere" where one could browse titles of a less academic nature. No textbooks were permitted, and if a notebook was brought into the room, it was to be left at the desk near the door.

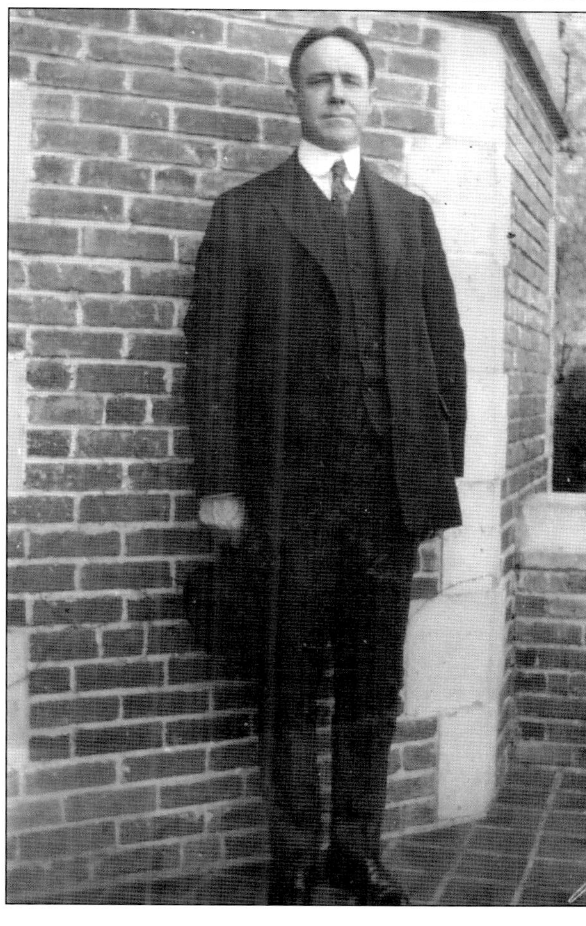

William G. Dodd joined the faculty at Florida State College for Women as head of the English department in 1910 and was made dean of arts and sciences in 1913. By the mid-1930s, Pres. Edward Conradi was relying heavily on Dodd, described as "prime minister of the deans," to maintain the college's academic direction. Dodd continued to provide invaluable service to the college until his retirement in 1944.

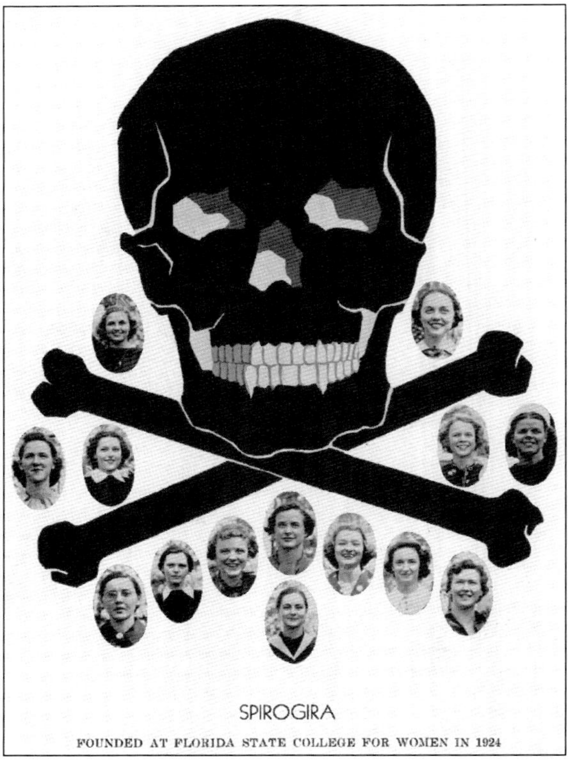

Spirogira, the Odd team's honorary society, was founded on October 24, 1924, and its members were chosen for their outstanding leadership, loyalty, and devotion to service. The name *Spirogira* came from a genus of algae. The skull and crossbones was selected for the society's emblem, and black and white for their colors. On certain days, members wore their tiny gold skull and crossbones pins on black blouses with white skirts. On December 14, 1930, the Evens created their own honorary organization called Esteren, for "the perpetuation of Even traditions, class loyalty, and friendship." Its colors were green and white, and its symbol was a large cauldron over an outdoor fire. Both groups enjoyed the support of the college faculty. After the college transitioned to coeducational in 1947, the new university honor society Garnet Key considered Spirogira and Esteren members its alumnae.

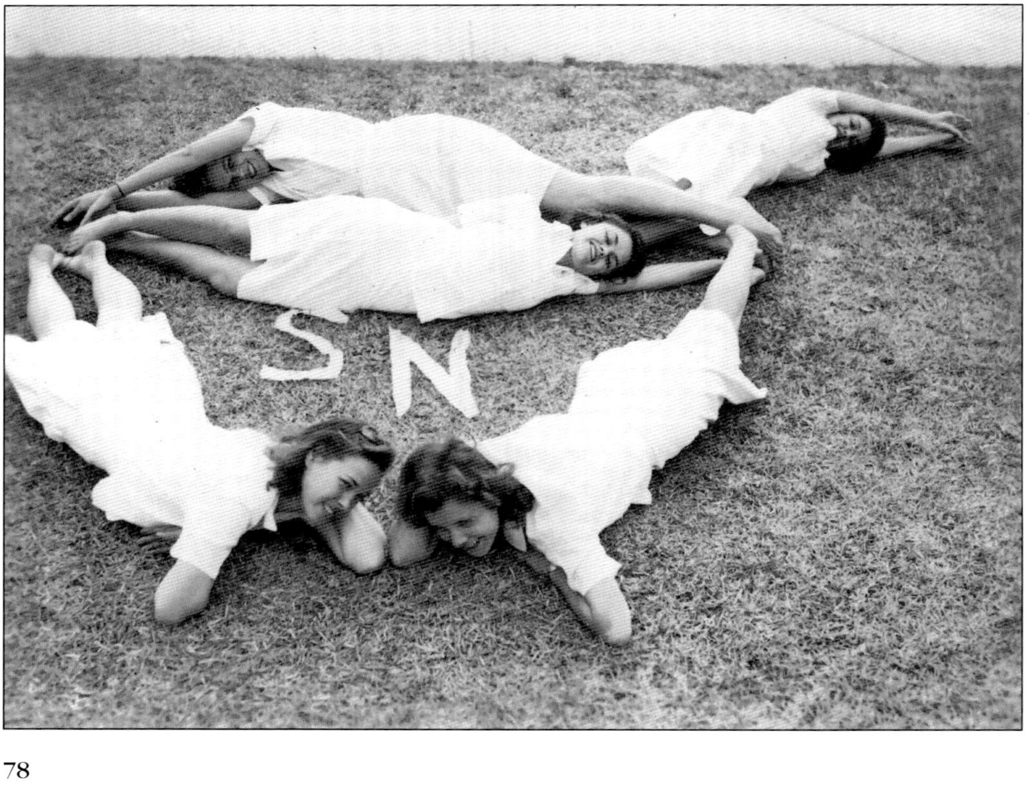

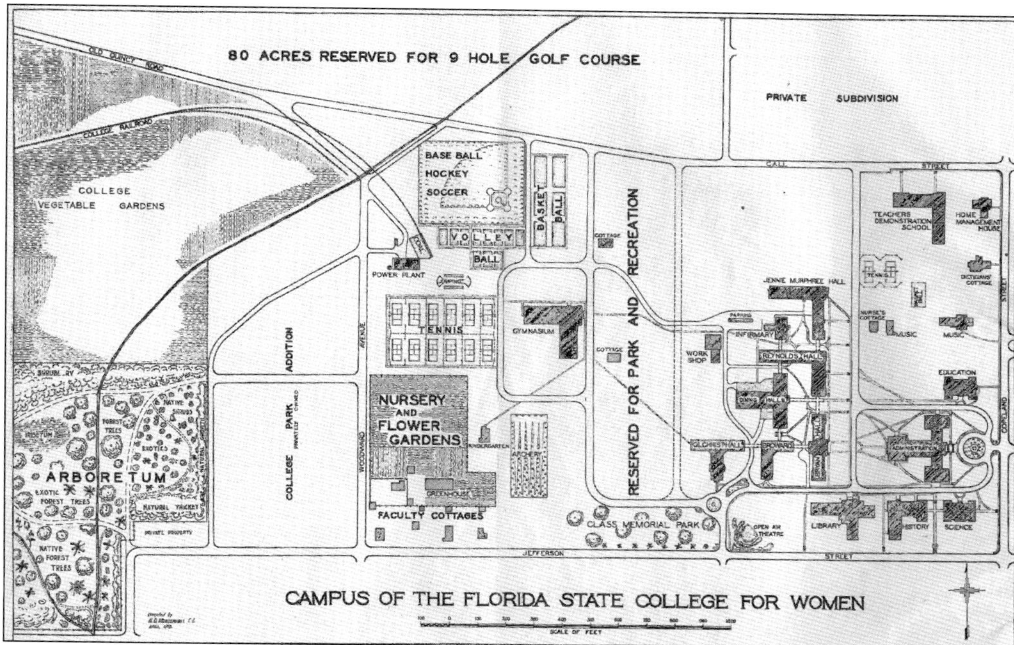

This 1932 Florida State College for Women Campus Map was created by college engineer H.D. Mendenhall and was included in the College Catalog until the mid-1930s. The map shows the westward development of the campus, along with the college vegetable gardens, arboretum, and nursery and flower gardens. The area noted as "Reserved for Park and Recreation" would become Landis Green.

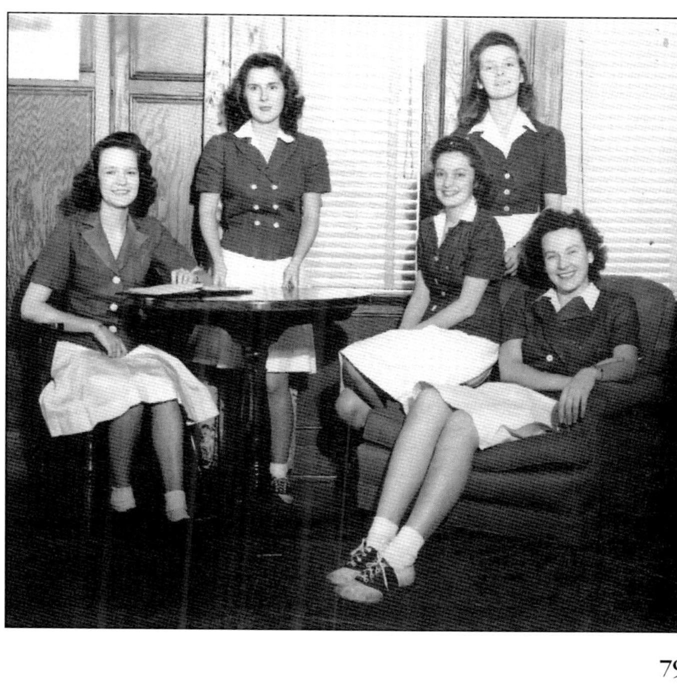

In the spring of 1936, the Freshman Commission and the Freshman Cabinet were merged to create the Sophomore Council. Dressed in their white skirts, blue jackets, and blue-and-white beanies, the Sophomore Council members were the Florida State College for Women incoming freshmen's best friends. They helped the bewildered newcomers move into their dormitory rooms, assisted them with registration during Orientation Week, and serenaded them after light flash (or lights out).

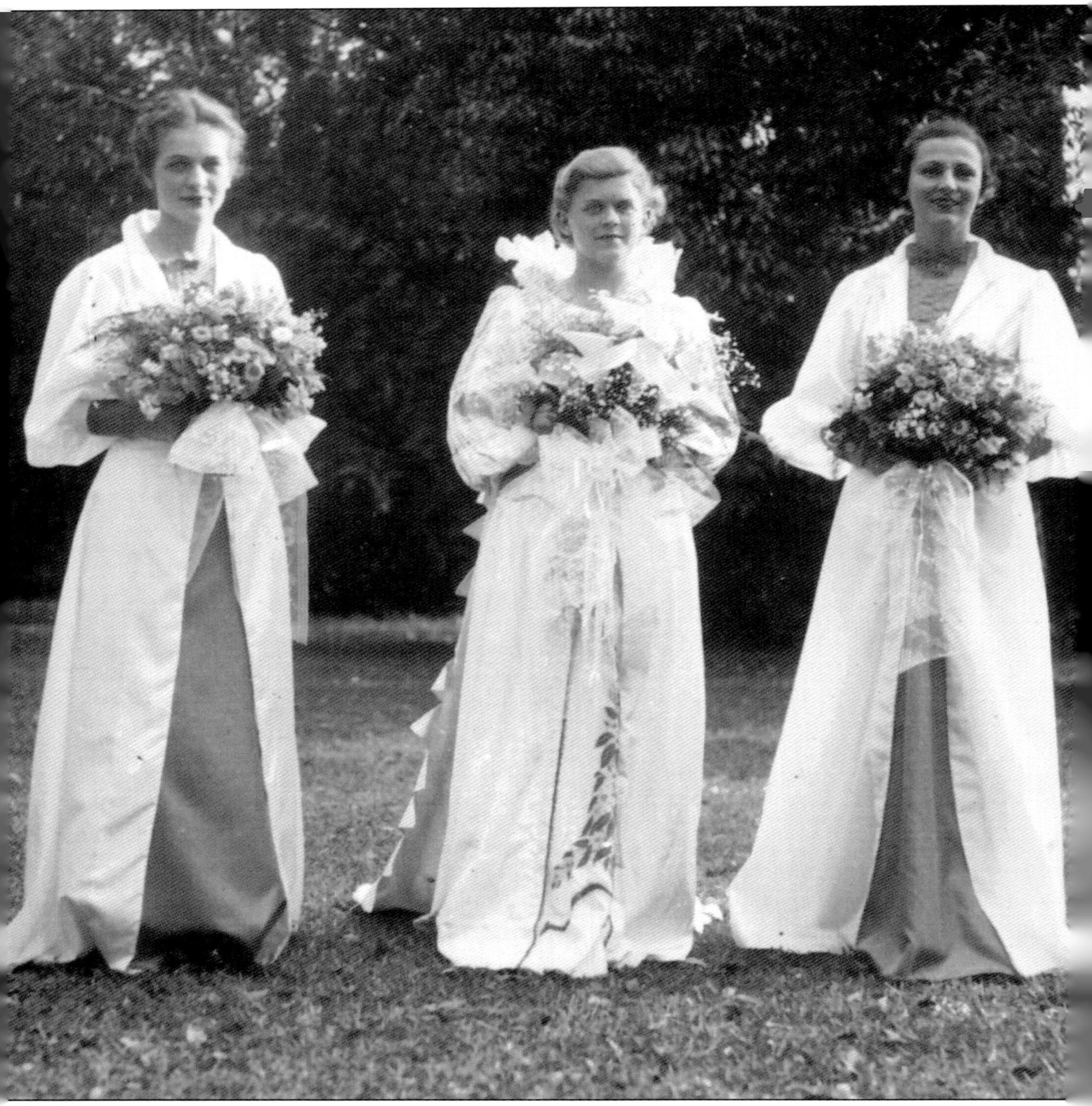

Katherine "Kitty" Blood Hoffman's (class of 1936) relationship with FSU stretches from the Great Depression to the 21st century. Her tuition was paid with oranges from her father's grove. Hoffman was an honor student, athlete, and leader. Earning advanced degrees, she returned to FSCW in 1940 as a chemistry teacher. Retiring in 1984, her extraordinary service continued. In awarding her an honorary degree in 2007, Pres. T.K. Wetherell noted, "Beginning as a student, Kitty Hoffman became a tireless alumna and, for more than four decades, a distinguished faculty member and administrator. We all owe so much to this award-winning academician and teacher, gracious colleague and beloved mentor who has made countless contributions to our university's great heritage." In the May 2, 1936, photograph above, May Queen Katherine Blood is accompanied by her maids of honor, Minna Dunn (class of 1936) on the left and Betty Manning (class of 1936) on the right.

With WPA funding, Florida State College for Women began construction of the much-needed new dormitory Landis Hall. The five-story, *U*-shaped structure, which opened in 1939, included elevators and intercom telephones in each room, as well as a men's cloakroom and guest sleeping quarters suitable for male guests. On the top floor, in addition to a lounge and club room, was a sundeck where the girls sunbathed in little or no clothing, which pilots at Dale Mabry Air Field quickly discovered. (Archives of Florida.)

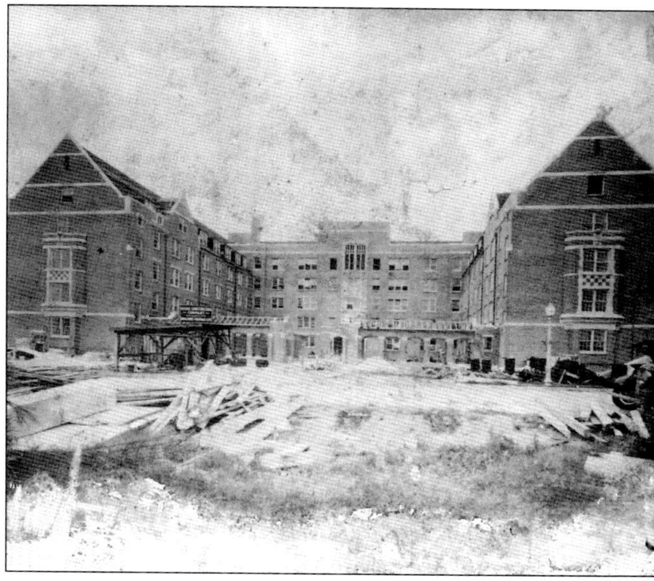

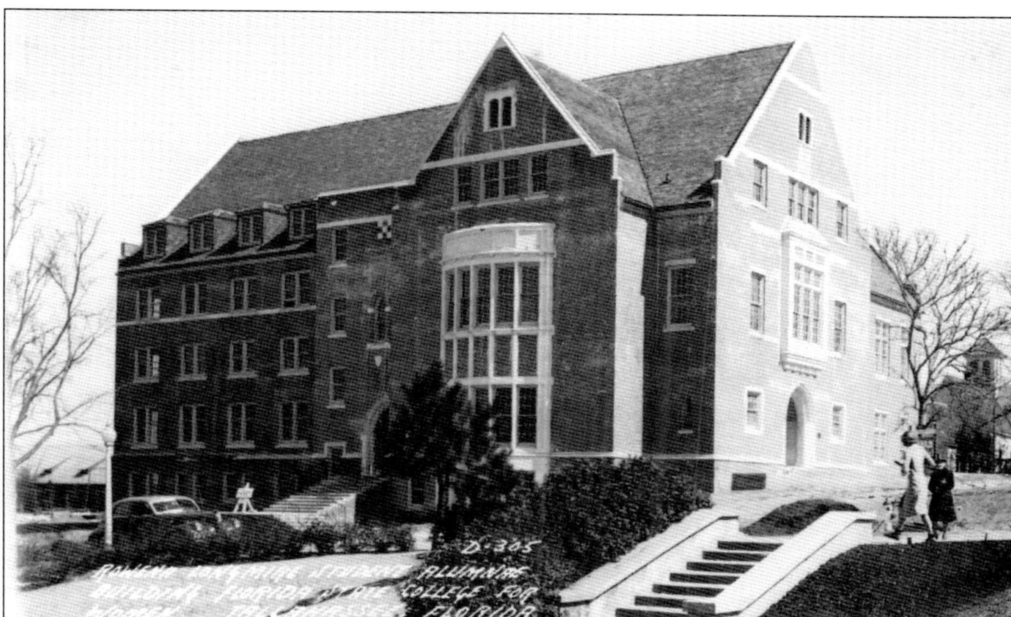

In 1939, Florida State College for Women constructed a student and faculty activities center. In addition to a student lounge and locker room for day students, the Rowena Longmire Student Alumnae Building housed the Alumnae Association, Student Government Association, YWCA, and campus publications plus third-floor accommodations for visiting alumnae and distinguished guests. The building was named in honor of Rowena Longmire, who founded the Alumnae Association in 1909.

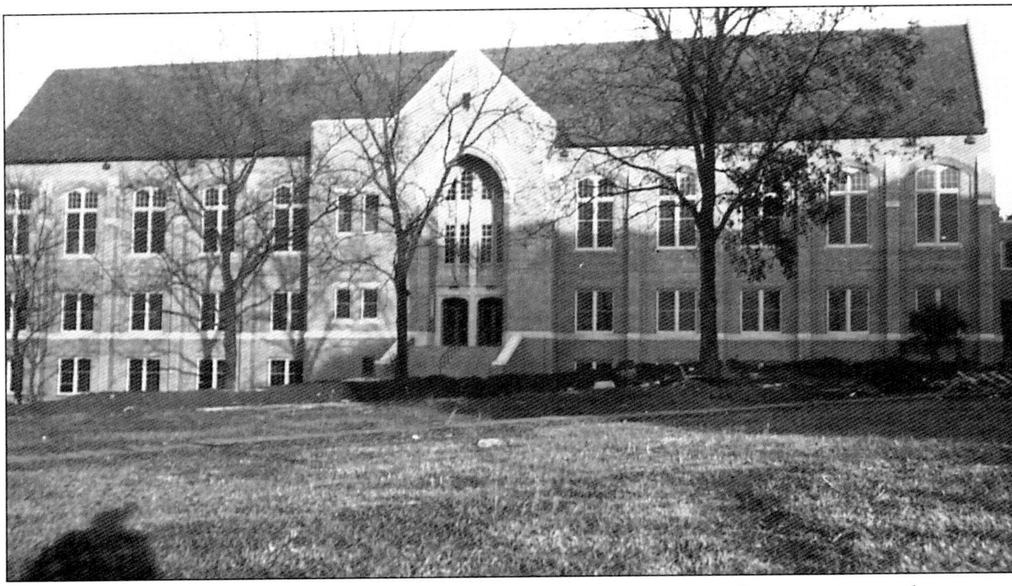

Constructed in 1938, the new dining hall was notable because the prominent three-story entrance faced the west side of campus, emphasizing campus growth in that direction, away from the original cluster of buildings. Connected to the west side of the older dining hall, the new two-story structure brought the dining hall complex to its final *H*-shaped design. The four dining rooms, two upstairs and two downstairs, could accommodate 700 diners. It was renamed the William Johnston Building in the 1980s.

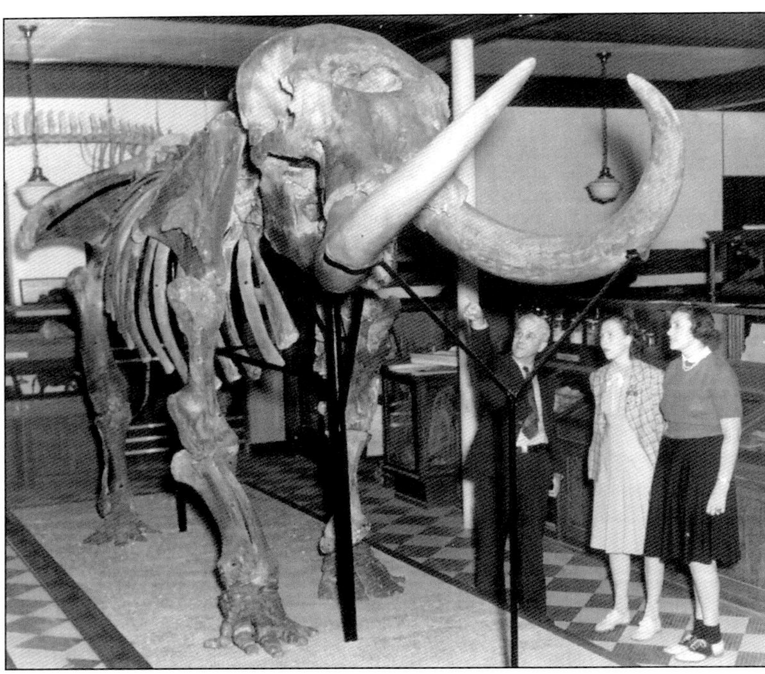

Completion of the new dining hall relieved some of the pressure on the old dining facility, and the college permitted State Geologist Herman Gunter to move his equipment and museum specimens to the unused lower dining area in December 1939. Soon, a mastodon skeleton, found at Wakulla Springs in 1934 and christened Oscar by the students, guarded the entryway.

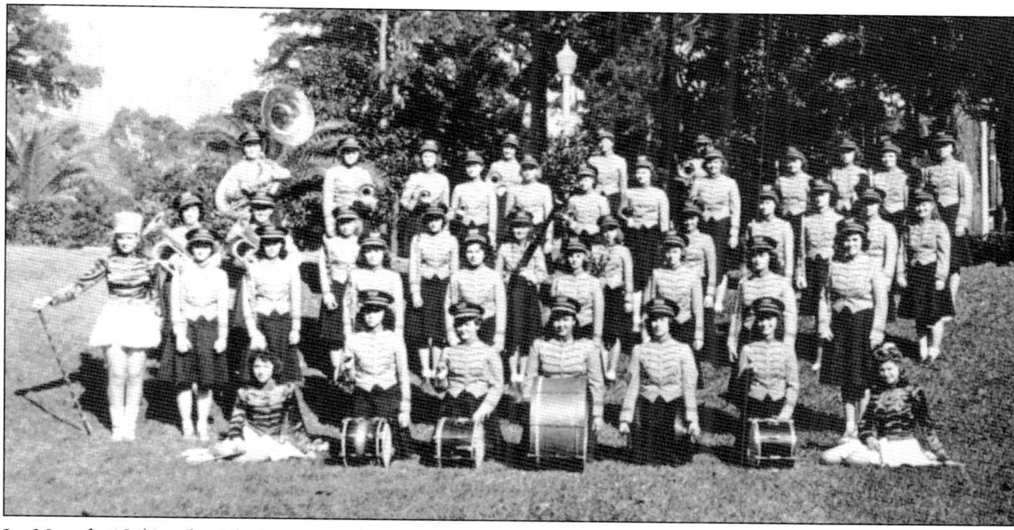

In March 1940, Florida State College for Women students formed the college's first marching band. Without authorization from the School of Music, they held tryouts and practice sessions, and the FSCW Marching Band made its debut on Thanksgiving Day 1941. The band proved so popular that the administration came through with funding for garnet and gold uniforms, which musicians wore when they played for the inauguration of Pres. Doak S. Campbell. (Archives of Florida.)

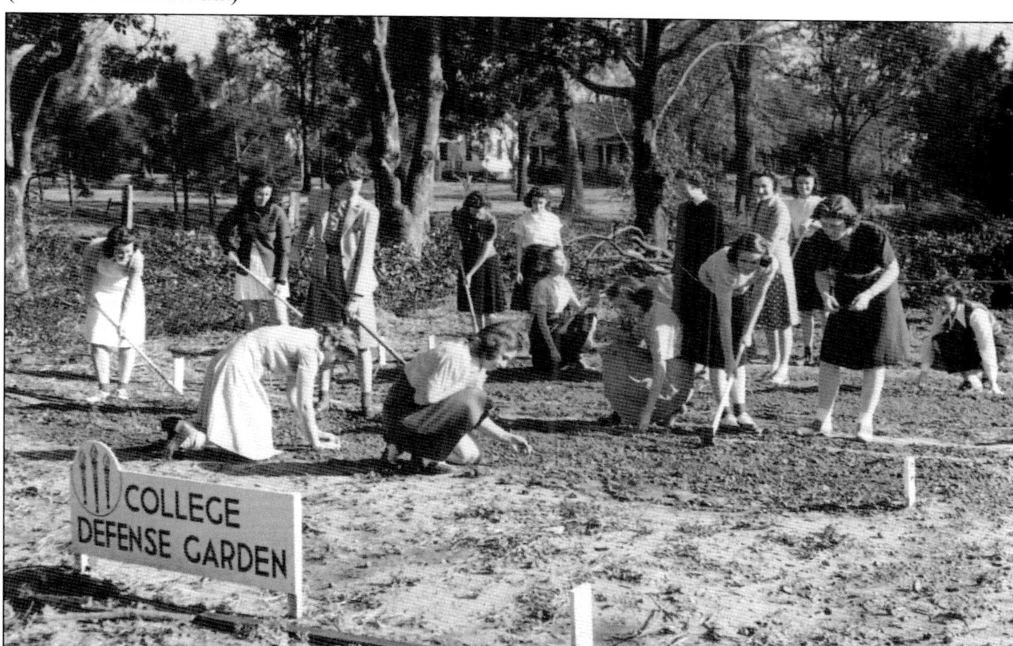

During World War II, the students were heavily involved in war-related projects and activities. Those activities of "impractical or of little comparative value were quickly weeded out, leaving Florida State a streamlined organization which placed high on national defense ratings." Between rolling bandages, staffing the information center at the library with international relations students, and rationing food and clothing, defense was an "all-year job" for FSCW students.

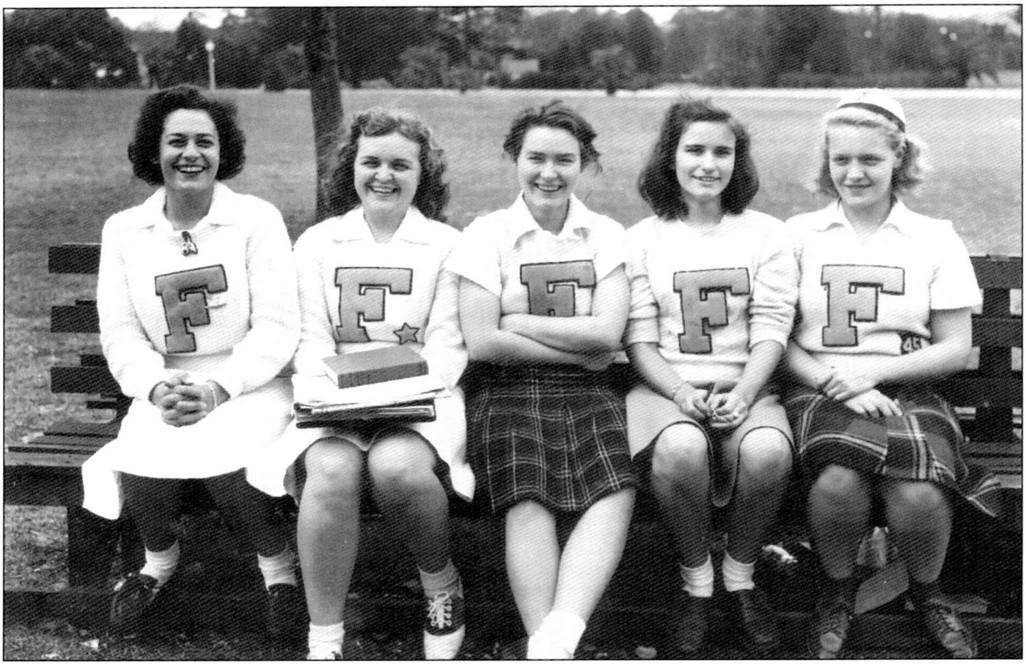

Founded in 1919 by the Florida State College for Women's Athletic Association, the F Club encouraged athletic participation and honored those students with multiple outstanding athletic achievements. The initiation ritual of the new inductees, or F Club Goats (wearing their *F*s upside down), was a campus-wide spectacle. Members, along with the Goats, wore white with their F Club letters on Friday and sang in front of the dining room after the evening meals, raising F Club's visibility on campus and making it a regular part of everyday college life, even for those who were not members. The initiation ceremonies culminated at Camp Flastacowo, which served like a second home for the popular athletic fraternity. To be a member, a student was required to play on two Odd or Even teams where she earned a varsity letter in one school term. In the photograph above are, from left to right, Vicki Lewis (class of 1944), Jean Lloyd (class of 1944), Elizabeth Jeffries, Winnifred Harding (class of 1945), and Evelyn Berry (class of 1945).

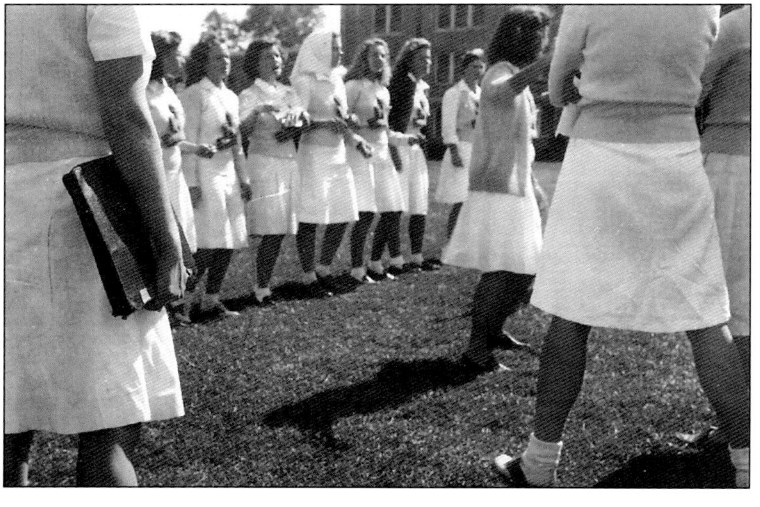

Doak S. Campbell, dean of the Graduate School at George Peabody College for Teachers, became president of Florida State College for Women in 1941. Campbell's research had included studies on women's colleges, and his recent reports on the subject placed him in an ideal position to assume the presidency. Campbell directed the college through the lean war years and through the transition to coeducation before retiring in 1957.

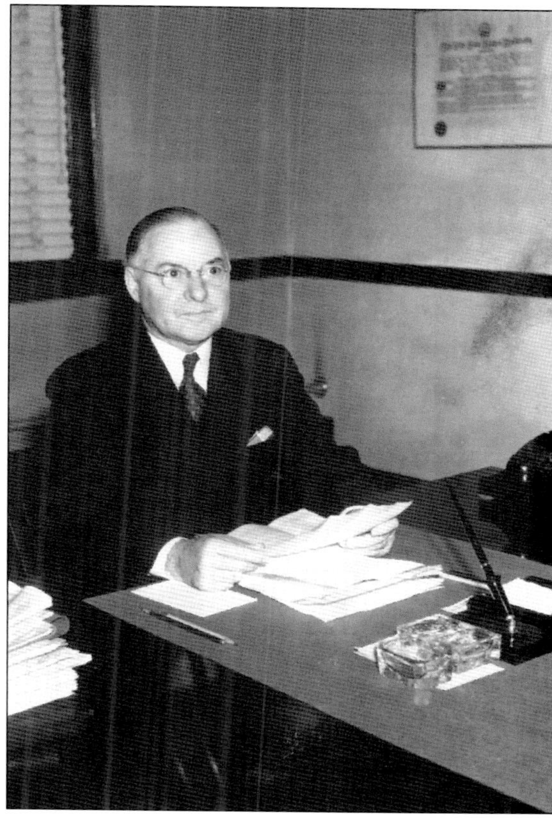

From left to right, this photograph is of Florida State College for Women students Martha Stroberg (class of 1942), Janet Wells (class of 1942), Grace Bail (class of 1942), and Mart Pierson (class of 1942) in the Spic and Span on the day of Doak S. Campbell's presidential inauguration, February 21, 1942. After serving in the Navy from 1944 to 1946, Wells earned her master's of arts and doctorate in education before returning to FSU in 1957 to teach physical education where she remained until her retirement in 1989.

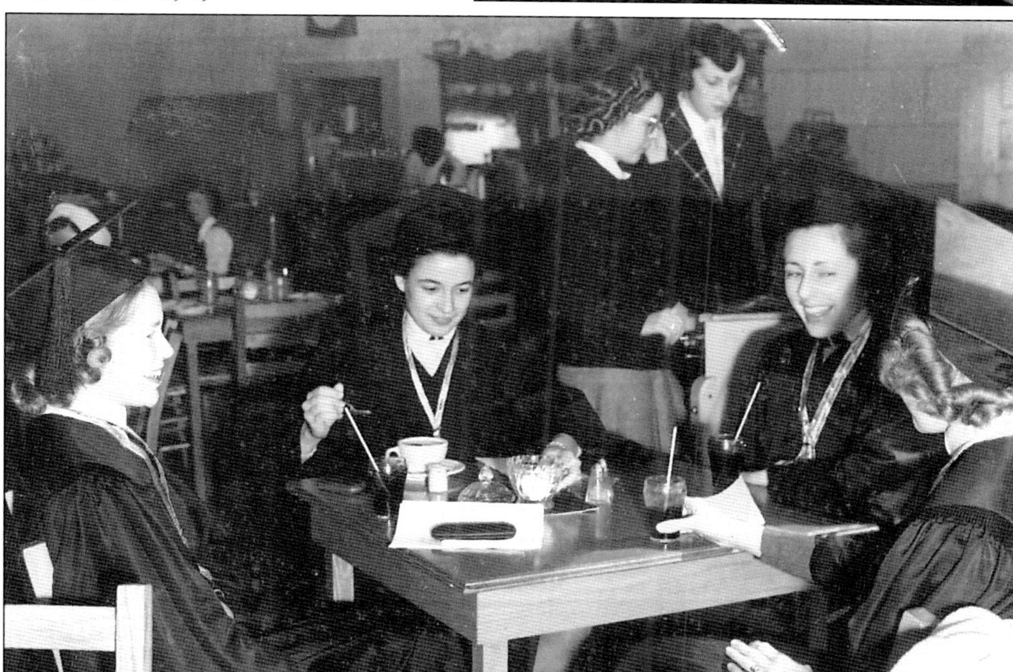

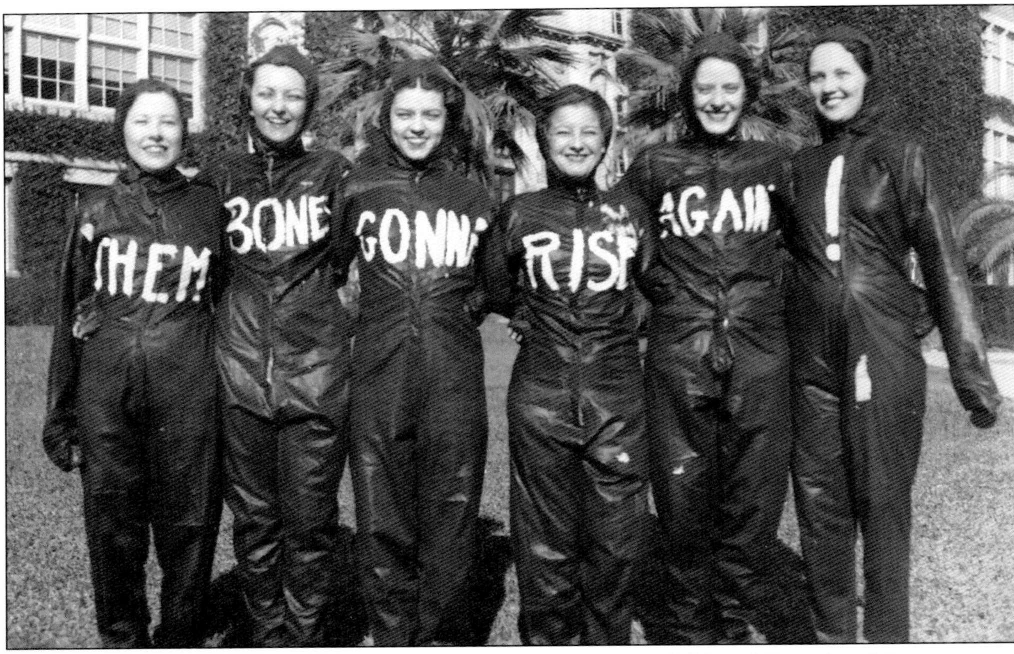

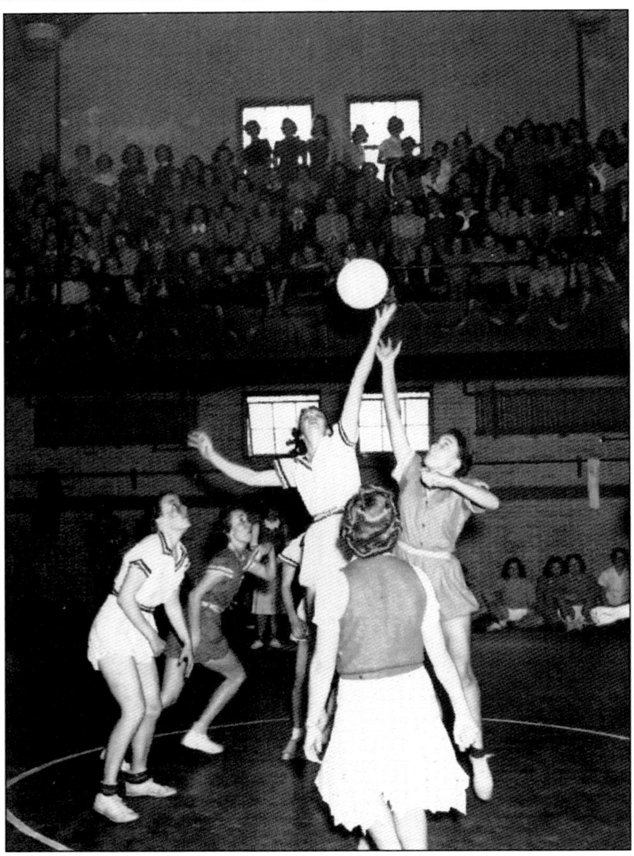

Odd and Even loyalties permeated every aspect of the Florida State College for Women students' social and cultural existences. Some competitions took the form of elaborate student productions (or demonstrations), which, over the years, evolved from simple skits used to introduce the teams to incoming students to full-blown musical events. The photograph above is from a 1933 Evens Demonstration.

The genesis of the Odd and Even teams' athletic competitions continued to expand into other major and minor sports. By the 1940s, the Odd-Even rivalry reached its pinnacle of creative and exuberant cheers and pep songs. The FSCW students were acutely aware of and loyal to these traditions.

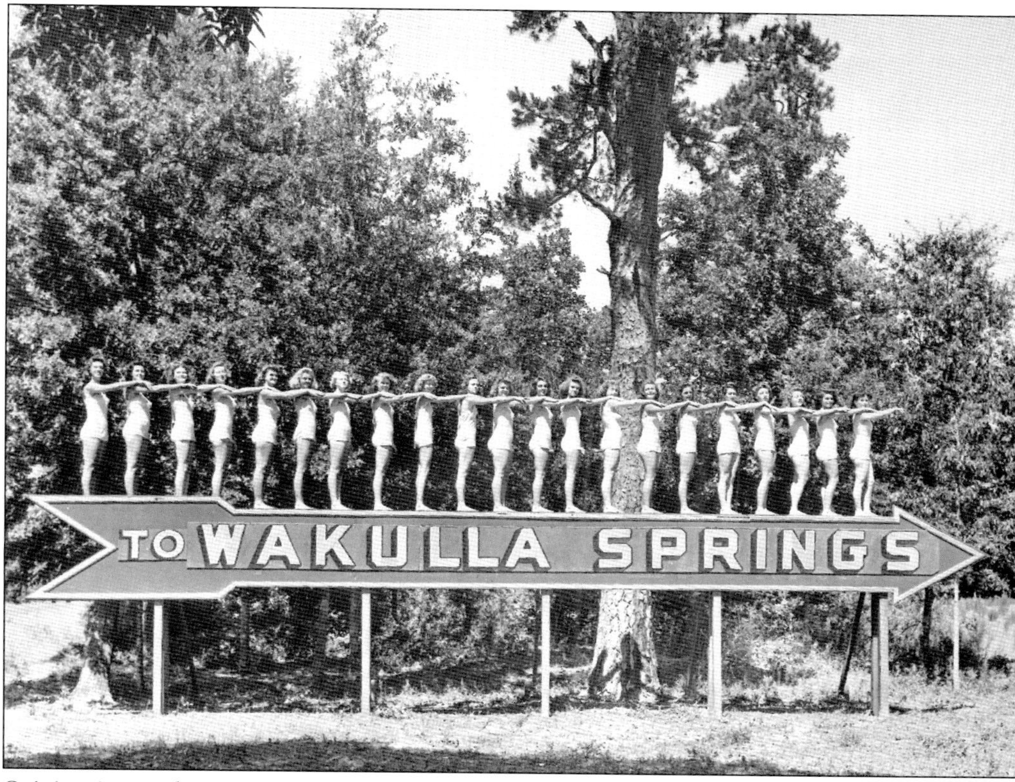

Originating with aquatic demonstrations by the Florida State College for Women Life Saving Corps in the 1920s, members formed the Tarpon Club in 1937 and began presenting "water pageants." These performances featured swimming and floating patterns with musical accompaniment. Over time, the group gained an international reputation for its performances. Sportswriter Grantland Rice featured the Tarpon Club three times in his Sportlight series of short films: *Aqua Rhythm*, filmed at Wakulla Springs in 1939; *Campus Mermaids*, also filmed at Wakulla Springs in 1945; and *Water Swimphony*, filmed at both Wakulla Springs and Cypress Gardens in 1953. Members also appeared in several Tarzan movies and as supporting cast for Esther Williams's feature films shot at Florida's Cypress Gardens. (Archives of Florida.)

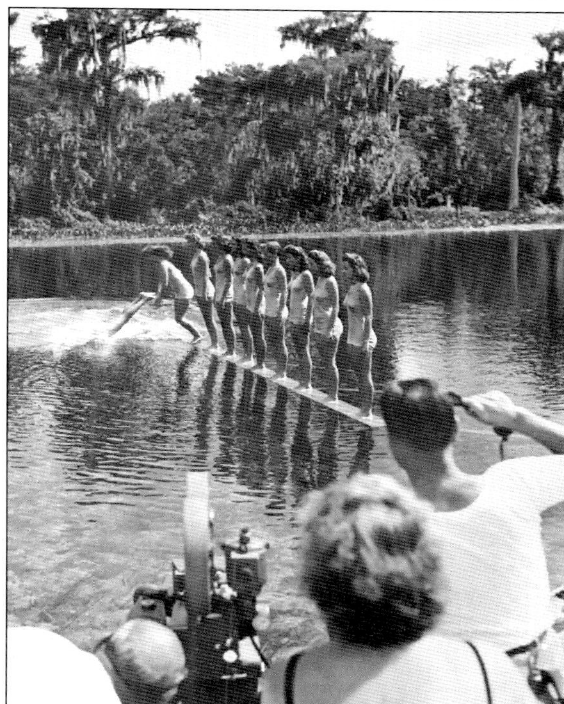

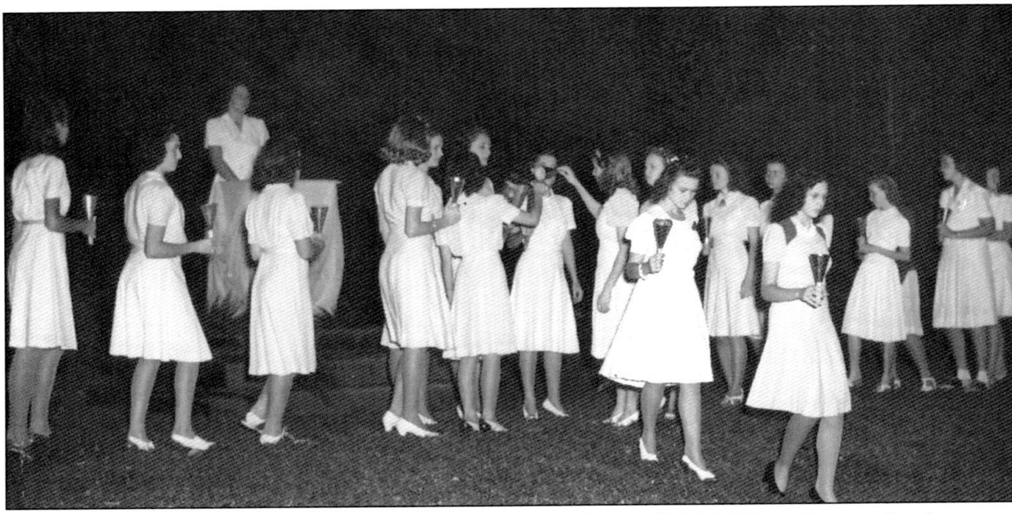

Established in 1925, Torch Night was one of the most beautiful FSCW traditions. Sophomores passed to freshmen the torch that had been handed down to them symbolizing the three torches of the college emblem, "Vires, Artes, Mores"—strength, skill, and character. The ceremony occurred each fall at dusk and remained unchanged from year to year. The ritual has been reestablished in recent years and is now part of convocation. The photograph above is from the 1945 ceremony.

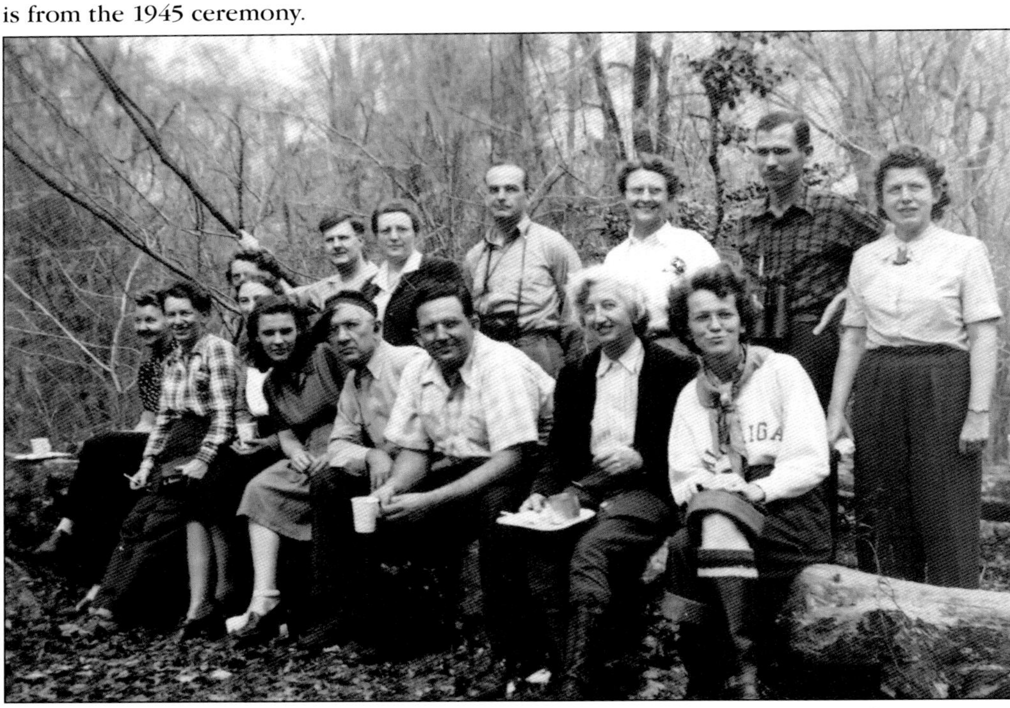

Herman Kurz arrived at the Florida State College for Women as a botany professor in 1922 and remained through the transition to Florida State University before retiring in 1956. His fun-loving good nature was legendary, as were his Saturday botanical field trips, for which there was always a waiting list of students. In the photograph above, Kurz sits with his hat cockeyed in the center next to education professor Hugh Stickler.

Peggy Barfield, Dottie Bryant, Vicki Lewis, Jean Lloyd, and Jeanne Eyman, known as the "Fearless Five," were daring and fun-loving friends. They sneaked out at night to skate on the dark campus streets or rendezvoused on dormitory rooftops, among a number of unsanctioned adventures. After graduating in 1944, they all went on to successful careers in education. In the photograph at right, Vicki Lewis stands on a dormitory rooftop.

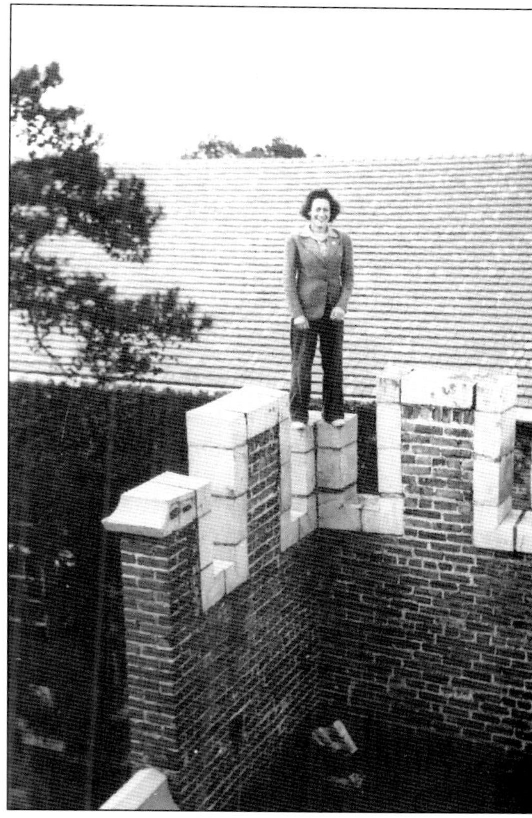

This view of the western side of the campus is from the site of the tree that is today known as the James P. Love Oak, in front of Strozier Library. Love, who worked as the FSU farm and dairy operations manager, at one time lived in a cottage that stood beside the ancient tree. The building next to the new dining hall once housed the journalism department.

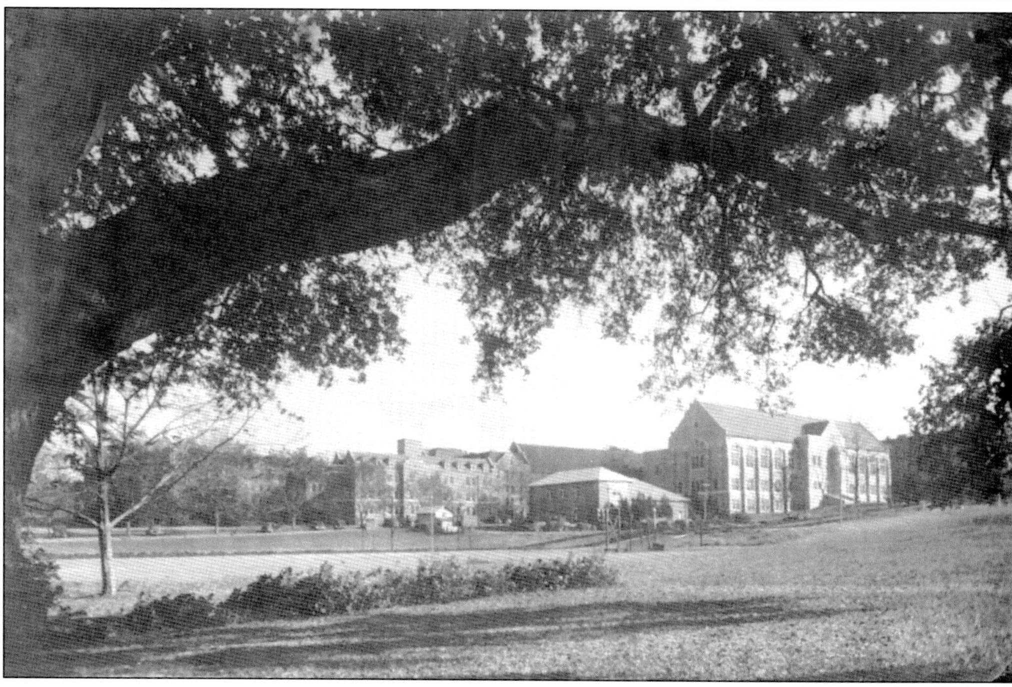

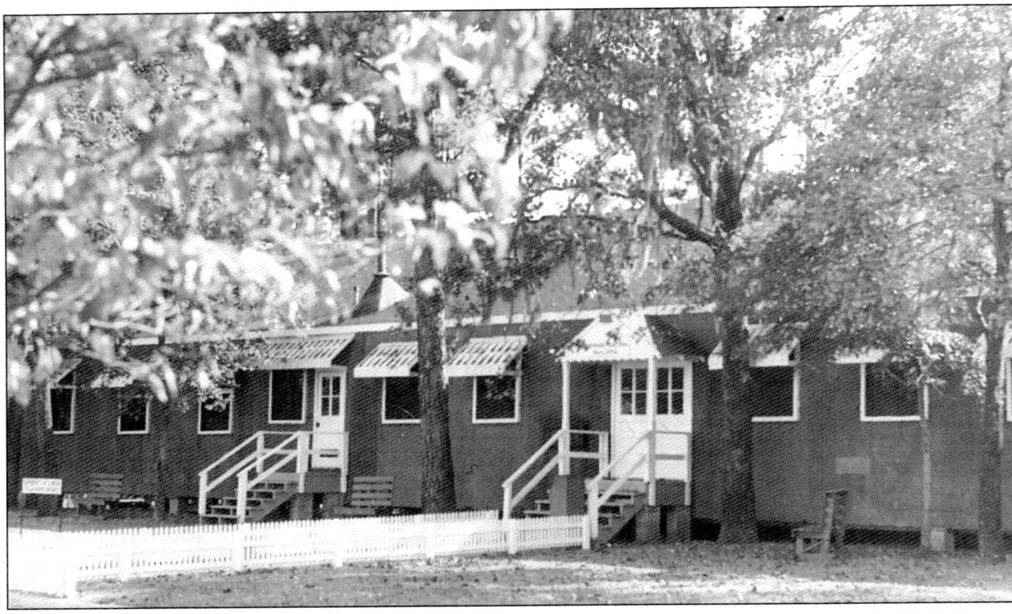

To accommodate the influx of returning veterans into the education system, the Tallahassee Branch of University of Florida (TBUF) was established in 1946, permitting male students to attend classes at Florida State College for Women. The issue of housing was temporarily solved by the use of the barracks at the decommissioned Dale Mabry Air Field southwest of the campus. Bus service on regular schedules covered the five miles between the men's West Campus and the FSCW campus. TBUF student James Tippin—a true freshman and not a veteran—described his dormitory Building No. 614 as a "typical, generic US Army structure, sitting high in the air atop cinder-block pylons." Walls were erected within the buildings to divide them into individual rooms. The men took their meals on the FSCW campus. The photograph below is of TBUF student Harold Boyd at West Campus in April 1947.

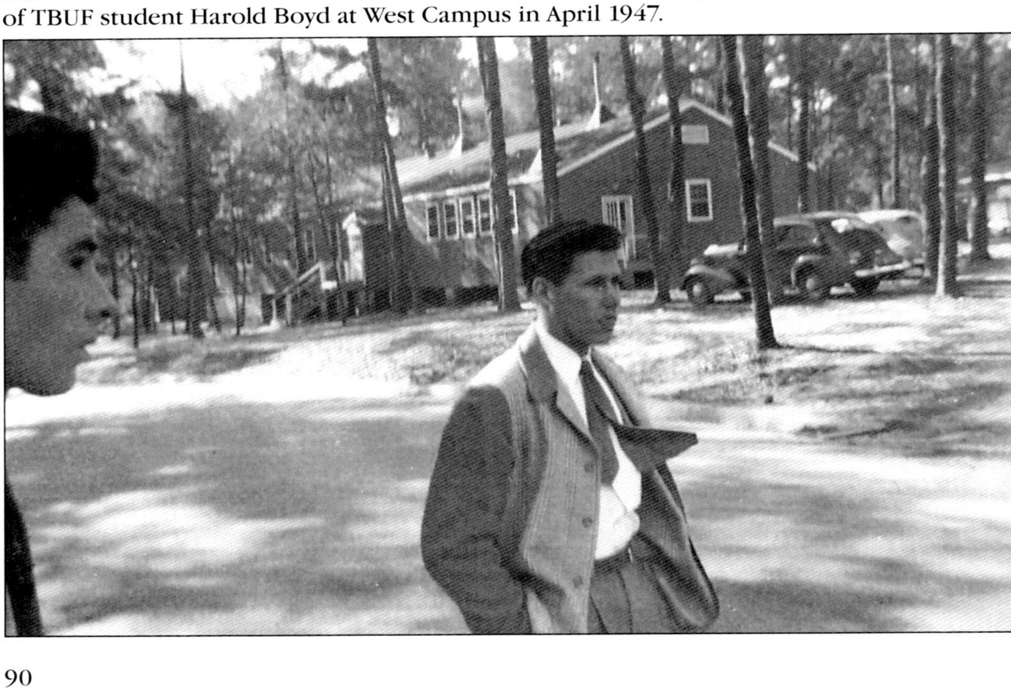

Four

Florida State University 1947–Today

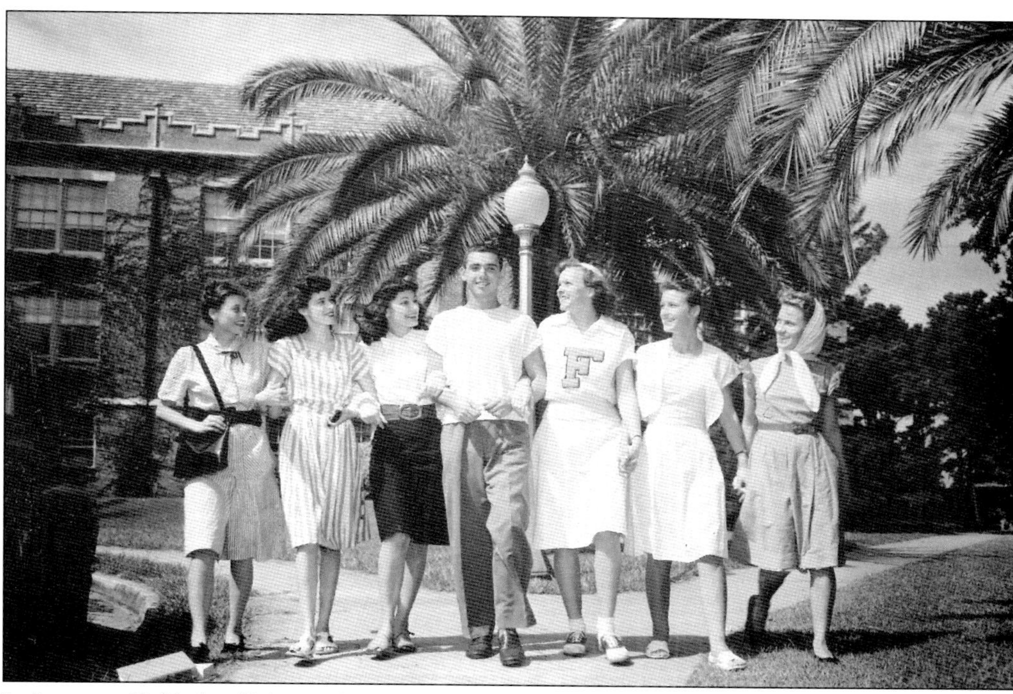

In January 1947, the Citizens Committee on Education reported in favor of coeducation for both the University of Florida and Florida State College for Women, a change that FSCW students overwhelmingly supported. On May 15, 1947, Governor Caldwell signed the new legislation, returning the two universities to coeducational status and renaming FSCW the Florida State University.

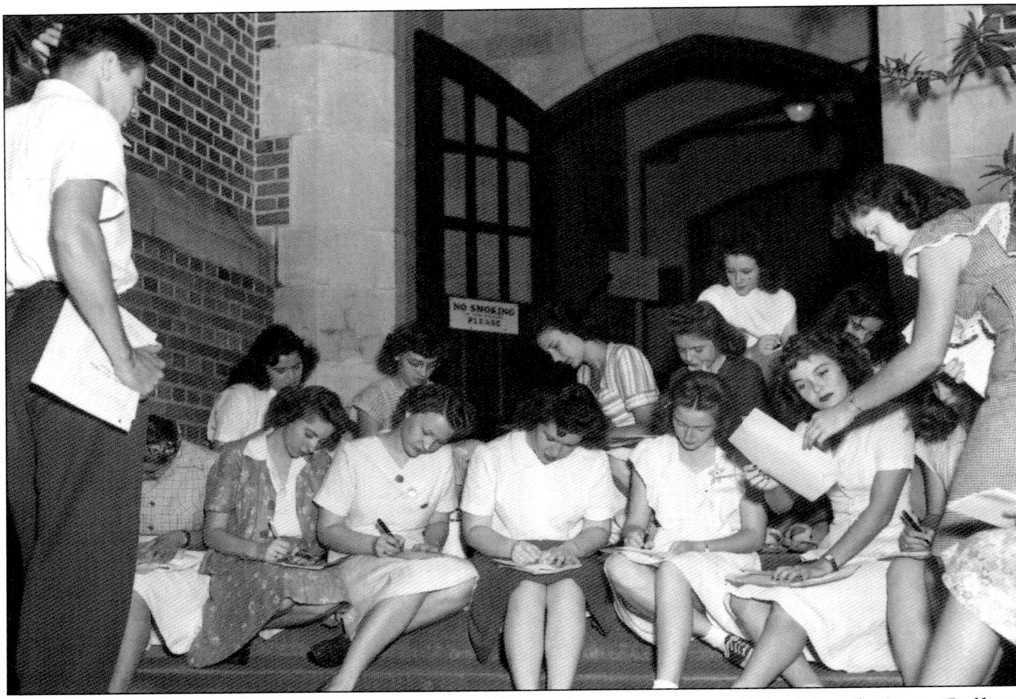

The well-established, nationally recognized liberal arts program of the Florida State College for Women was the institutional foundation for the curriculum of the new university. The university wisely retained the three torches and the motto, "Vires, Artes, Mores," for the FSU seal, but the words *femina perfecta* were removed for obvious reasons. The June 9, 1947, commencement ceremony marked the graduation of 431 women and 12 men, completing the transition to coeducation.

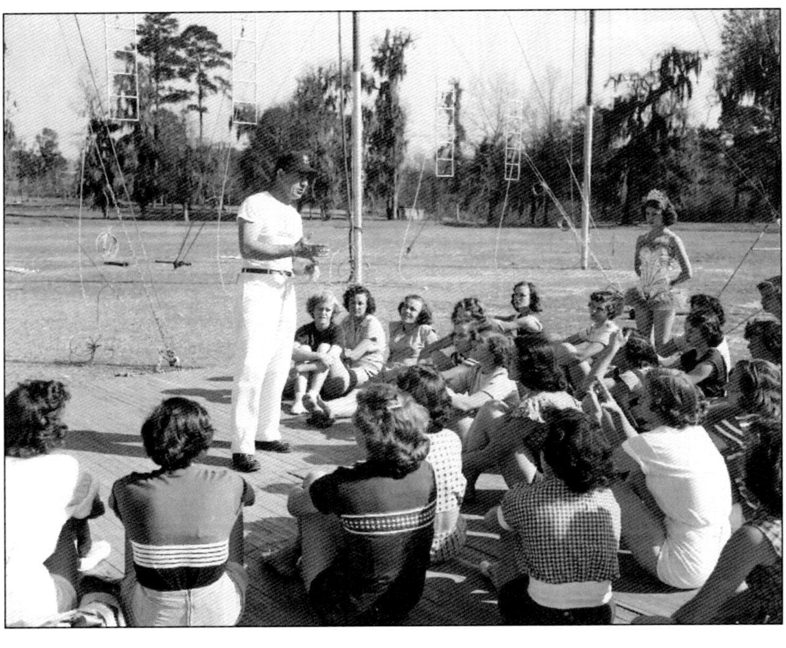

The Florida State University Flying High Circus was founded in 1947 by Jack Haskin as a coeducational activity that male and female students could participate in together. In the photograph at left, Haskin instructs student performers at the old circus lot on West Campus.

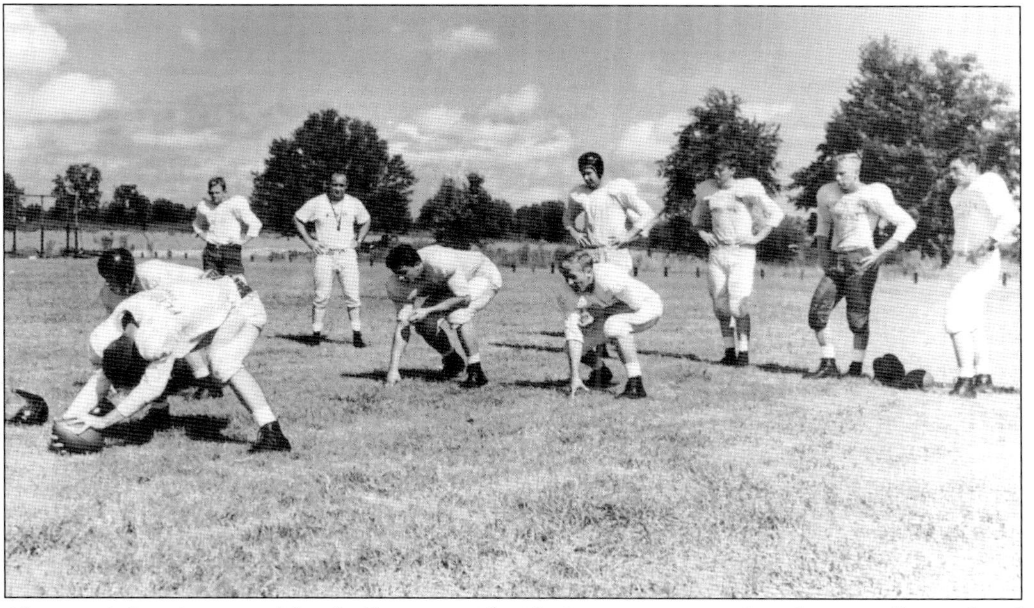

After a winless inaugural football season, Florida State University hired Don Veller as head coach in 1948. Veller (standing in the rear, second from left) went 31-12-1 during his five seasons at the helm, establishing a winning tradition that would be difficult to maintain as the team transitioned to playing major college football teams. Veller stepped aside in 1953 but spent the rest of his life in service to FSU, much of that time as golf coach. (FSU Athletic Department.)

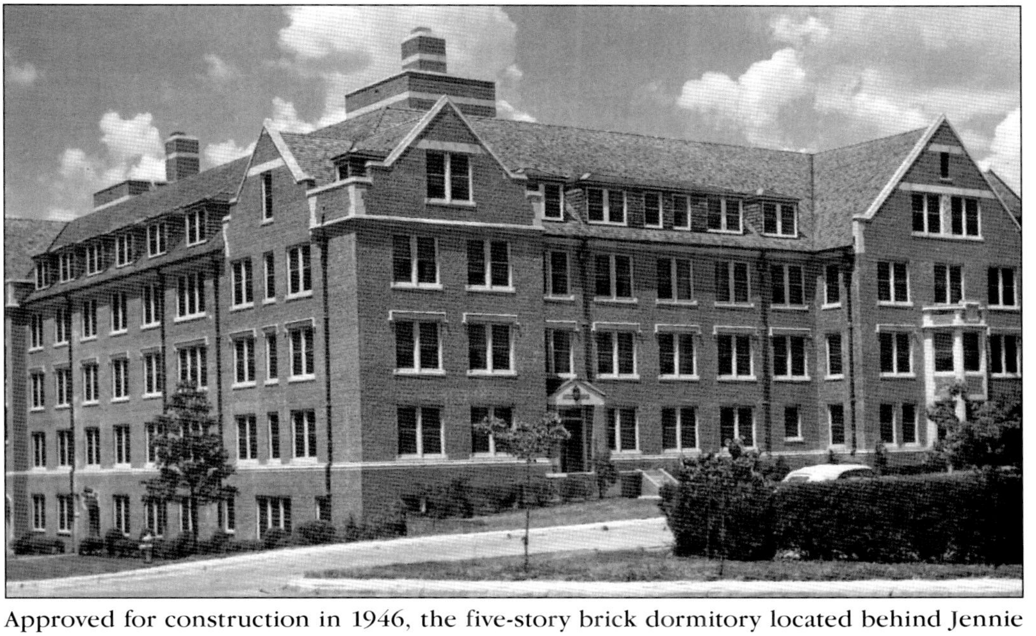

Approved for construction in 1946, the five-story brick dormitory located behind Jennie Murphree Hall was the last of that era to conform to the campus Collegiate Gothic design. A stone relief with the letters "FSCW" is visible at one entrance, even though the building was not completed until 1948. The new residence hall was named after the first FSCW Dean of the College Home, Sarah Landrum "Tissie" Cawthon.

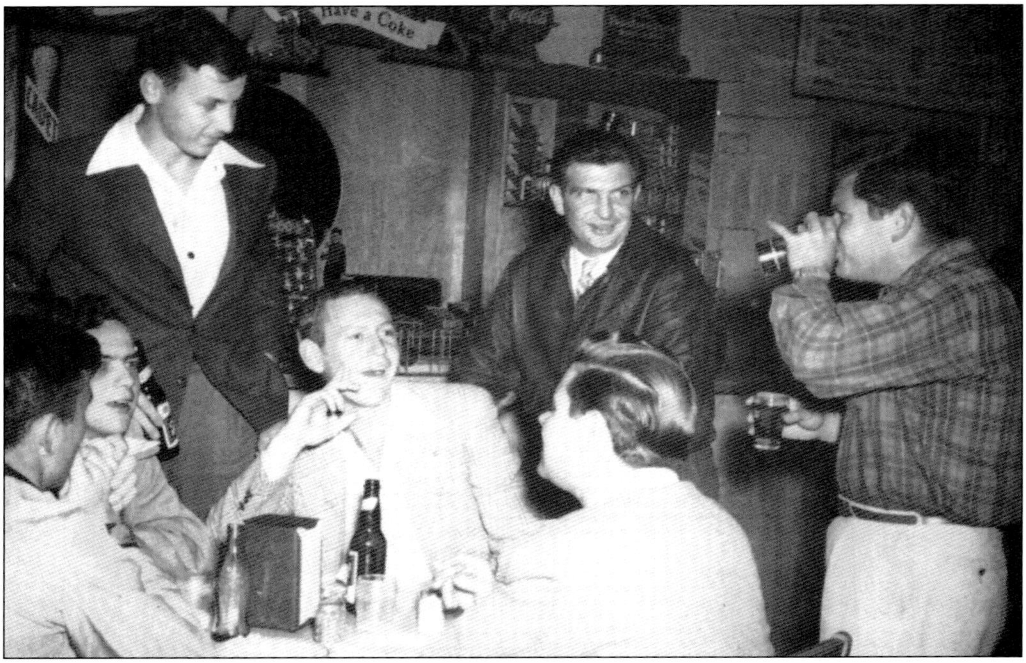

Men on campus brought notable change to the character of the former all-women's college. The Florida State College for Women's student handbook, known as the *Gold Book*, had been full of strict guidelines on how students should behave. With the arrival of the men, the rule book was drastically revised, and the thick student handbook shrank to a slim booklet almost overnight. This photograph is from the *Tally-Ho*, the 1949 yearbook.

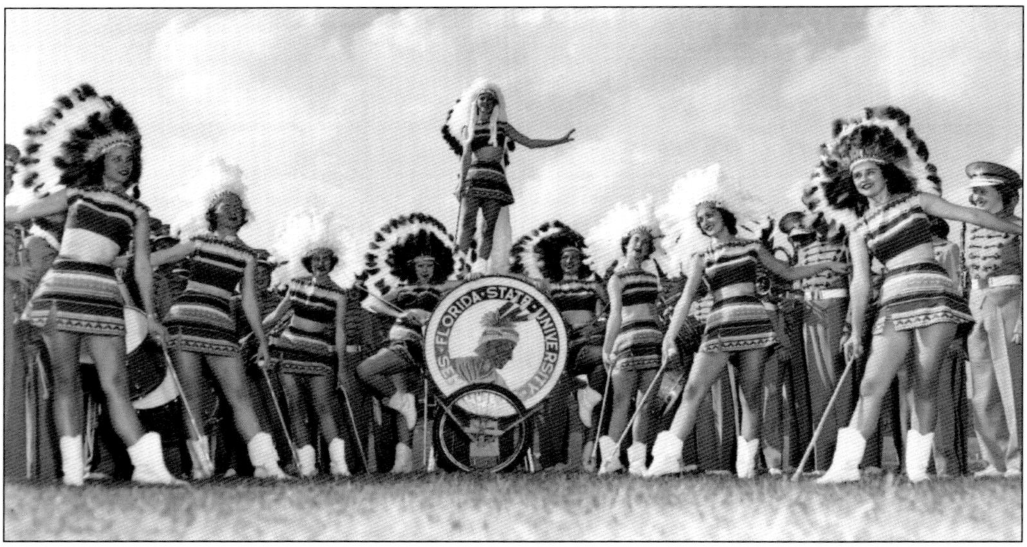

In 1950, Florida State University's marching band officially adopted the name Marching Chiefs and made its first appearance under that name at the FSU football game against Sewanee on October 28, 1950. The band became so highly regarded that when the football team was invited to play in the 1955 Sun Bowl game, a reporter suggested that the Marching Chiefs were responsible for sealing the deal. The photograph above was taken in 1952.

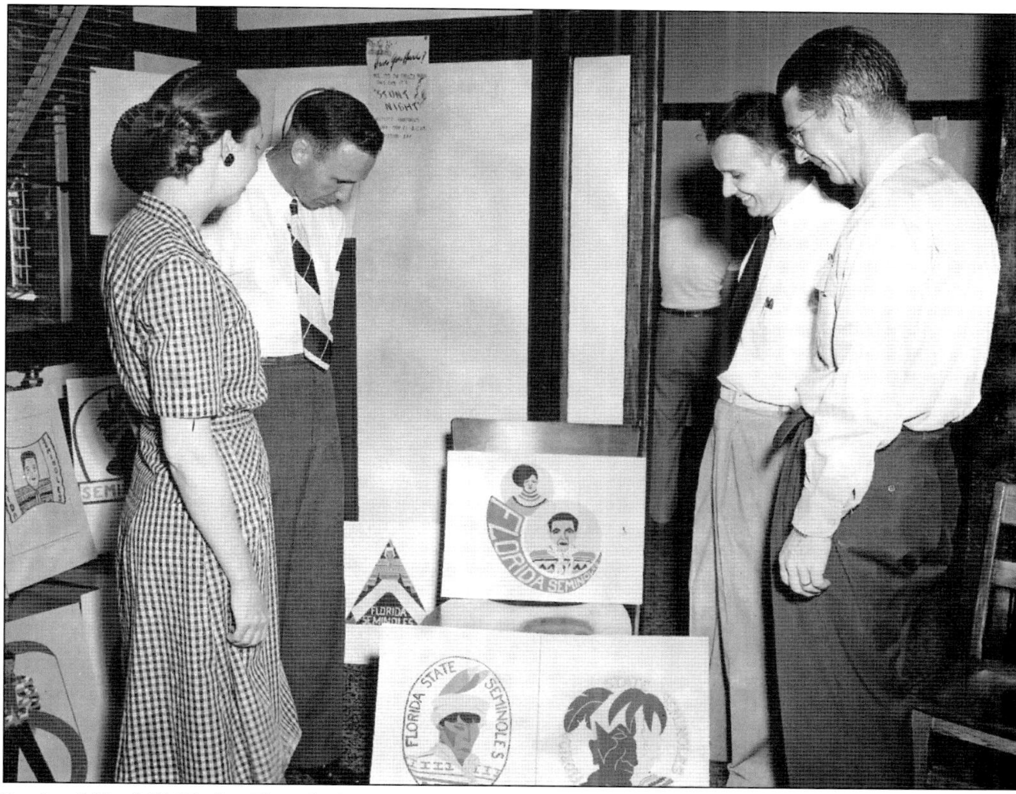

In the fall of 1947, the Florida State University student body voted that the athletic symbol of the university should be the Seminole Indian. In April 1948, the *Florida Flambeau* announced the "Design a Seminole" contest, with entries to be judged by faculty and staff. Unable to decide which of the two finalists were best, the judges declared a tie with Priscilla Carter (class of 1949) and Marseille Dell Donne (class of 1949) sharing the honor and splitting the $25 prize. Aspects of the two designs were combined into one, and this symbol was used until the early 1960s. In the photograph at right, from 1949 Freshman Week, students John Smith and Ima Jean Hartsfield (right) view items with the new design in the school bookstore.

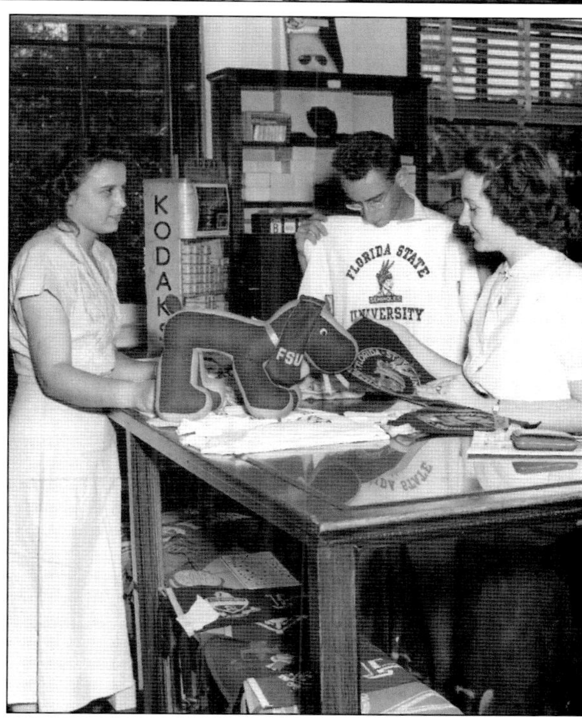

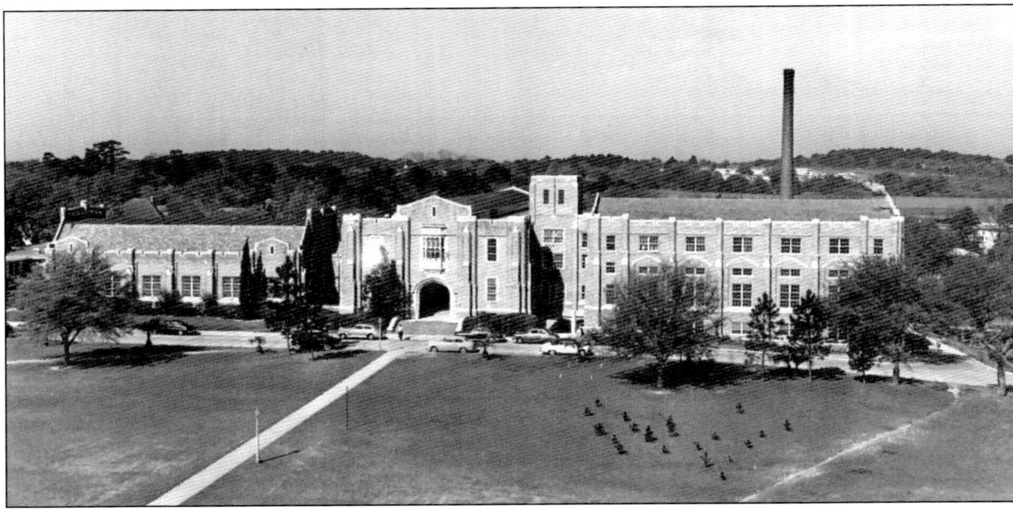

The north wing of the Physical Education Building was added in 1949. The gymnasium served as headquarters for the Florida State University Physical Education Department and, in addition to a basketball court, included a bowling alley and swimming pool. In 1959, the building was named to honor former director of physical education Katherine Montgomery. In 2004, Montgomery Hall was renovated and is now the home of the school of dance.

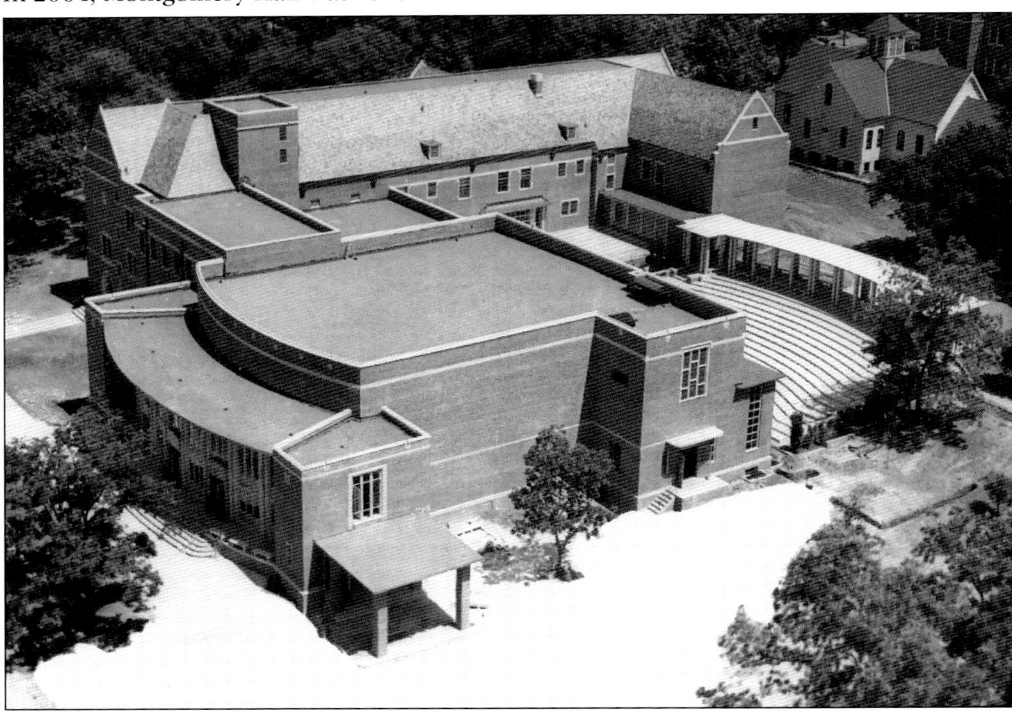

Opening in 1949, the new music building reflected the transition from the traditional Collegiate Gothic style to the Modern. At the time of its construction, it was declared one of the best in the country. In 1952, the building's performance hall was renamed in honor of Ella Scoble Opperman, the director of the School of Music from 1911 to 1944. The old gymnasium can be seen at the far right.

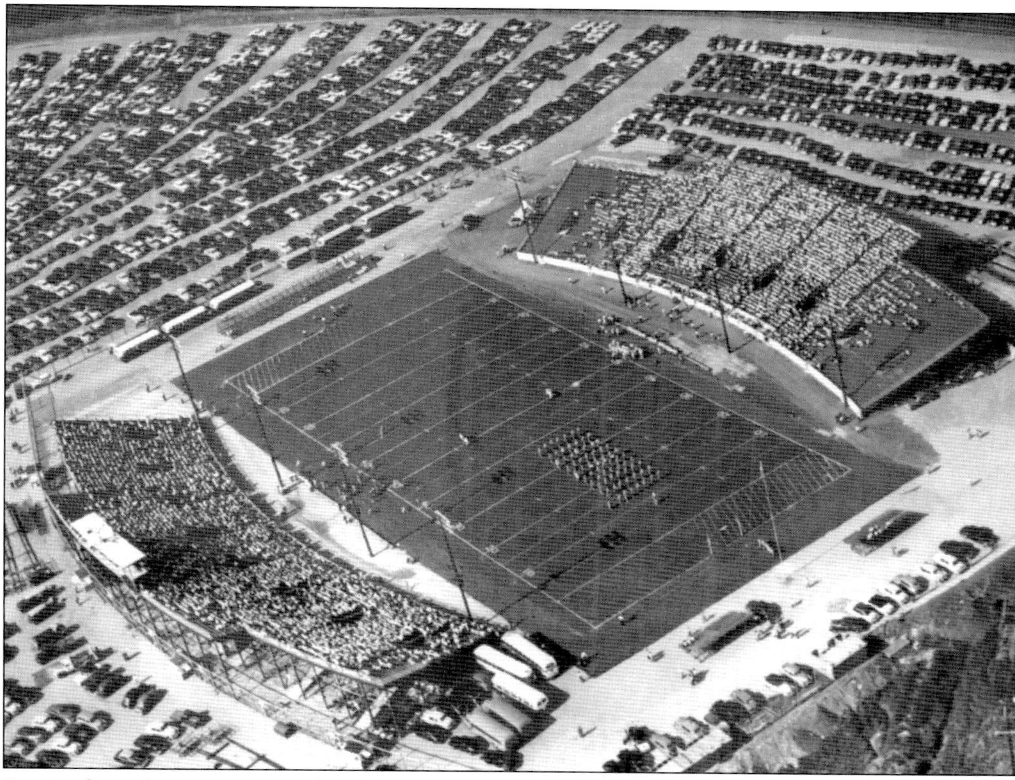

For its first three seasons, the Florida State University football team played all of its home games at Centennial Field near the state capitol. That changed in 1950 when Doak Campbell Stadium was constructed. From its humble and distinctive skeletal metal design, the structure would undergo numerous expansions. The photograph above is from its Dedication Day Game on October 28, 1950.

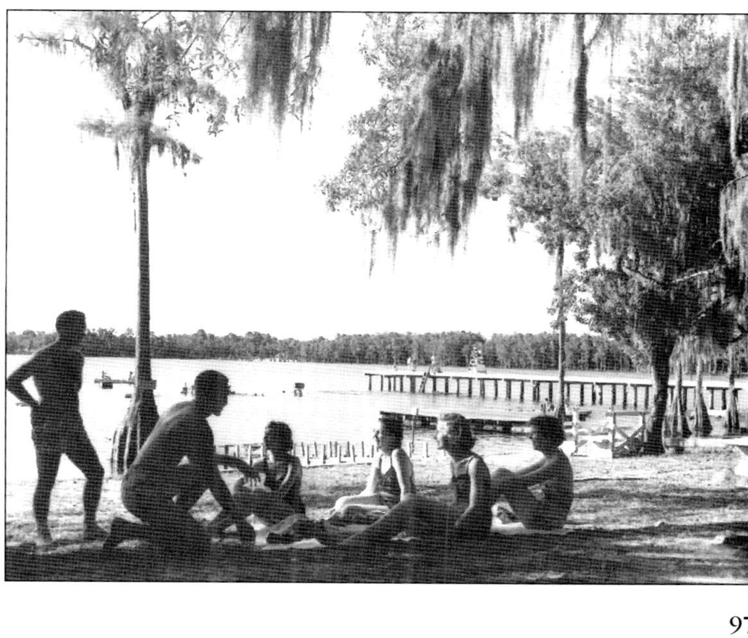

Camp Flastacowo continued to grow over the years and remained a popular retreat for students, faculty, and staff through the transition from Florida State College for Women to Florida State University. In 1954, after a campus-wide search for a new name, the recreational facility was renamed the FSU Reservation.

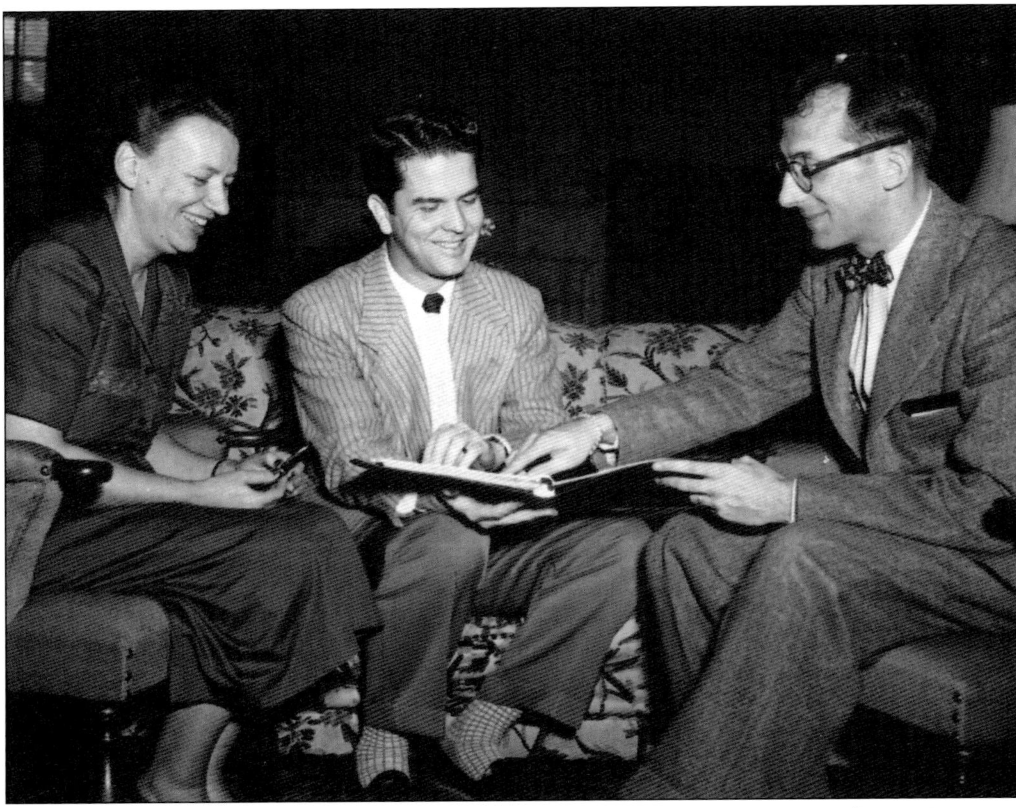

Modern languages professor Eva May Atwood, English professor Lester Moore, and geology professor Stephen B. Winters were officers in the Tallahassee Playmakers, a Florida State University faculty and staff theater group. Winters was later a popular dean of basic studies, notorious for his jokes and bow ties.

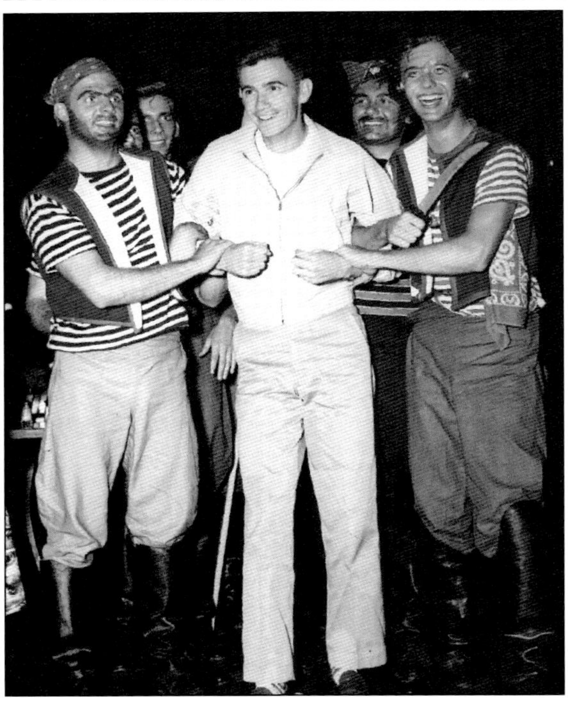

After being discharged from the military, future Florida governor Reubin Askew attended Florida State University from 1948 to 1951 where he served as student body president. In this photograph, the Pirates of Penzance are about to throw Askew into the fountain on the night of his engagement to his future wife, Donna Lou Harper. (Archives of Florida.)

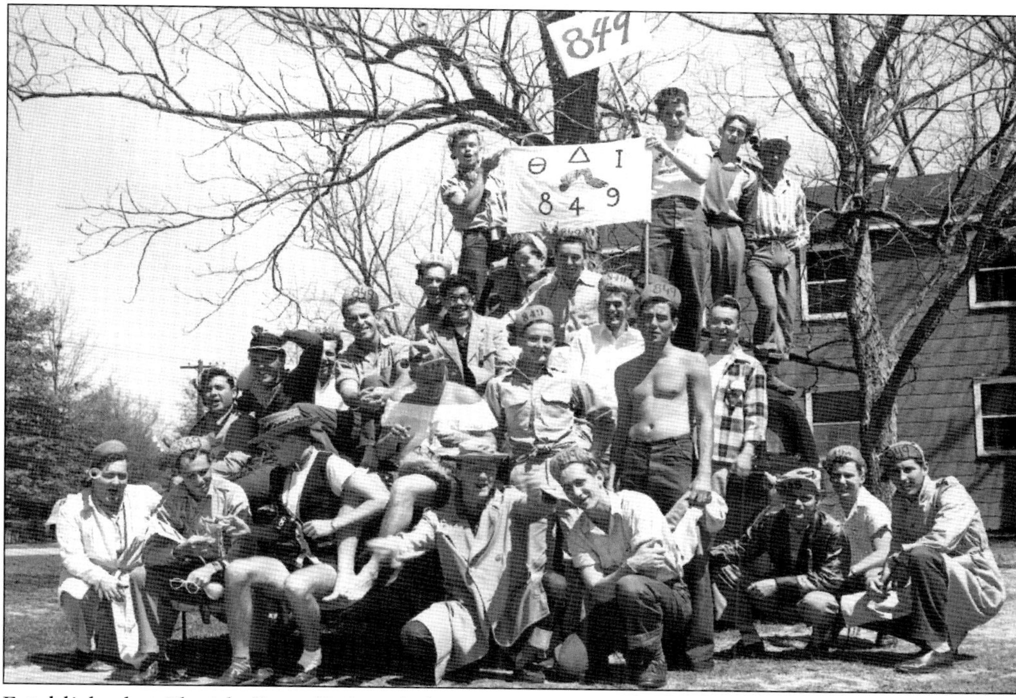

Established at Florida State University's West Campus in the fall of 1951, the "849ers" were residents of barracks 849 at the former airfield. The "849ers" bonded together in a pseudo-fraternity they called Theta Delta Iota. After repeatedly being told that they should go national, the group held a parade where they marched from campus to the National Shirt Shop on Monroe Street.

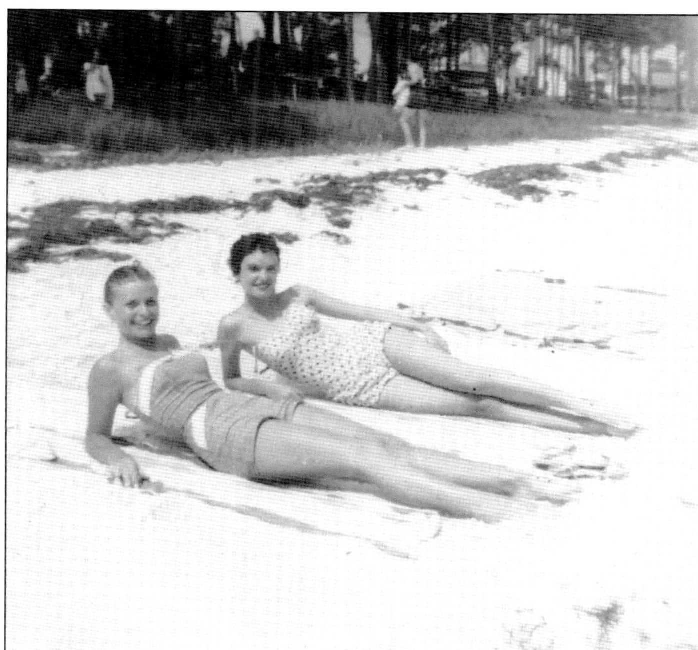

After her appearance on the December 15, 1952, cover of *Life* magazine, coed Marlies Gessler was probably Florida State University's most famous student. The photograph spread documented her life at FSU, from her Flying High Circus practice to her work at the soda shop to her participation as homecoming queen. In this photograph, she is on the left with a friend at a Gulf Coast beach.

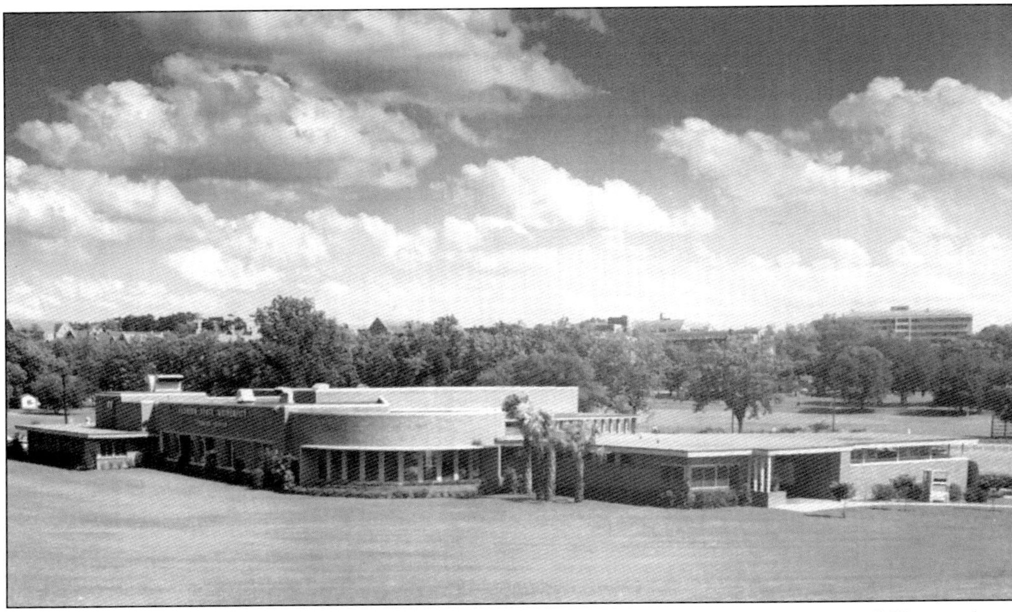

Prior to the completion of the Florida State University Student Center in 1952, students would gather at the Longmire Building and at the student O club (the former officers' club) on West Campus. Located on the far western extremities of campus, the new Student Center contained the post office, a snack bar, and a room for dancing. Florida Hall, also completed in 1952, can be seen in the background to the right.

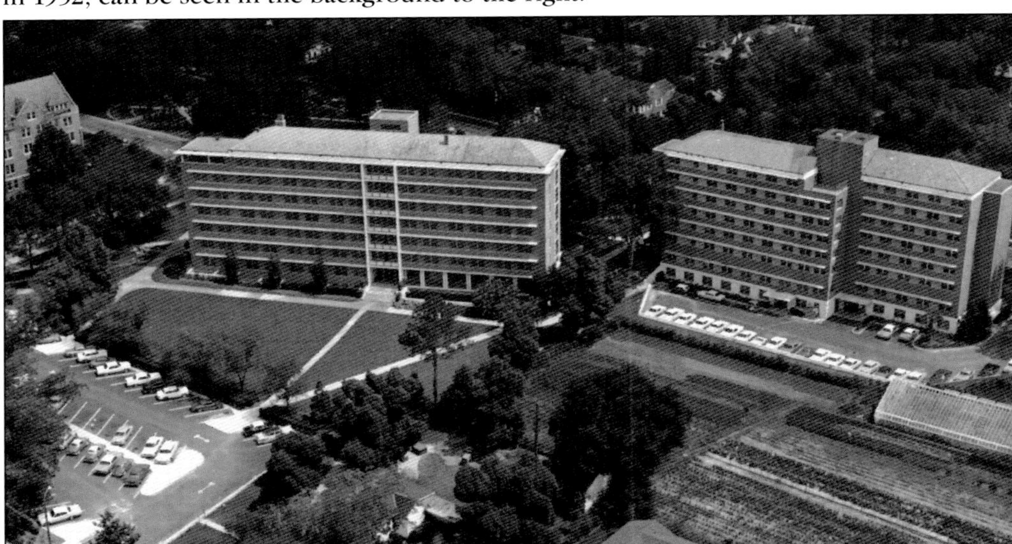

After the completion of Cawthon Hall in 1949, newer dormitory and classroom buildings at Florida State University took on a more contemporary design. Completed in 1950, DeGraff Hall was the first to exhibit this architectural trend. Typical also of this design were Florida and Dorman Halls, pictured above. Located west of Landis Hall and constructed in 1952, Florida Hall was later renamed Deviney after longtime zoology professor Ezda May Deviney. Completed in 1959, Dorman Hall was named after former classics professor and dean of students Olivia Dorman.

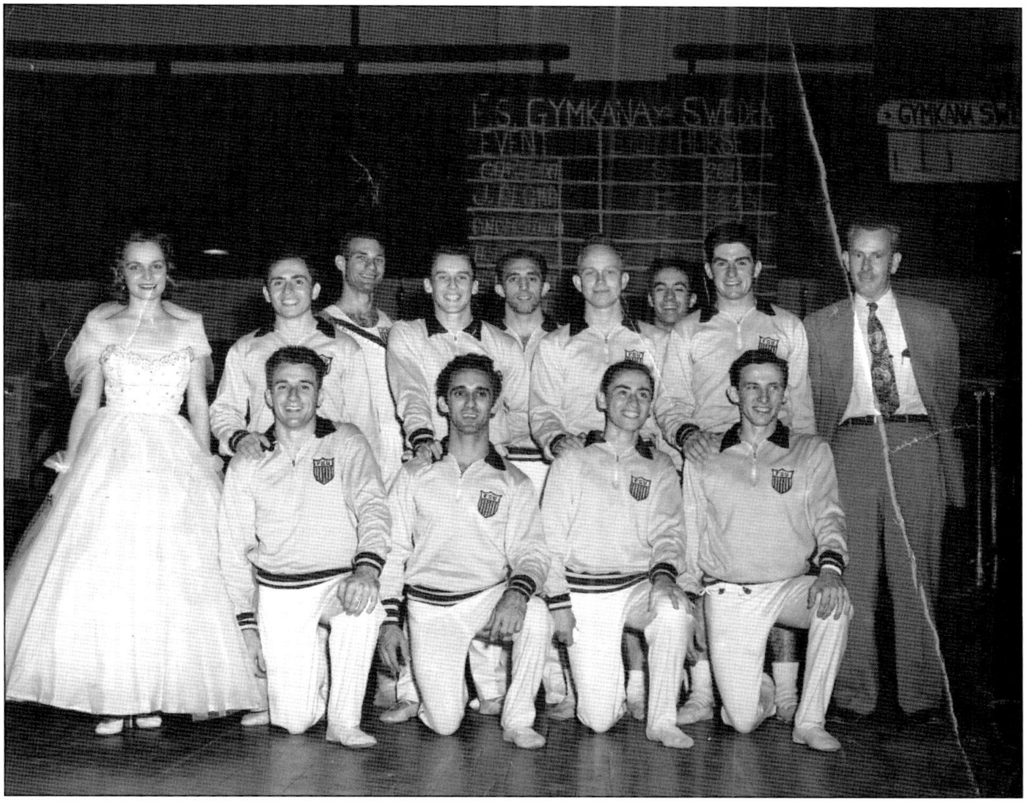

The Florida State University men's gymnastics team had a very impressive record throughout the 1950s. Their 1951 National Collegiate Athletic Association (NCAA) championship was the first collegiate national championship of any team from the state of Florida. They would go on to repeat the next year as NCAA champions, win three national Amateur Athletic Union (AAU) championships (1951, 1953 and 1955), and numerous other competitions. Coach Hartley Price (right) appears in this photograph taken after FSU defeated the Swedish national team in February 1954.

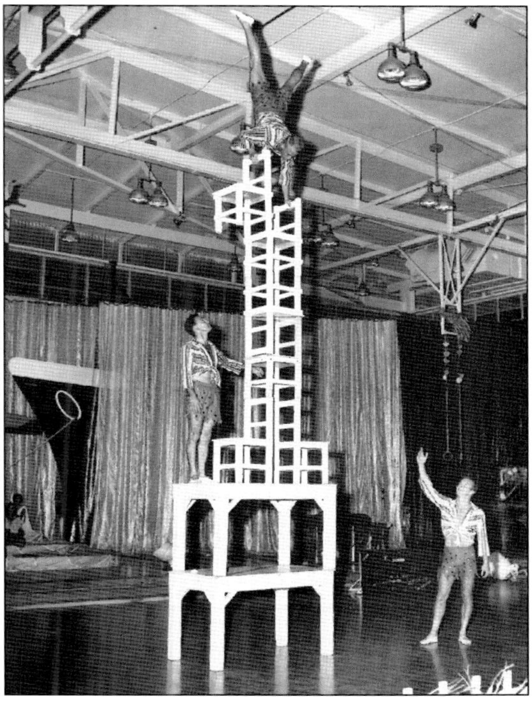

Many of the athletes who participated on Florida State University's gymnastics teams also took part in Gymkana productions at FSU. Gymkana was an entertaining acrobatic exhibition, and the events often involved elaborate themes and costumes. This photograph is from a 1956 production titled *Aloha*.

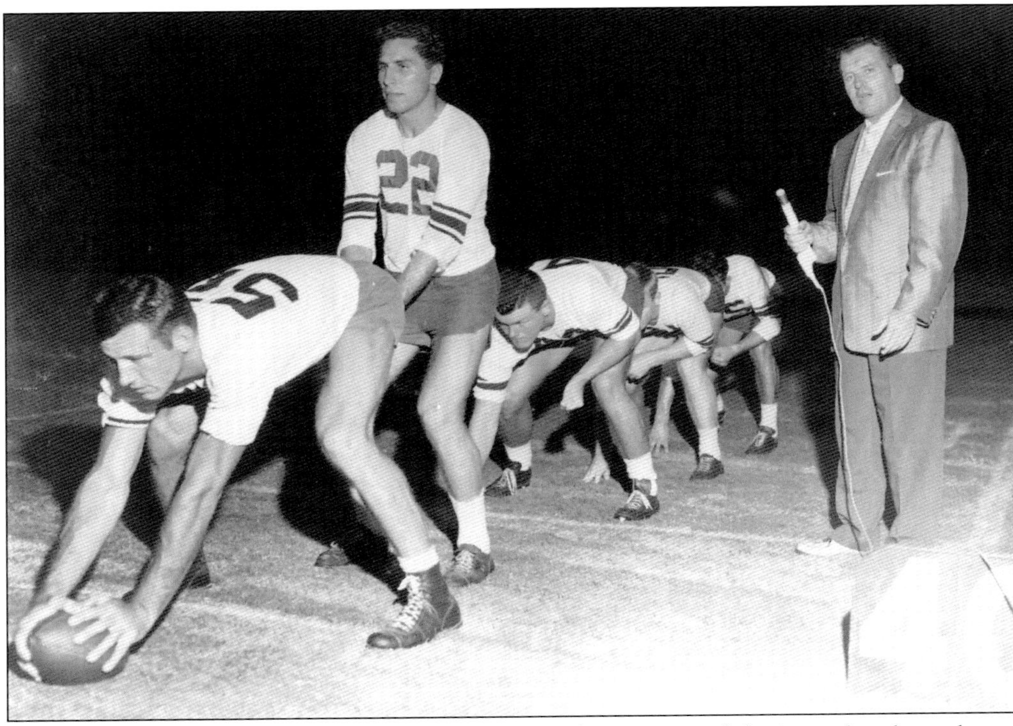

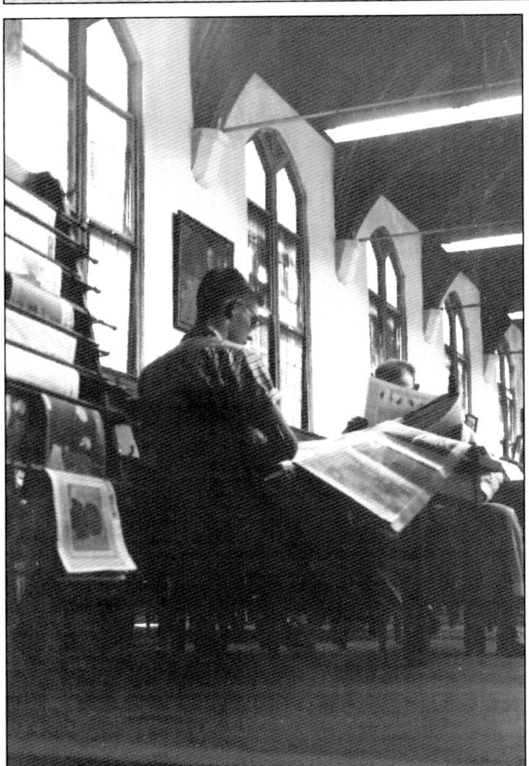

After a successful stint as head coach at Virginia Military Institute, where he developed the I formation, Tom Nugent took over as FSU's head football coach. Nugent remained at FSU from 1953 to 1958, guiding the team to a 34-28-1 record with two bowl appearances. During his tenure, Nugent (right) coached Burt "Buddy" Reynolds and Lee Corso (class of 1957). Corso is pictured wearing the No. 22 jersey. (FSU Athletic Department.)

After the transition to coeducation, the library reading room became even more overcrowded and busy, in part because of the influx of men but also because the library became a campus social center. After the new library opened in 1956, the former library housed, at various times, the College of Arts and Sciences, the philosophy department, and WFSU-TV. In 1961, it was renamed Dodd Hall in honor of the former dean of Arts and Sciences. The FSU Heritage Museum is now located in the former reading room.

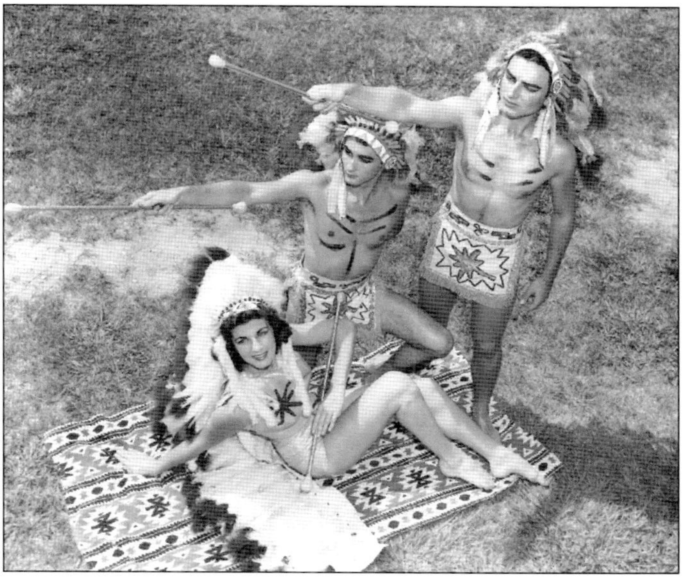

Dick Puckett (class of 1958) and Ed Franklin (class of 1962) came to Florida State University in 1953, and for the next four years, they were known as the "Flying Seminoles." Although highly recruited by other schools for their baton twirling, dance, and acrobatic abilities, they chose FSU, where they performed with the Marching Chiefs. In the 1956 photograph at right, Puckett (kneeling in the middle) and Franklin pose with majorette Paula Parsons (class of 1958).

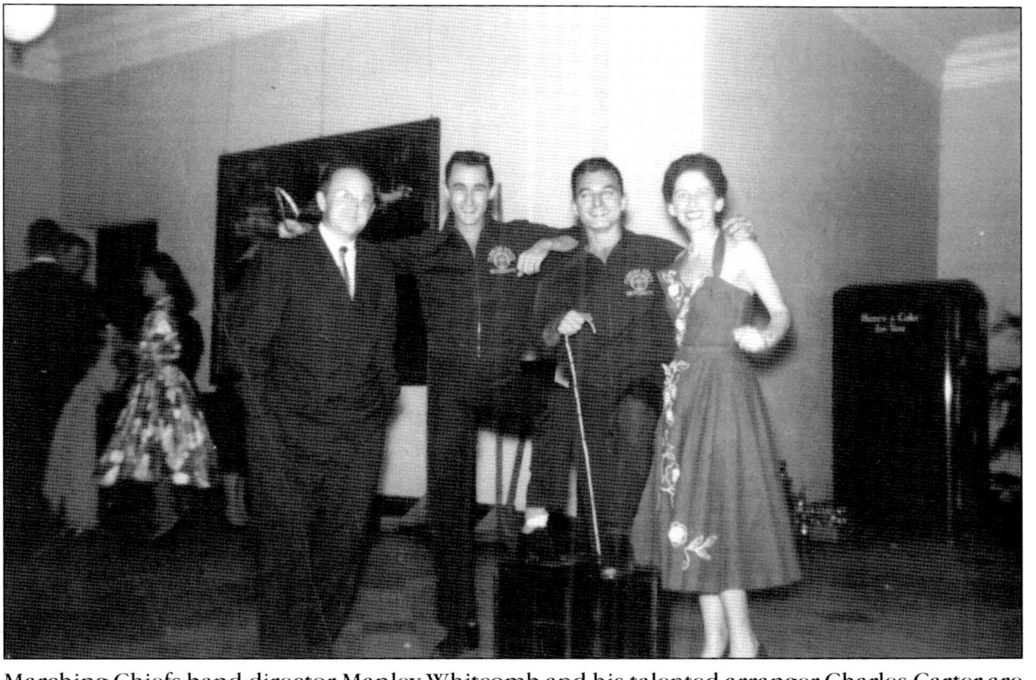

Marching Chiefs band director Manley Whitcomb and his talented arranger Charles Carter are credited with revolutionizing the Florida State University marching band. Arriving at FSU in 1953, Whitcomb instituted fast marching tempos and the high step with an arm swing known as the Chiefs' Step; he also introduced the concept of marching eight steps to five yards. In the photograph above, Dick Puckett (class of 1958), second from the left, and Ed Franklin (class of 1962), second from the right, pose with Doctor Whitcomb (left) and his wife, Leah.

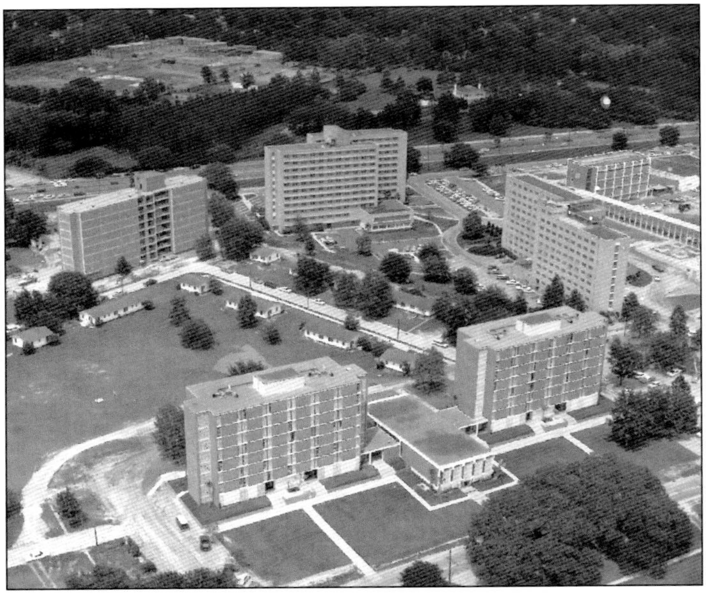

Constructed in 1952, West Hall (later renamed Smith Hall) was the first dormitory built on the western side of the campus and became the nucleus around which other western residence halls were constructed. The 11-story building was the largest dormitory on the campus, housing over 550 men. It was followed by Kellum in 1959, Salley in 1964, Rogers in 1965, and McCollum in 1975. Salley Hall was the university's first coed dormitory.

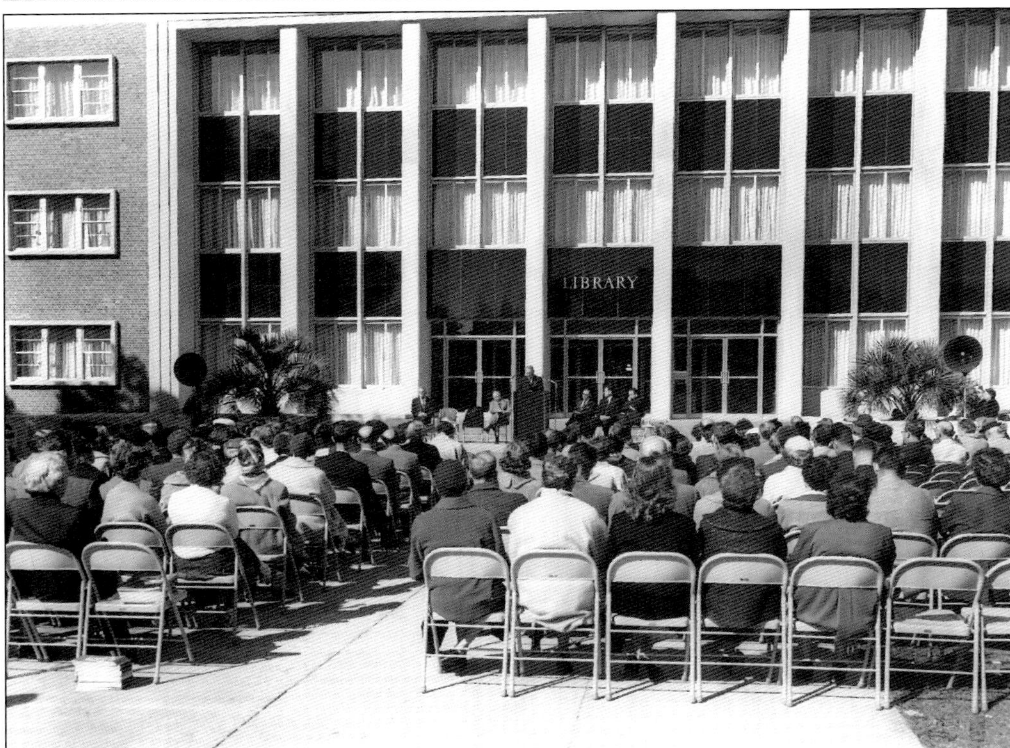

The new Florida State University library building was dedicated on November 9, 1956. The three-story structure had many modern conveniences, including a smoking lounge, faculty and student carrels, and air conditioning. In 1961, it was named in honor of Robert Manning Strozier, FSU president from 1957 until his untimely death in 1960. In 1967, a five-story annex was added in the rear. It still serves as the main campus library.

After the school's transition to Florida State University, the Gulf Coast continued to be a recreational destination for students. The photograph at right is from an Alpha Gamma Delta Weekend at the Avant's beach cottage at Alligator Point in May 1956. From left to right are Sam Moore, June Grant (class of 1957), Edwin Moure, Joan Cunningham (class of 1957), Lou Griffin, and Rollin Davis.

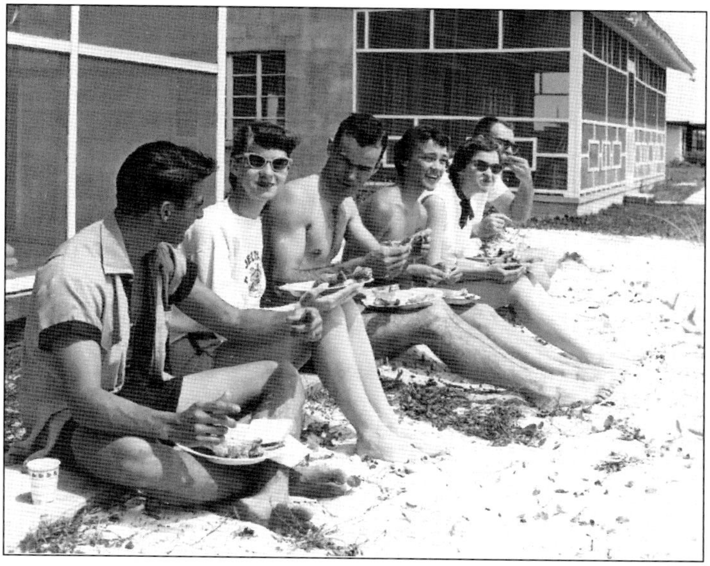

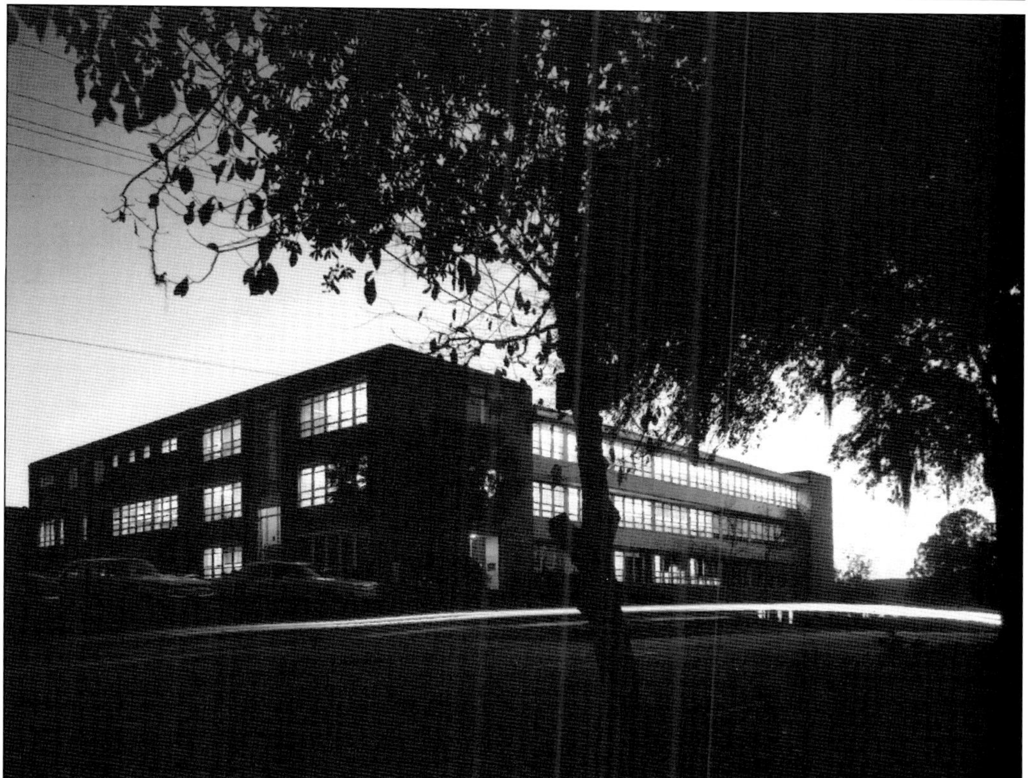

Built in 1956 to house the School of Home Economics, the Sandels Building has recently undergone extensive renovations, including a new east facade that blends the Collegiate Gothic style of the surrounding buildings into its original 1950s Modern architectural design. Named in honor of Margaret Sandels, the former head of the school, the School of Home Economics now functions as the College of Human Sciences.

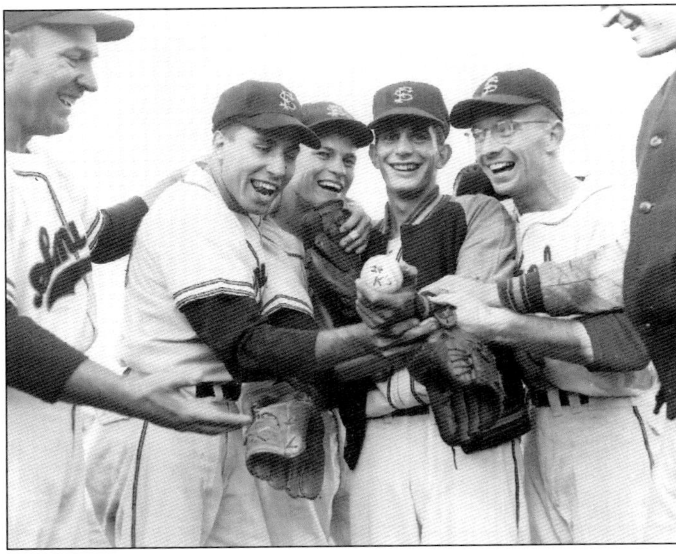

Florida State University's baseball team became a national powerhouse in the late 1950s, reaching the NCAA tournament in 1956 and the College World Series in 1957. In addition to his other achievements, pitcher Tony Avitable's 1956 feat of striking out 24 Furman University batters is a school record that may never be broken. In the photograph at left, Avitable (center) holds a ball commemorating his accomplishment. Lee Corso is second from the left. (FSU Athletic Department.)

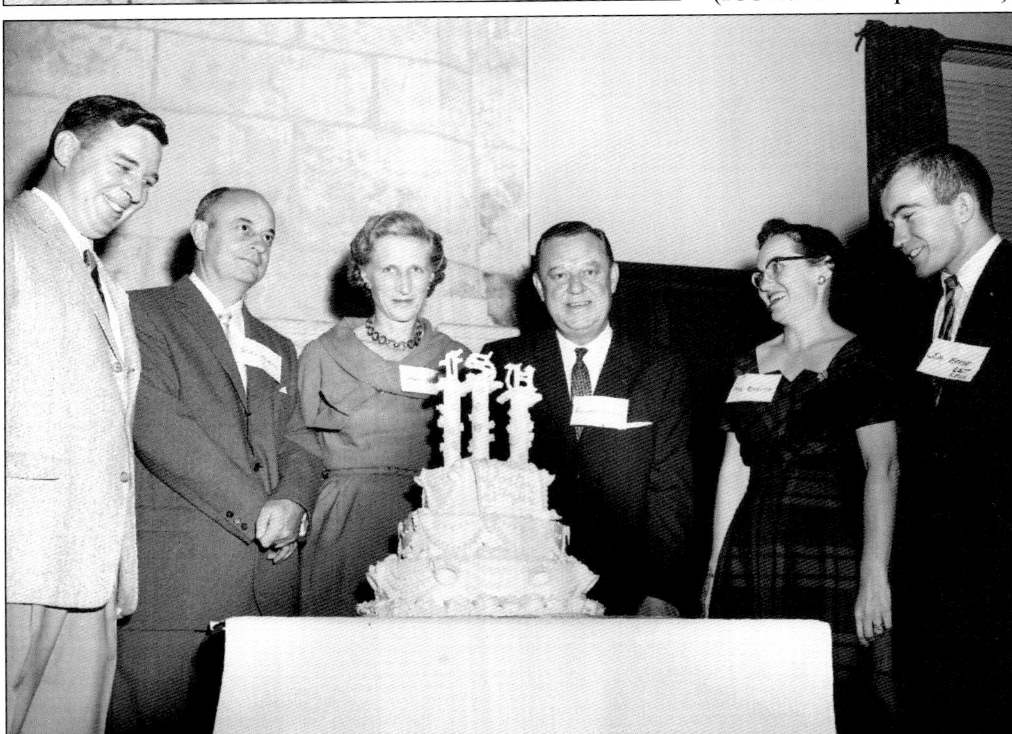

When Robert Manning Strozier arrived at Florida State University in 1957, his goal was to make "Florida State a great university." A serious academic, students appreciated his humor, and he established a great rapport with the faculty. He died suddenly from a heart attack on April 20, 1960, at age 53. The university's main library is named in his honor. Included in the photograph above are Strozier (fourth from left) and his wife, Margaret (fifth from left), and dean of the School of Business Charles Rovetta (second from left) and his wife, Mary (third from left).

Freezing weather and threats of snow in Tallahassee are not unheard of, but they are always considered unusual. Students loved to take photographs of the Administration/Westcott Fountain when it froze over, and it was in fact considered good luck for the fountain to freeze at least once during an FSCW student's four years on campus. The February 1958 snowstorm takes the cake for overall photographic documentation.

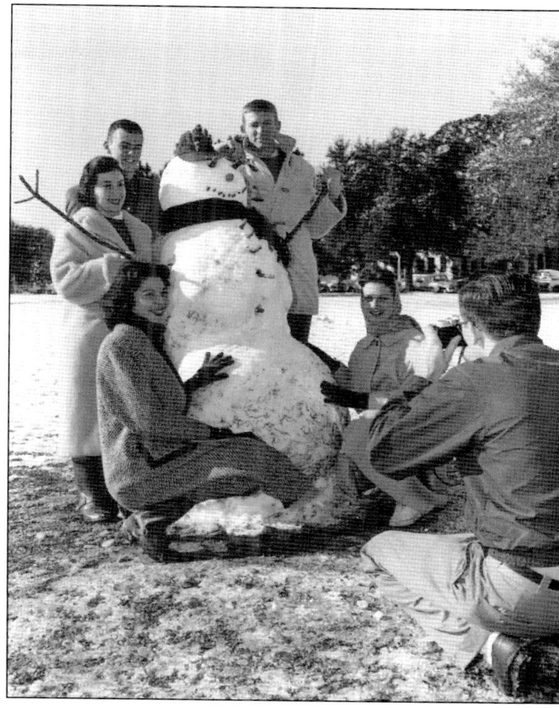

As a freshman, Tallahassee native and Florida State University student Faye Dunaway was active in campus productions. Dunaway, an education major who later became a famous actor, was on the 1959 Miss FSU Court and a member of Pi Beta Phi sorority. The photograph below is from the fall of 1958 FSU speech–theater department production of *The Hairy Ape*.

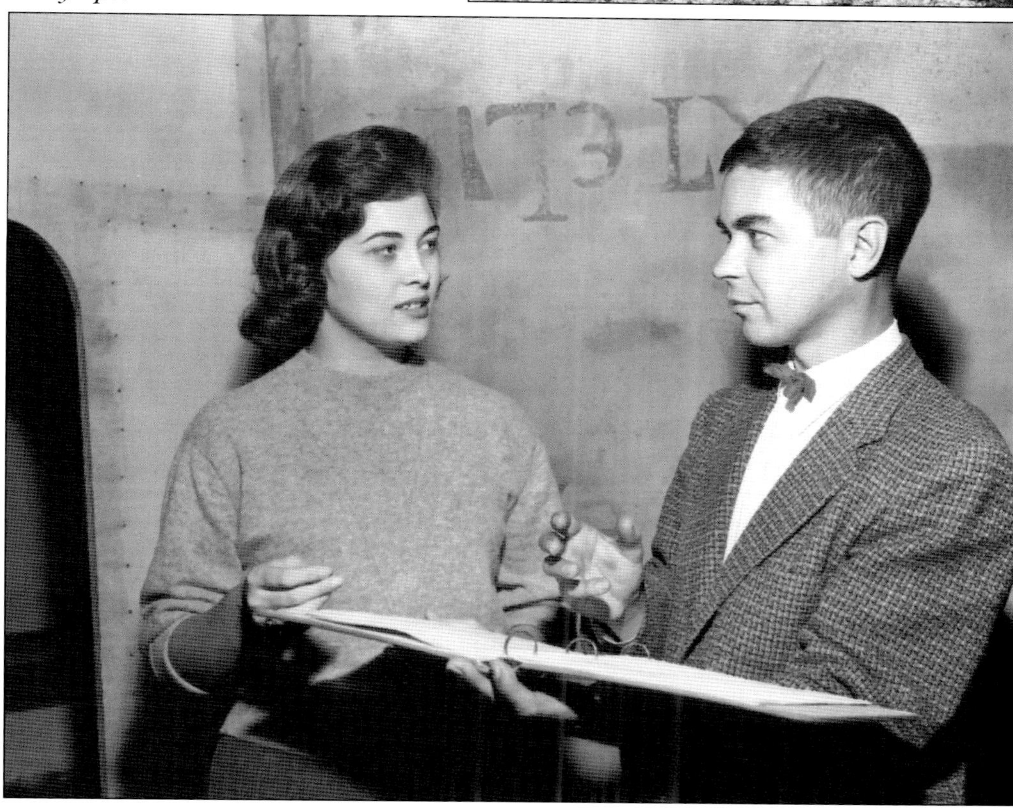

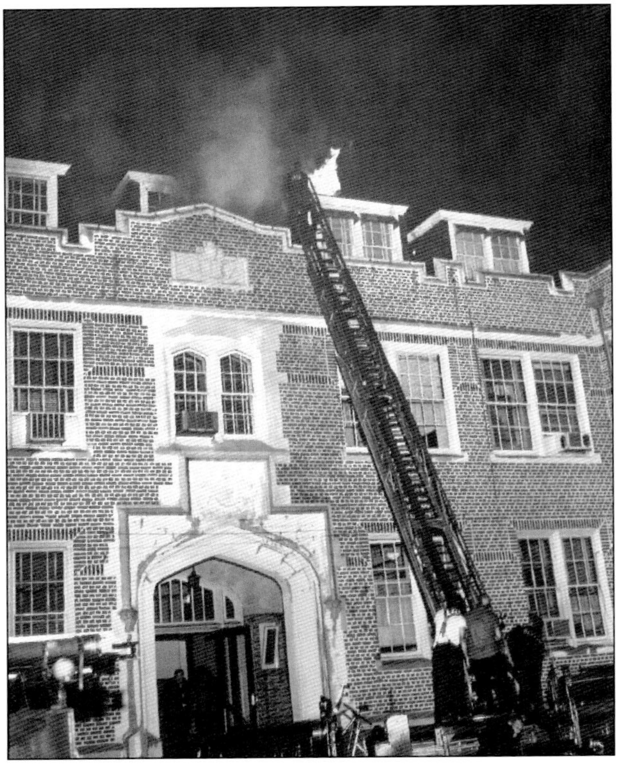

On September 23, 1960, fire raged through the upper floors of the Psychology Building, causing extensive damage. The blaze, which started in the attic, took fire crews two and a half hours to control. No one was injured, but approximately 100 graduate students who used the space lost nearly all of their equipment. (Archives of Florida.)

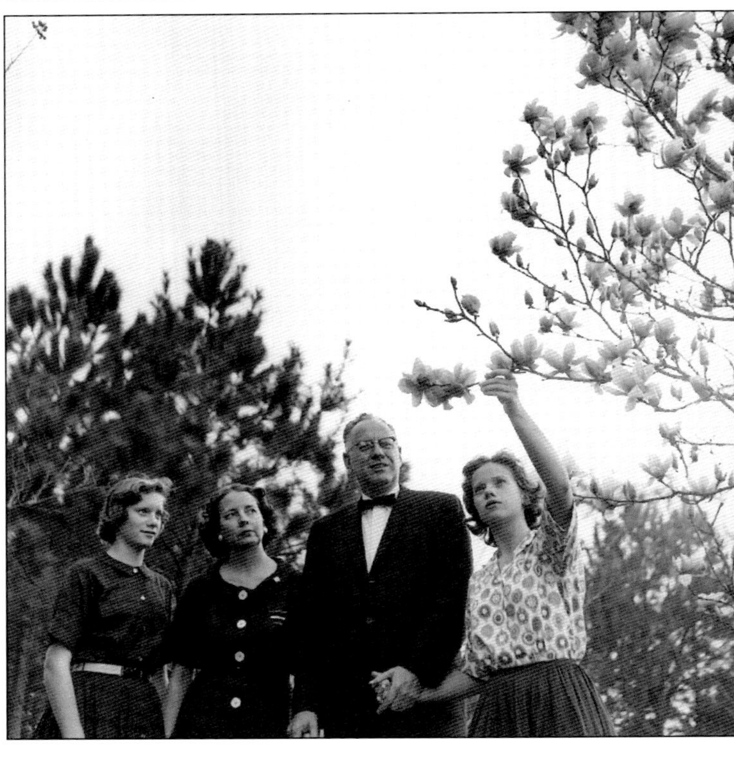

Academic program development, building construction, and development of a well-rounded athletics program were the major accomplishments of Gordon Blackwell's tenure as Florida State University president from 1960 to 1965. He also played a vital role in the integration of the university, with the first African American students enrolling during his presidency.

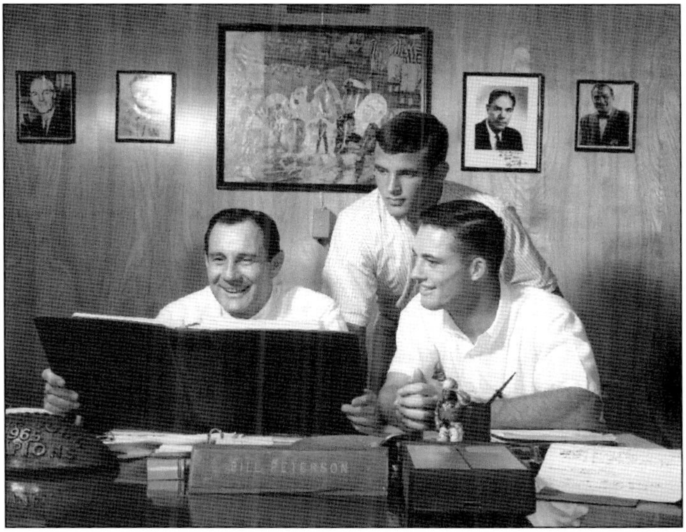

Bill Peterson was Florida State University's head football coach from 1960 to 1970, compiling an overall record of 62-41-11, with four bowl appearances. In 1964, he was the first coach to guide his team to a victory over the University of Florida (UF). Before he left FSU, he had coached FSU's first All-American, Fred Biletnikoff, and hired several assistants who would go on to successful coaching careers, including Joe Gibbs, Bill Parcells, and Bobby Bowden.

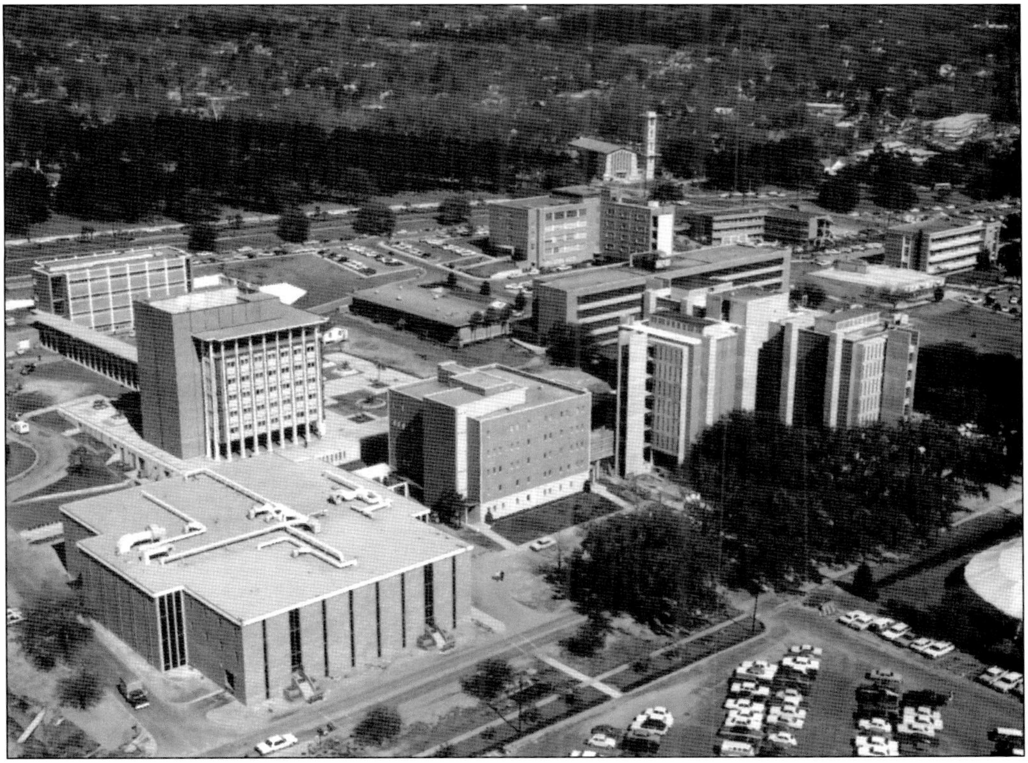

With the continued western expansion and growth in research, a complex of science buildings developed. Originating with the Carraway Building, Carothers Hall, and the Love Building, the area's development as the FSU Science Center began with the construction of the Molecular Biophysics Building in 1962. The Keen Physics Research Building and the Biology Building followed. These were eventually followed by other science buildings, including the Dirac Science Library in 1988. The first decade of the 21st century brought a true science quadrangle, including medicine, chemistry, and biology buildings.

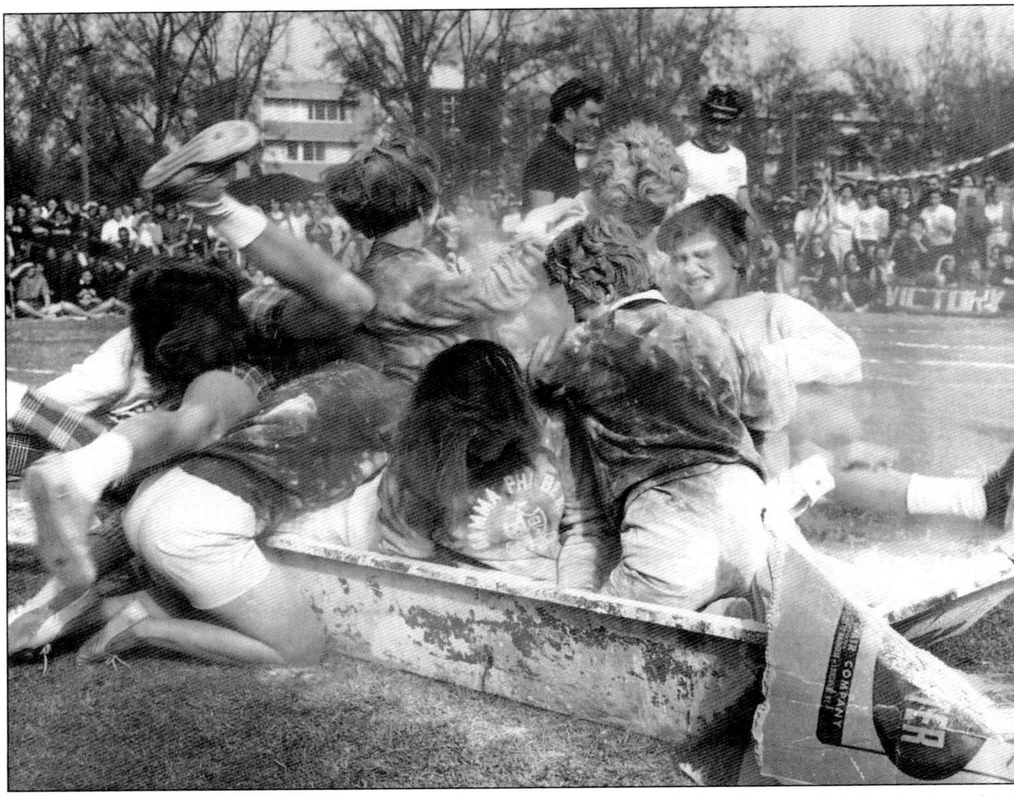

In the late 1950s and 1960s, Sigma Chi fraternity sponsored the Sigma Chi Derby in which sororities on campus competed in various contests of "skill," such as the key hunt, obstacle race, balloon pop, chicken chase, and egg drop. In some years, there might be a pie-throwing contest and other "contests," like the event shown in the photograph above. Funds raised through the event augmented the Campus Chest.

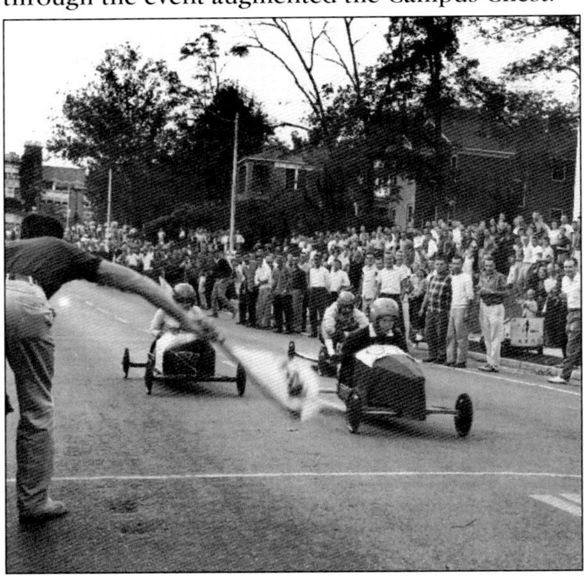

The annual soap box derby was another fundraising event with proceeds going to the Campus Chest. "Women drivers, sleek racers, and a perilous downhill descent" were not ingredients for disaster, but rather "FSU's challenge to the Indianapolis Speedway." Sponsored by Alpha Gamma Delta sorority and Phi Delta Theta fraternity, the race sent its participants speeding down the hill on College Avenue.

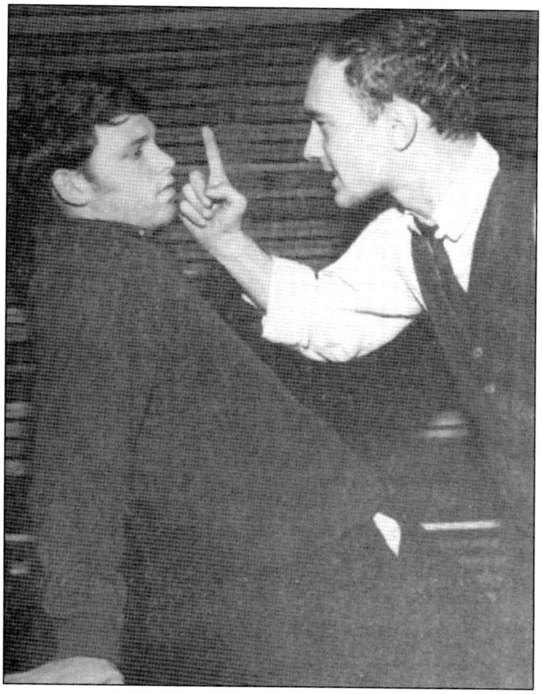

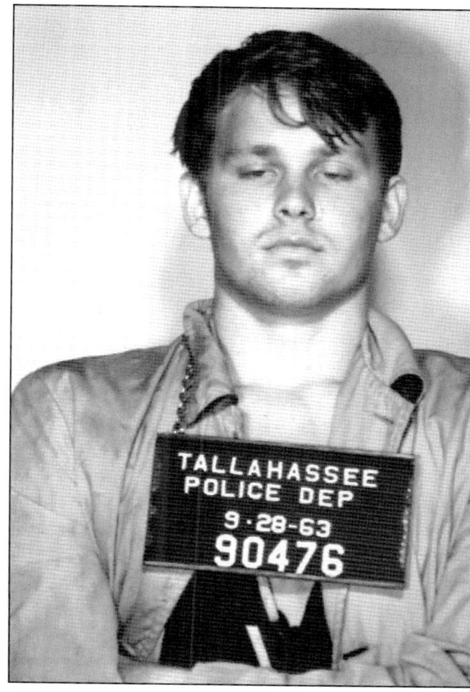

Rock star Jim Morrison attended Florida State University in 1962–1963. While Morrison was a good student, on at least one occasion he got into trouble with the law. On September 28, 1963, following a football game, he was arrested at the Pensacola entrance to Doak Campbell Stadium for disturbing the peace, public drunkenness, and attempting to steal a police umbrella and riot helmet. Morrison was interested in the arts and took Werner Vagt's cinematography course offered through the art department. Morrison appeared in at least one campus theater production, playing the role of Gus in Harold Pinter's *The Dumb Waiter* in December 1963 (above left). In 1964, Morrison left FSU and moved to California to attend film school at UCLA. (Below and above right, Museum of Florida History.)

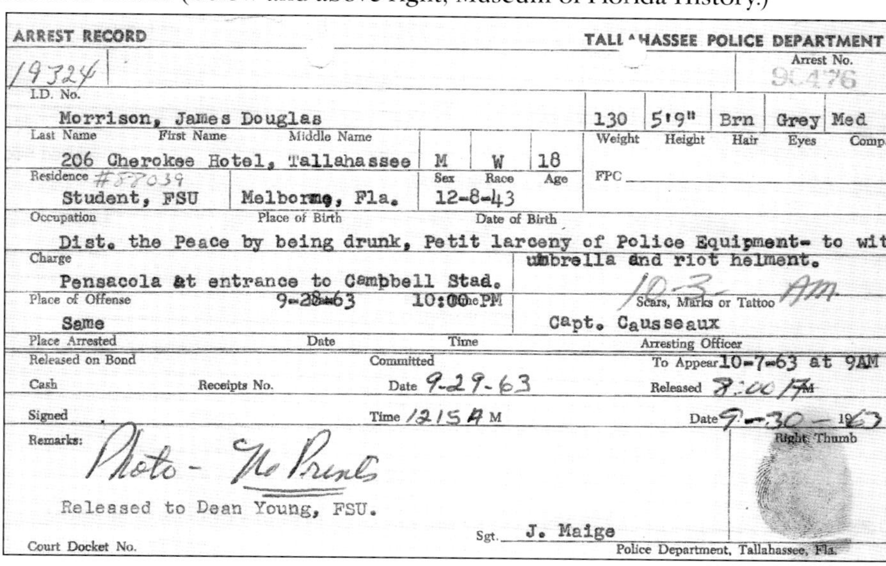

ARREST RECORD — TALLAHASSEE POLICE DEPARTMENT

I.D. No. 19324 — Arrest No. 90476

Last Name, First Name, Middle Name: Morrison, James Douglas
Weight: 130 — Height: 5'9" — Hair: Brn — Eyes: Grey — Comp.: Med

Residence: 206 Cherokee Hotel, Tallahassee #58039
Sex: M — Race: W — Age: 18
FPC

Occupation: Student, FSU — Place of Birth: Melborne, Fla. — Date of Birth: 12-8-43

Charge: Dist. the Peace by being drunk, Petit larceny of Police Equipment- to wit umbrella and riot helment.

Place of Offense: Pensacola at entrance to Campbell Stad. — 9-28-63 — 10:00 PM
Scars, Marks or Tattoo: 10:3- AM

Place Arrested: Same — Date — Time
Arresting Officer: Capt. Causseaux

Released on Bond — Committed — To Appear 10-7-63 at 9AM
Cash — Receipts No. — Date 9-29-63 — Released 8:00 AM
Signed — Time 1215 AM — Date 9-30-1963

Remarks: Photo - No Prints
Released to Dean Young, FSU.

Right Thumb

Court Docket No. — Sgt. J. Maige — Police Department, Tallahassee, Fla.

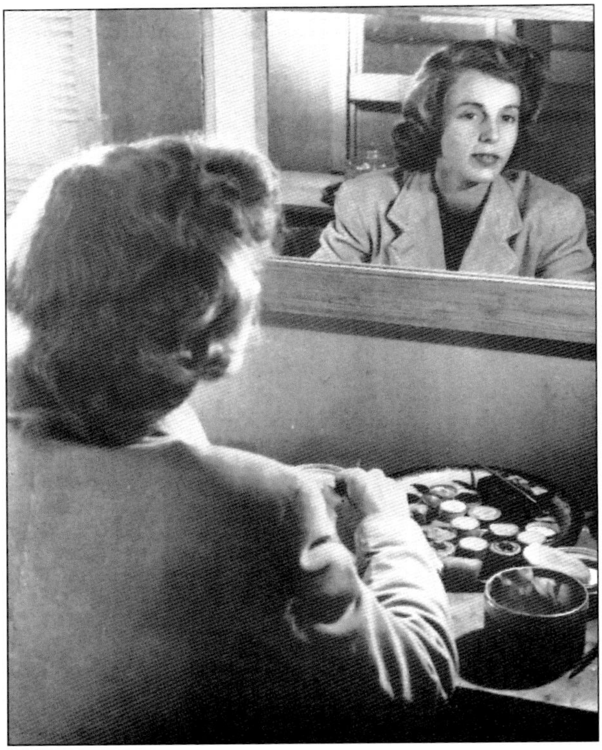

Florida State College for Women graduate Nancy Kulp (class of 1943) was the master of ceremonies for the 1963 FSU Homecoming Hootenanny. The Miami Beach native earned her bachelor's of arts degree in journalism and was active in the Odds and Spirogira, Tarpon Swim Club, and Mortified. She was voted the "show-off" of her senior class, with "a heap of brains and an overpowering sense of humor that deserves to be shown off." She later achieved fame as a character actress and was most notable for her performance as Jane Hathaway in situation comedy *The Beverly Hillbillies*, receiving an Emmy Award nomination for that role. In the photograph below, *Beverly Hillbillies* costar Irene Ryan waves goodbye to Kulp as she heads off to her 1963 homecoming engagement. (Below, *Tallahassee Democrat*.)

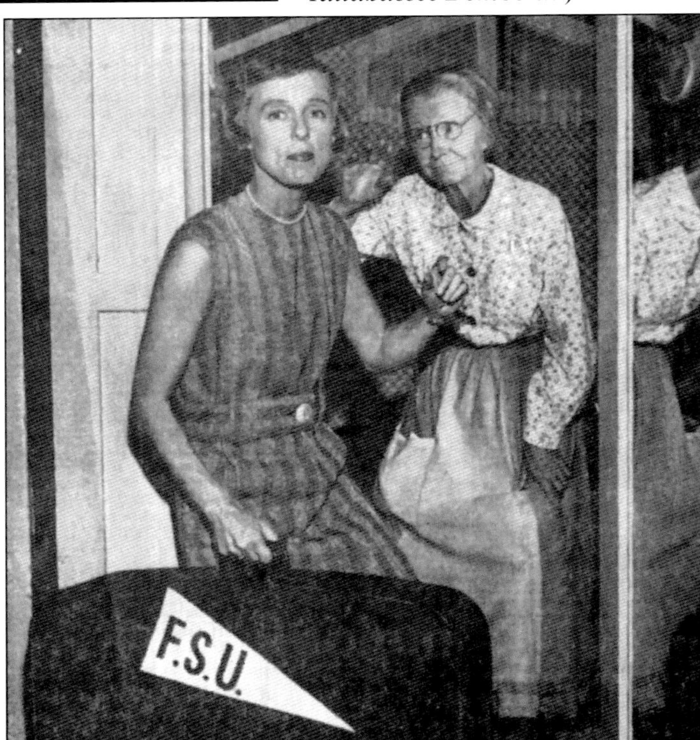

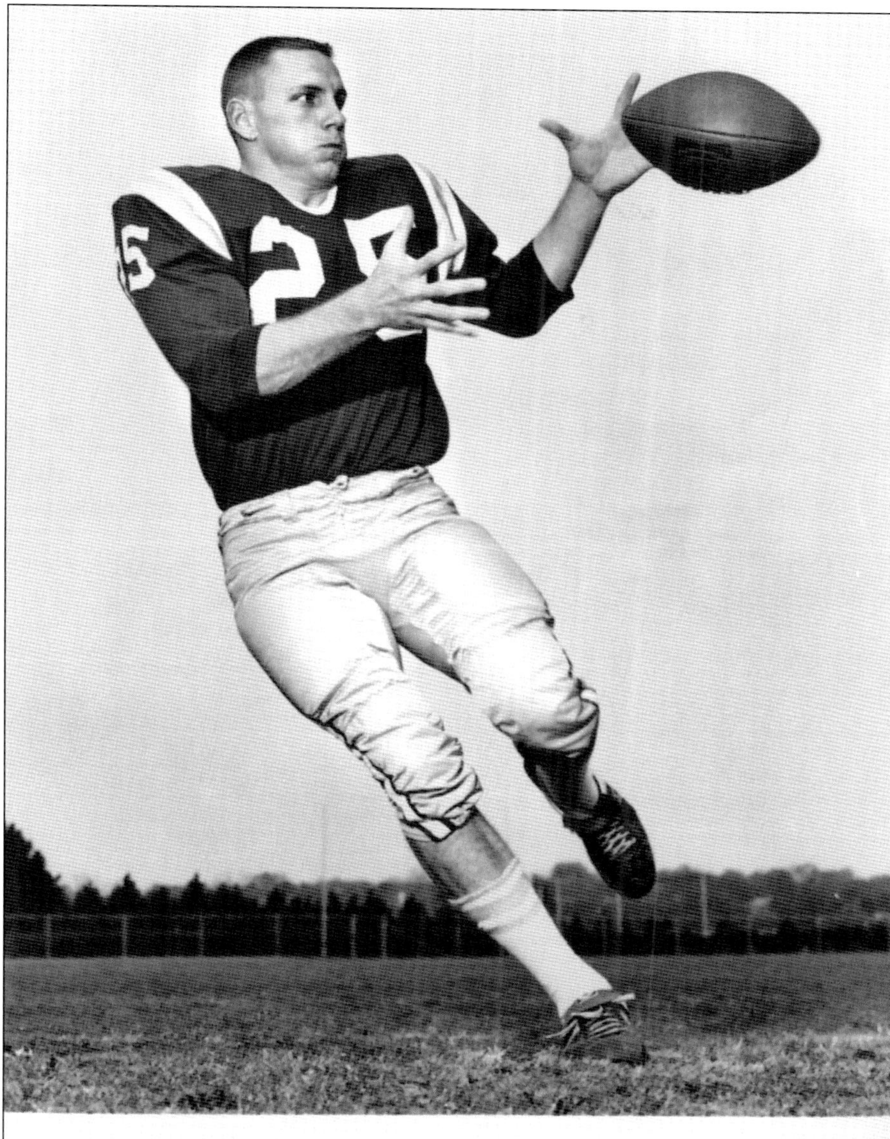

T. K. WETHERELL FLORIDA STATE

Daytona Beach native Thomas Kent "T.K." Wetherell attended Florida State University on a football scholarship from 1964 to 1967. He was a durable two-way player and over the course of his career played receiver, punt/kickoff returner, and defensive back. He went on to earn his master's of science and his doctorate in educational administration, all from FSU. He served in the Florida State Legislature from 1980 to 1992, the final two years as Speaker of the House. A lifetime educator, he served as president of Tallahassee Community College and then president of FSU from 2003 to 2010, the first alumnus ever to do so. Under his leadership, FSU enrolled the most academically talented students in the history of the university, increased the number of doctoral degrees awarded, set new records for research dollars, and experienced a boom in campus construction. On his retirement from the presidency, Wetherell became a professor in the College of Education. He is in the FSU Sports Hall of Fame.

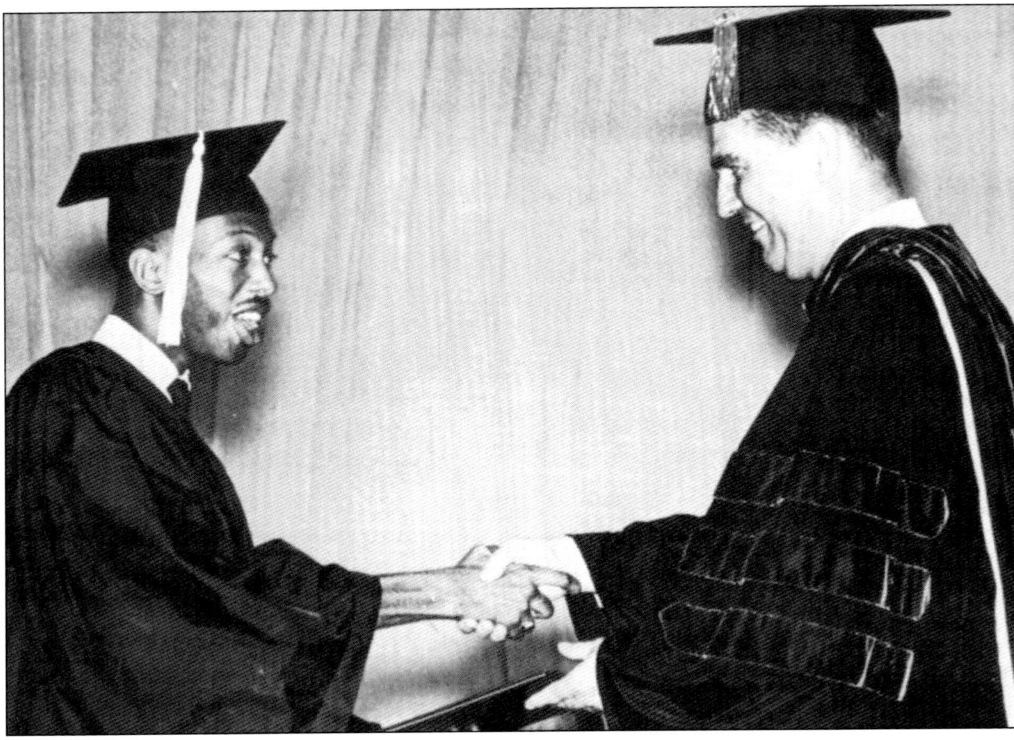

Tallahassee Lincoln High School graduate Maxwell Courtney was the first African American student to attend and graduate from Florida State University. His achievement, along with those of Fred Flowers, the first African American athlete at FSU, and Doby Flowers, FSU's first African American homecoming princess, are celebrated today on the Integration Statue near the Student Union. In the photograph above, Courtney receives his mathematics degree in 1965 from Pres. John Champion. (FSU Alumni Association.)

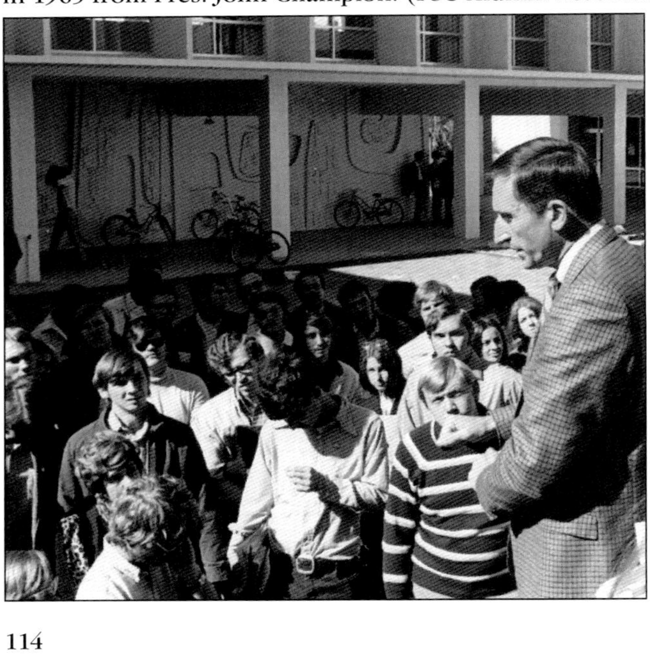

During his presidency from 1969 to 1976, J. Stanley Marshall guided Florida State University through the tumultuous 1960s, largely without incident. There were protests and demonstrations, but there was no violence at FSU. The fact that Marshall was the president of FSU during this turbulent period sometimes overshadows the progressive achievements his administration made in racial integration at the school.

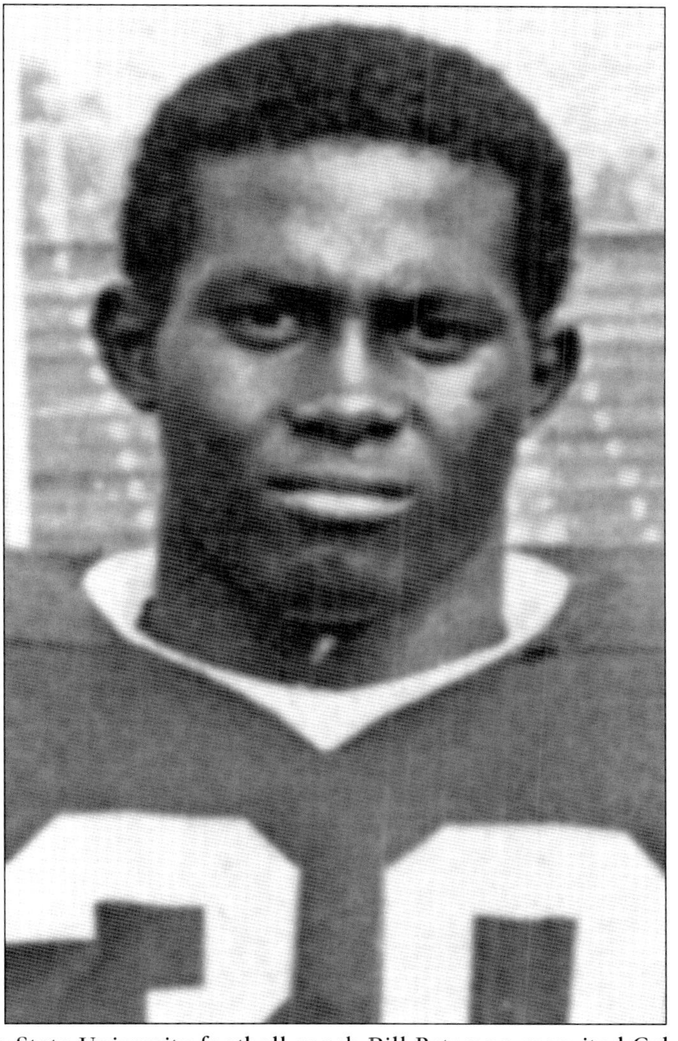

In 1968, Florida State University football coach Bill Peterson recruited Calvin Patterson, a fleet-footed running back from Palmetto High School in Miami, as the first African American on the team. After three years of struggling in a racially charged environment on and off the field, his grades suffered and he was forced to leave school. In 1972, in an effort to provide an excuse to his friends and family about why he would not be playing in his upcoming last year of eligibility, he shot himself, intending only to wound. Patterson's plan backfired, and he accidently killed himself. Ignored by the FSU community from the time of his death, FSU in 2004 formally recognized the significance of his role at the university. This included an on-field ceremony at halftime with nearly 30 family members attending the event.

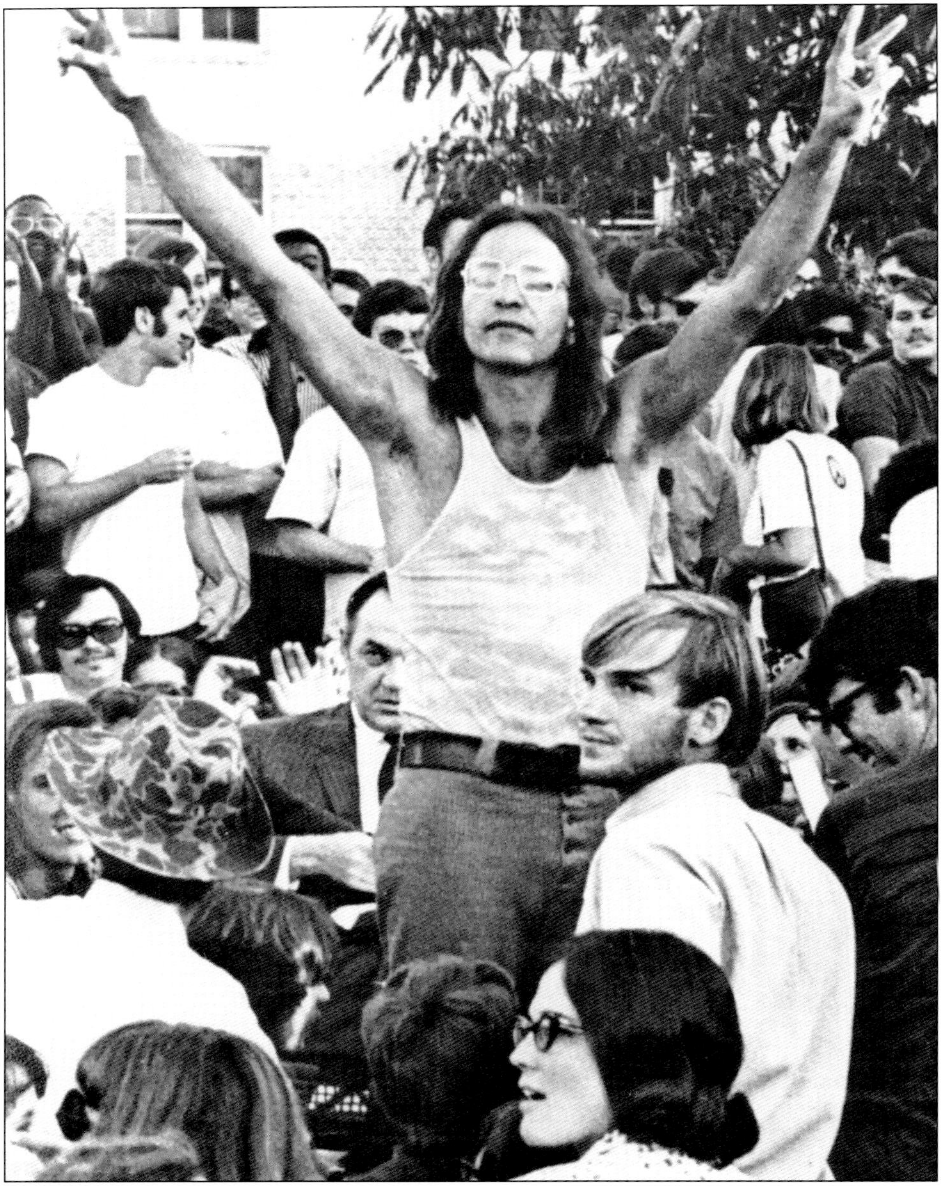

Campus dissent and protest at Florida State University reached its peak at the end of the 1960s. With active chapters of the Liberal Forum, the Grassroots Movement, and Students for a Democratic Society, the university had gained a reputation for activism and was known by some as the "Berkeley of the South." Students sought to effect change on campus and in academics, as well as in politics and community affairs. Their concerns included but were not limited to the Vietnam War, censorship, freedom of speech, and civil as well as women's rights. They also wanted a role in how the university was run. Pres. Stanley Marshall's administration believed that they maintained an open dialog, giving students room for expression without incidents on the campus. This iconic image is from a May 8, 1970, rally following the Kent State incident a few days earlier. In the background wearing a tie is Florida governor Claude Kirk.

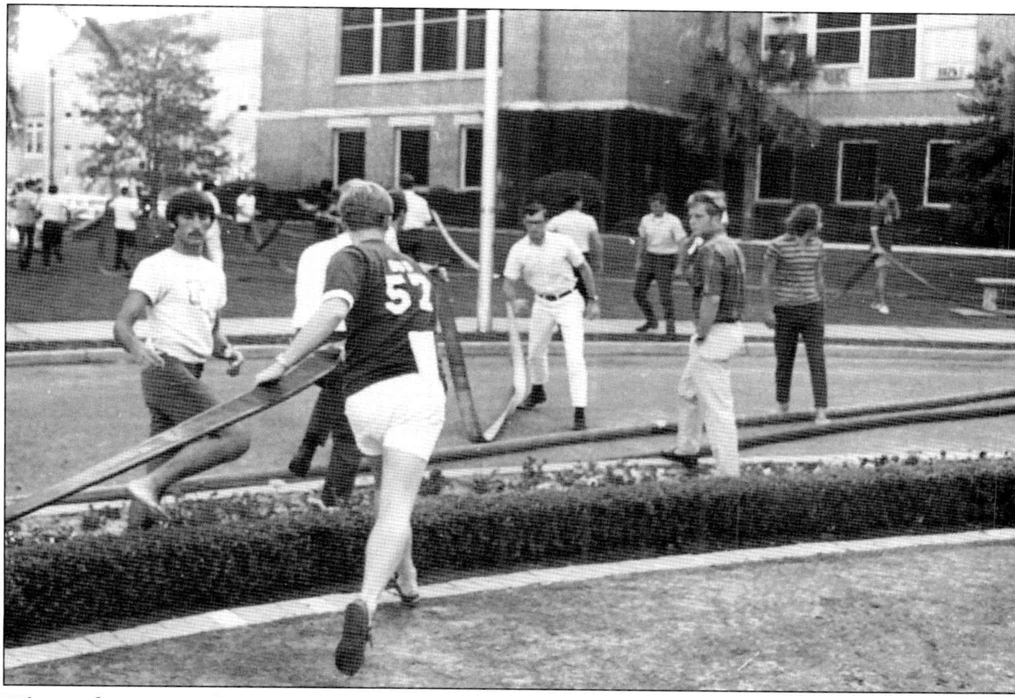

When a fire swept through the fourth floor of the Westcott Building on the afternoon of April 27, 1969, the university community rallied to save the building and its contents. Sweating students carried equipment and invaluable records from the structure, even as the fire ravaged the top floor. Coeds in bell-bottom pants and Bermuda shorts passed folders, books, and other materials in a human chain to a safe spot on the Westcott lawn, and newly appointed president Stanley Marshall directed the fire brigades. Firemen tossed typewriters and other office equipment from a third-story window to a taut tarpaulin held by students below. Some of the rescued materials included irreplaceable student transcripts as well as records that dated from the school's founding as the West Florida Seminary.

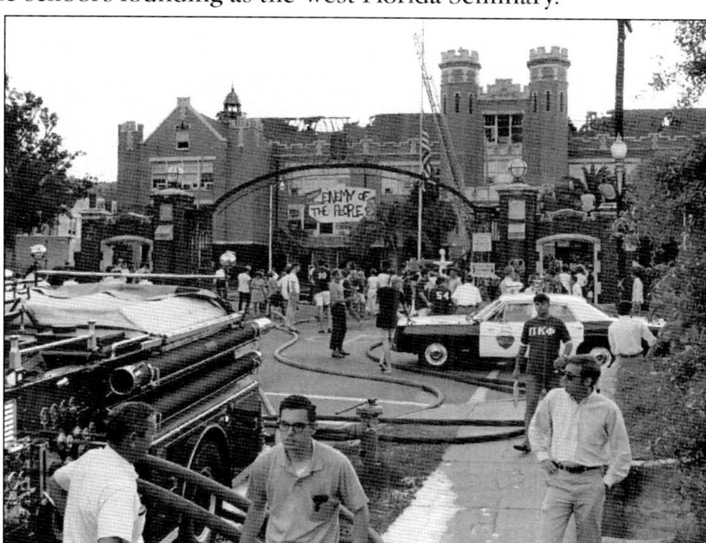

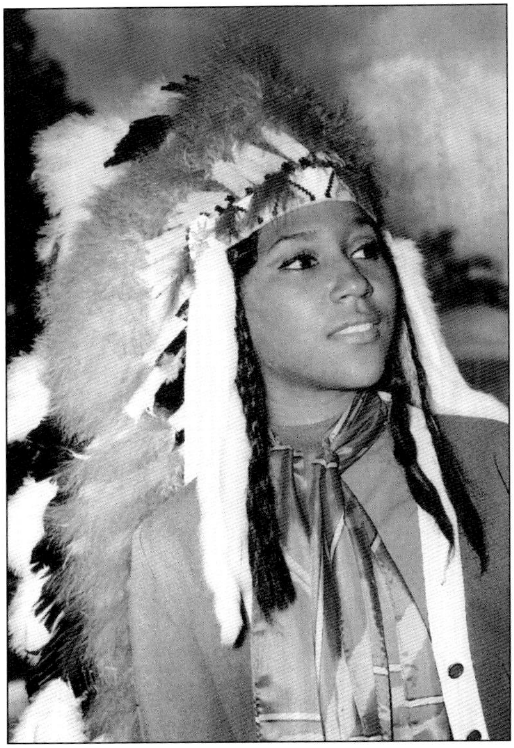

On November 13, 1970, Doby Flowers (class of 1971), a senior majoring in social welfare, became the first African American homecoming princess in Florida State University history. Her brother Fred Flowers (class of 1969) was a member of the baseball team and the first African American uniformed athlete at FSU. Their accomplishments, along with those of Maxwell Courtney, are celebrated today by the Integration Statue near the Student Union.

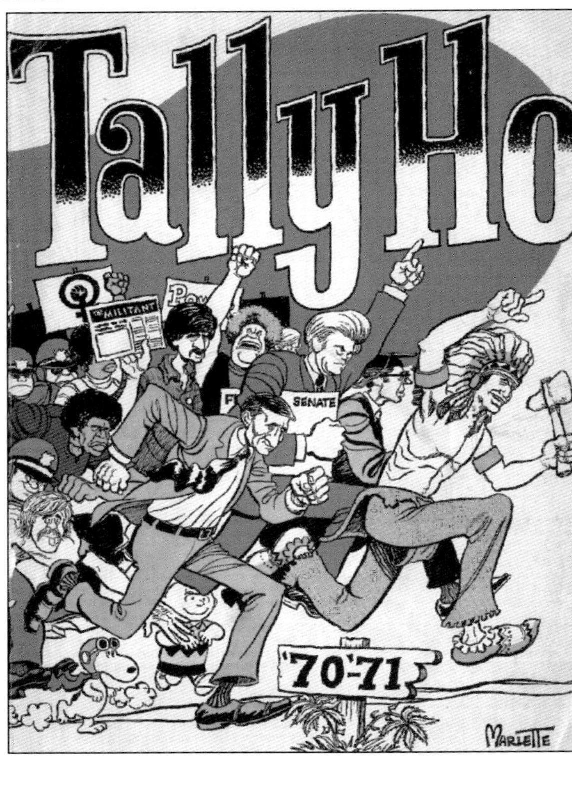

Florida State University alumnus and *Kudzu* cartoon creator Doug Marlette (class of 1971) is credited with "liberating" the FSU yearbook from its traditional format. In 1971, students took over the publication of the annual *Tally Ho* and decided to make a paperback version. The book contained no student portraits, but instead focused on campus current events, looking more like a giant pamphlet for student causes. After that, yearbook publications were sporadic.

The 1972 FSU men's basketball team was distinctive. The team was made up largely of African American players when few teams in the South had more than one or two. Also, under head coach Hugh Durham (class of 1959), the overachieving team made it to the national championship finals, losing to UCLA. In the photograph to the right, Lawrence McCray blocks a shot by UCLA center Bill Walton. (Bill Bolton.)

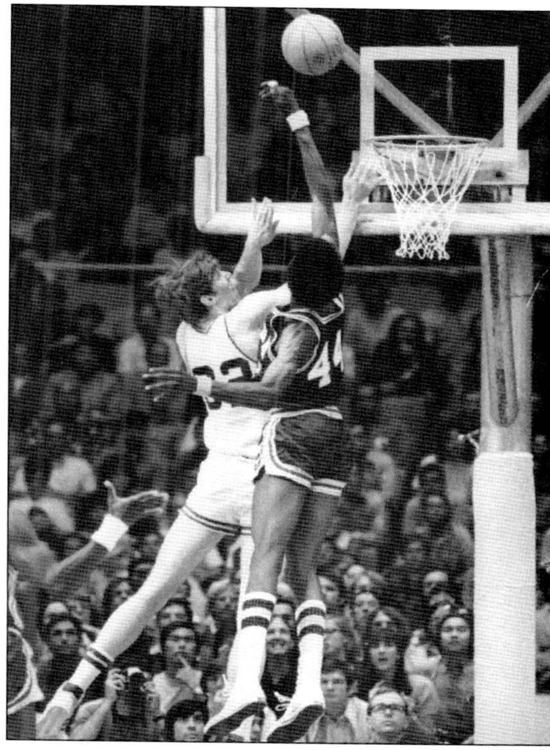

Legend has it that the streaking craze that swept the nation in the 1970s started at Florida State University. Some say that it began when about 200 students ran across the campus one evening in March 1974; however, some argue that it began a couple of months earlier and on a much smaller scale. Prior to streaking, it was just called "running naked." In the photograph below, streakers take their books to Strozier Library's circulation desk.

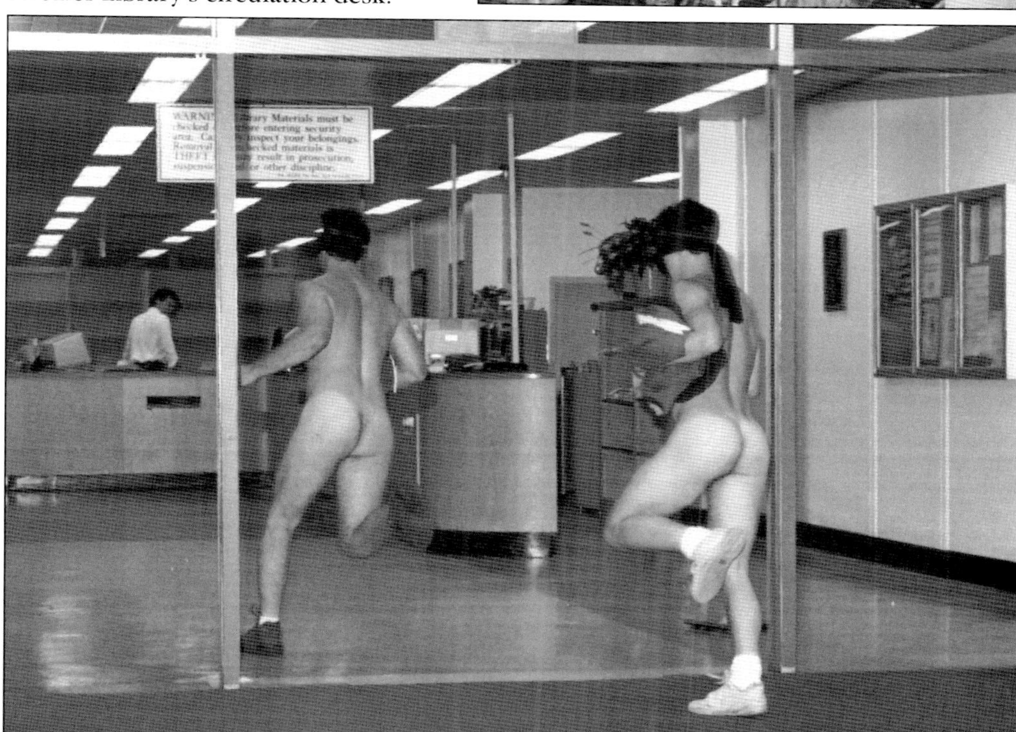

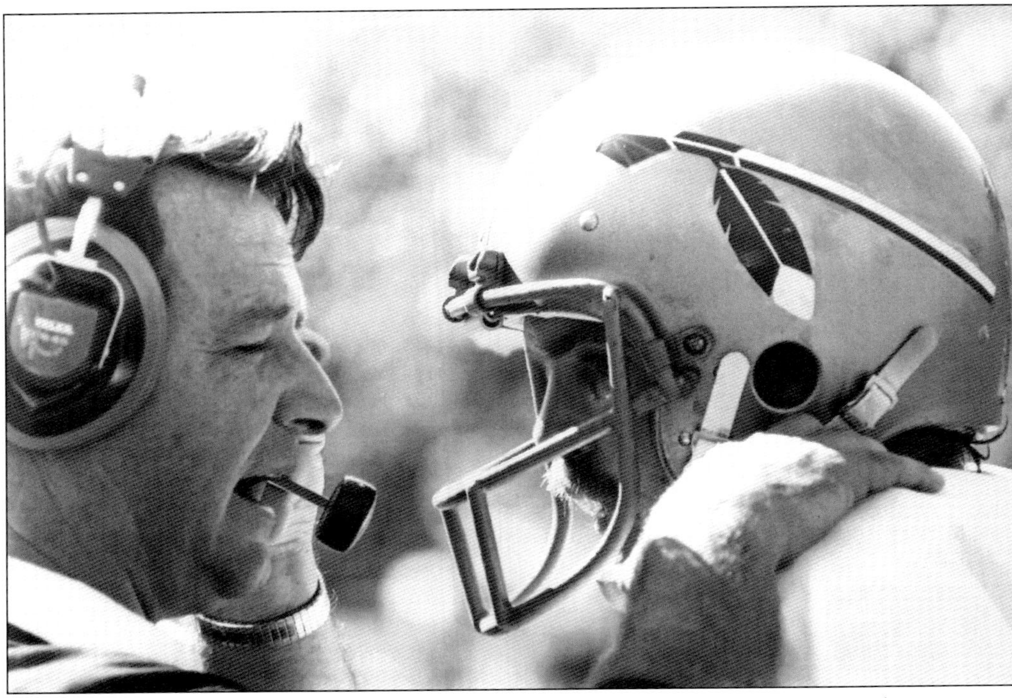

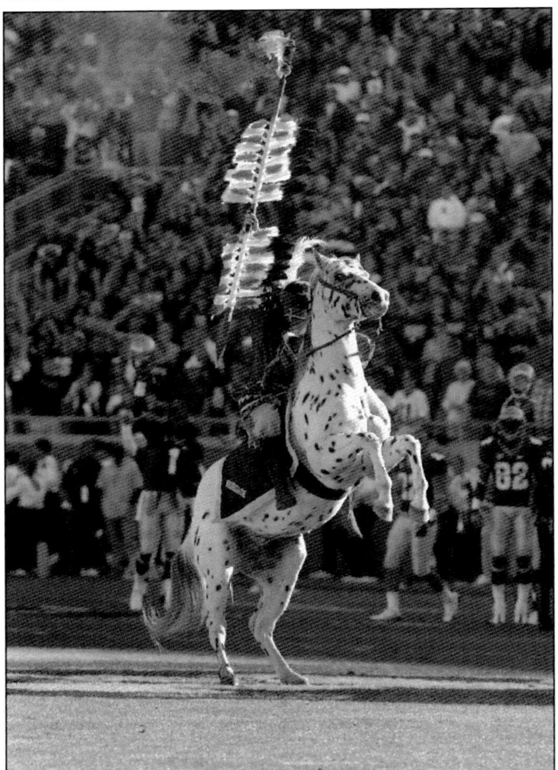

The arrival of Bobby Bowden as head coach for the Florida State University football team revitalized a program that was on the verge of being disbanded. In his second year at the helm, Bowden took a team that had gone 4-29 in the three years prior to his arrival to a 10-2 record and a 1977 Tangerine Bowl victory. In this photograph from his first season, he talks with quarterback Jimmy Black. (Jerry Sexton.)

One of Florida State University's most well-known and recognizable traditions is that of Osceola and Renegade leading the football team onto the field at all home games. In the legendary ritual, established in the fall of 1977, Osceola is dressed in authentic regalia designed by members of the Seminole Tribe of Florida and plants a flaming spear in the center of the field at the start of the game. (Ryals Lee.)

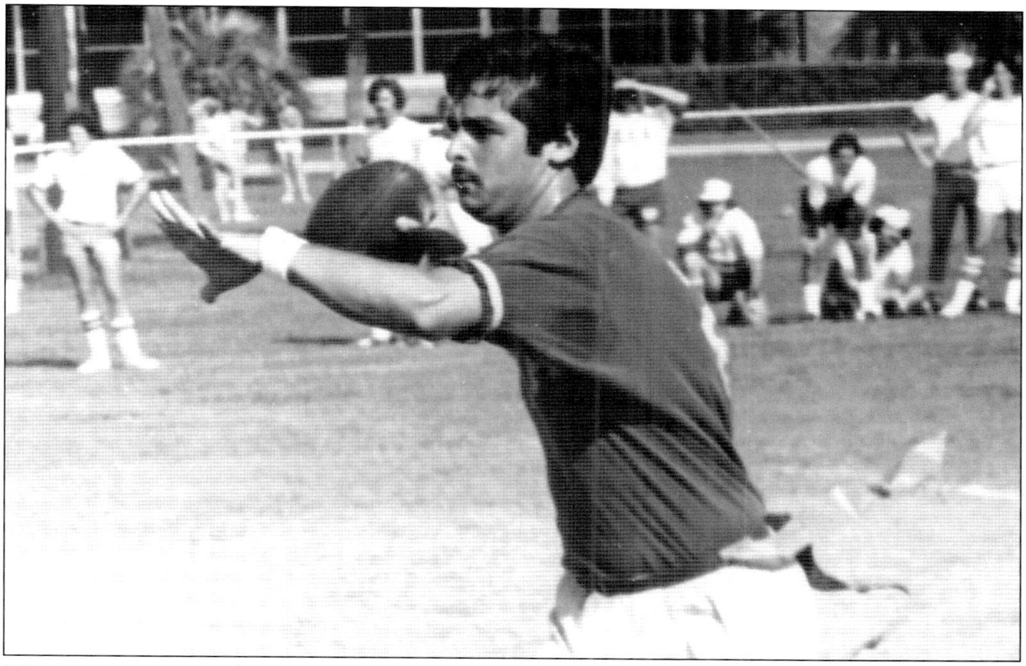

After two years at Wake Forest University where he played football, Charlie Crist transferred to Florida State University. He was vice president of student government and a member of Pi Kappa Alpha fraternity. He graduated in 1978 and then earned his law degree and worked as an attorney before taking up politics. Crist served as a state senator, education commissioner, and attorney general before he was elected Florida's governor, holding that post from 2007 to 2011. (Jerry Sexton.)

After a football injury sidelined him, Burt Reynolds, Florida State University's "most illustrious" former student, left FSU to pursue an acting career. However, he always remained loyal to FSU and would periodically make references to it in his films. On January 14, 1981, Reynolds received an honorary doctorate in humane letters from his alma mater. The following year, he was appointed an adjunct professor of theater at FSU.

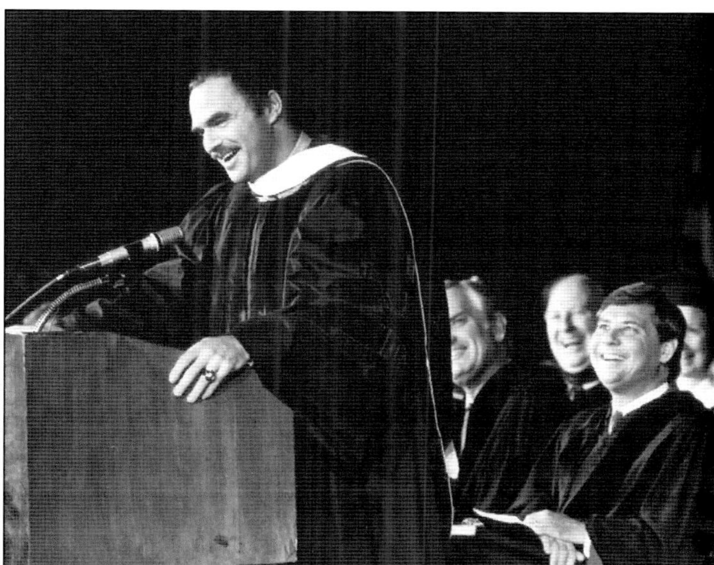

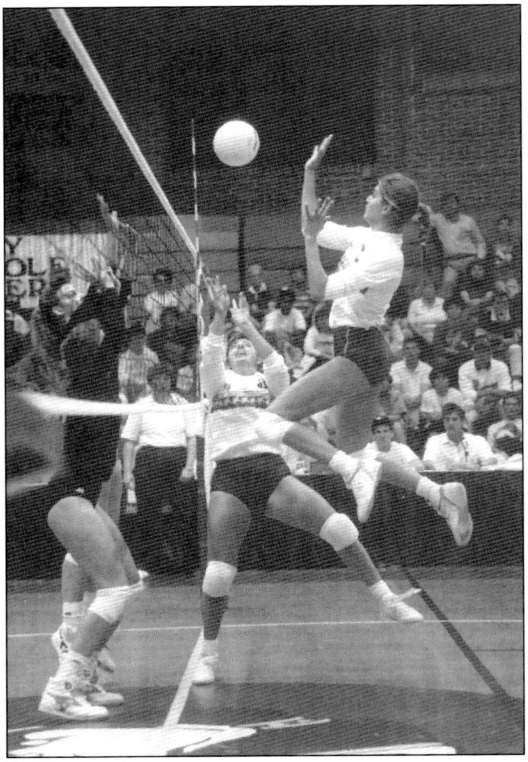

The 1980s marked the era when Florida State University arrived as a well-rounded sports powerhouse. Men's sports had already had moments of glory, but during this time, women's athletics became more competitive with women's golf, softball, and track and field all delivering national championships. FSU's most famous volleyball alumna, Gabrielle Reece, holds multiple solo records and garnered a number of all-star selections. She is in the FSU Sports Hall of Fame. (FSU Athletic Department.)

Pres. Bernie Sliger's 1976–1991 administration and his interim in 1994 saw unprecedented growth in academics and intercollegiate athletics. Noted for his friendly and easygoing manner, as well as his casual appearance, Sliger, known to all as "Bernie," did not drive and could frequently be found strolling across campus in his guayabera shirt and trousers. His annual President's Ice Cream Socials were much anticipated, and the tradition continues today.

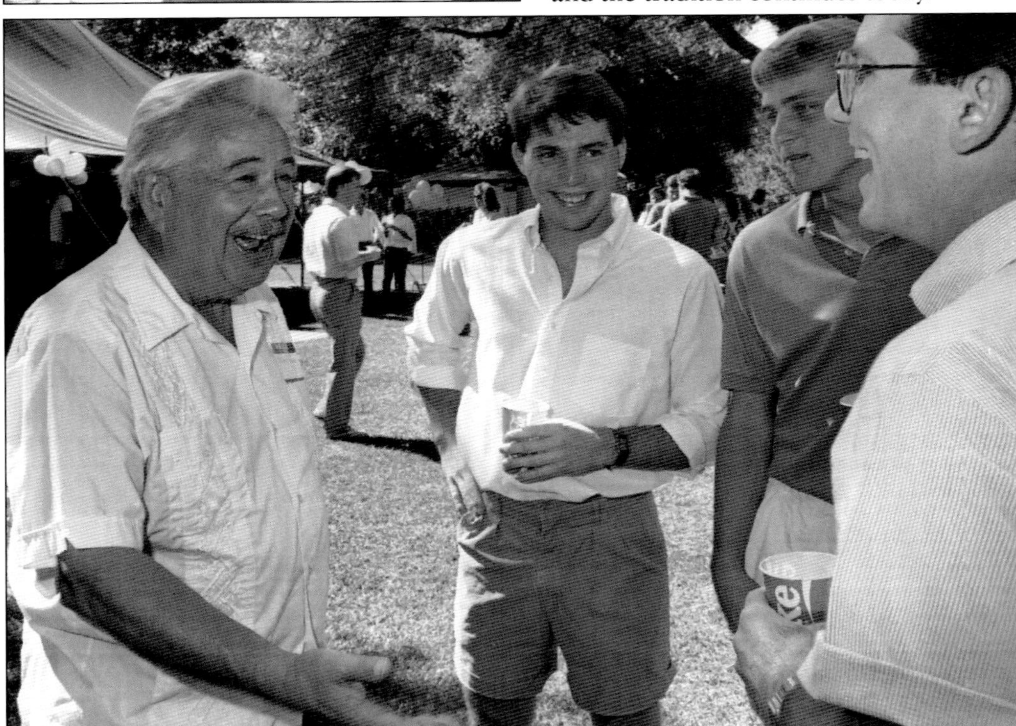

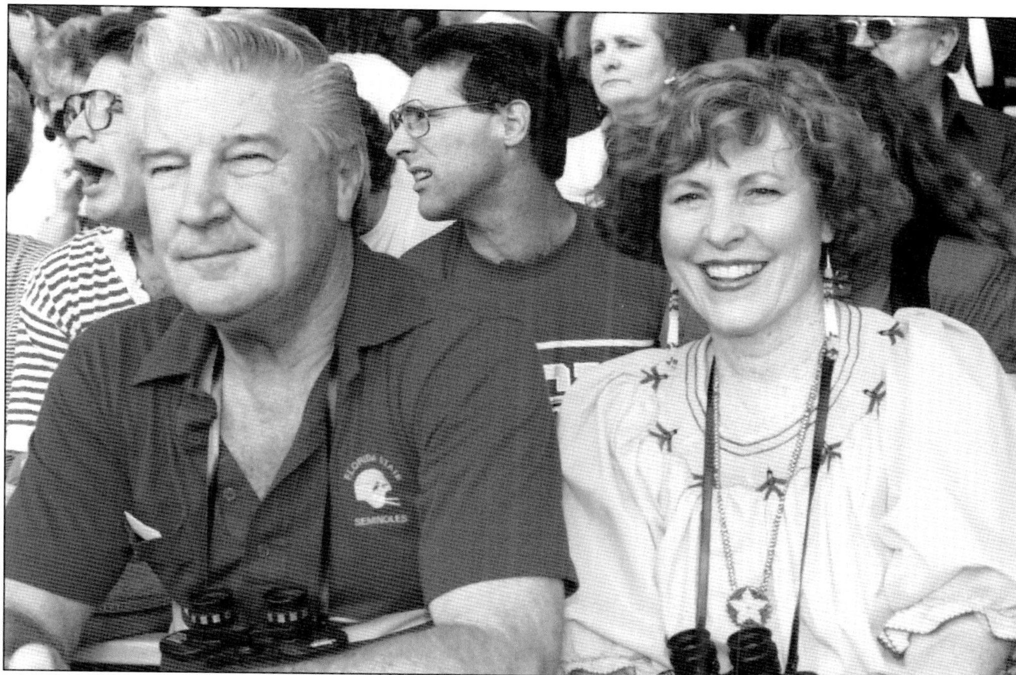

After graduating from Florida State University in 1957, Leonard Skinner became a physical education teacher in Jacksonville. One day, he sent student Ronnie Van Zant to the principal's office because his hair was touching his collar, a flagrant violation of the school's dress code. Van Zant honored his former authoritarian nemesis by renaming his rock band Lynyrd Skynyrd. Skinner was a longtime member of the Seminole Boosters. He died on September 20, 2010. Above, Skinner and his wife, Rosemary, attend an FSU football game. (Susie Skinner Moore.)

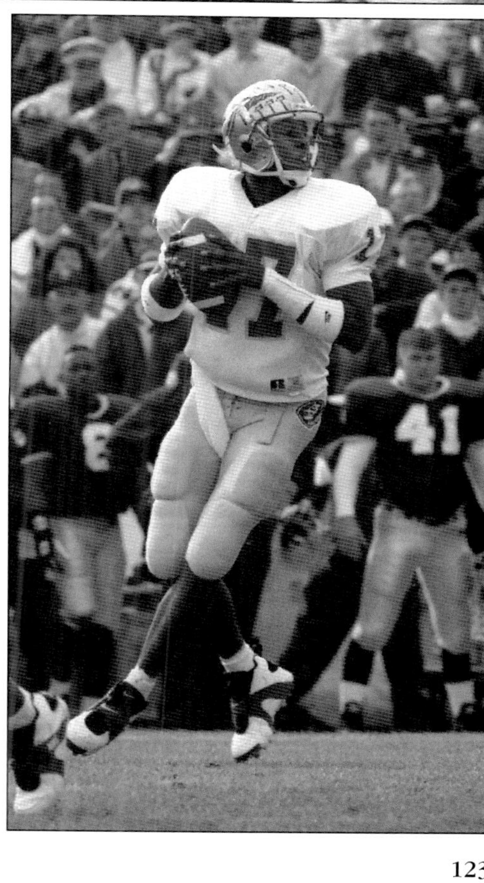

In 1993, quarterback Charlie Ward became the first Florida State University football player to be awarded the Heisman Trophy. That year, he led the Seminoles to their first national championship when FSU defeated Nebraska in the Orange Bowl. Ward was the model student-athlete and served as vice president of the Student Government Association. A multisport athlete, he was drafted into the NBA in 1994 and had a successful 12-year career. In 2000, Chris Weinke would be the second FSU player to win the Heisman Trophy. (Ryals Lee.)

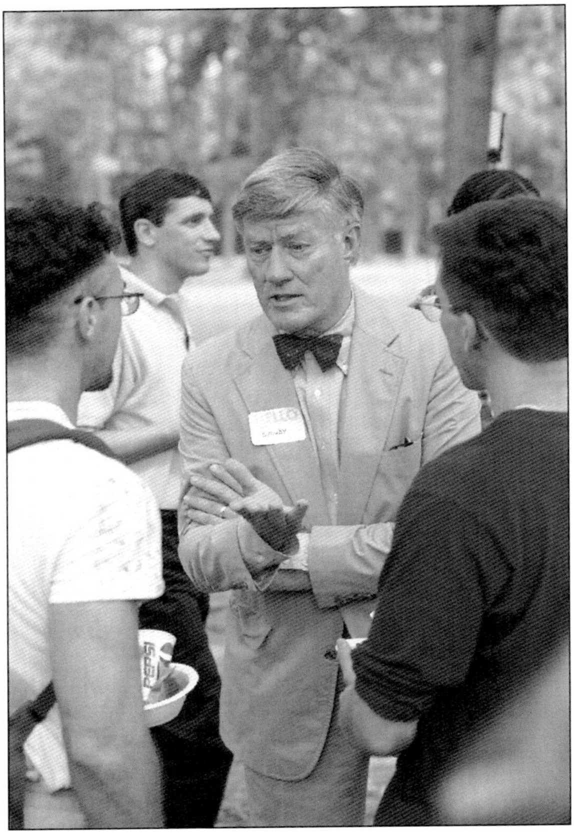

Talbot "Sandy" D'Alemberte, served as president of Florida State University from 1994 to 2003. Previously, he was dean of the FSU College of Law. Under his leadership, the College of Medicine was established, and the university became headquarters of the National High Magnetic Field Laboratory. With a grandfather who attended West Florida Seminary, and his mother an FSCW alumna, he is keenly aware of the importance of preserving the university's heritage. (FSU Photography Services.)

In 2003, Doak Campbell Stadium was expanded to 84,000 seats. Renovations to the structure included addition of the University Center, providing much-needed offices and classroom space. In the photograph below, the stadium can be seen behind the Heritage Tower, a gift of the classes of 1946, 1947, and 1948. The Heritage Tower was formally dedicated in 1998. (FSU Photography Services.)

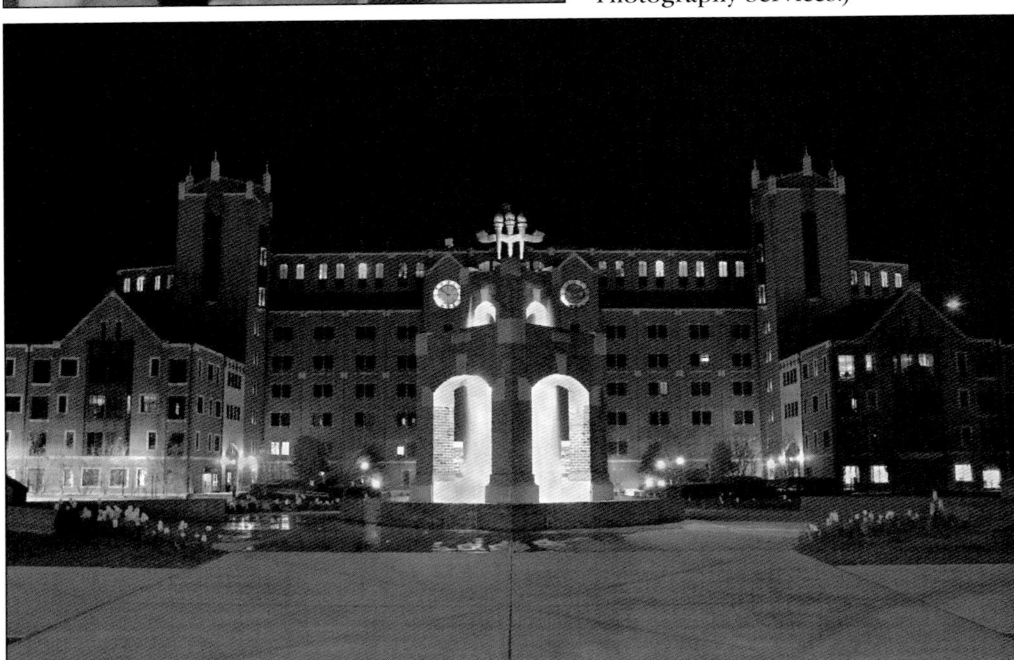

The Florida State University football team beat Virginia Tech 46-29 in the 1999 Sugar Bowl, capping off FSU's first undefeated season leading to an undisputed national championship. The Seminoles were also declared the 1993 national champions after their 18-16 victory over the University of Nebraska in the 1994 Orange Bowl. In the photograph to the right, durable, all-purpose FSU running back Travis Minor turns the corner in the 1999 Sugar Bowl victory.

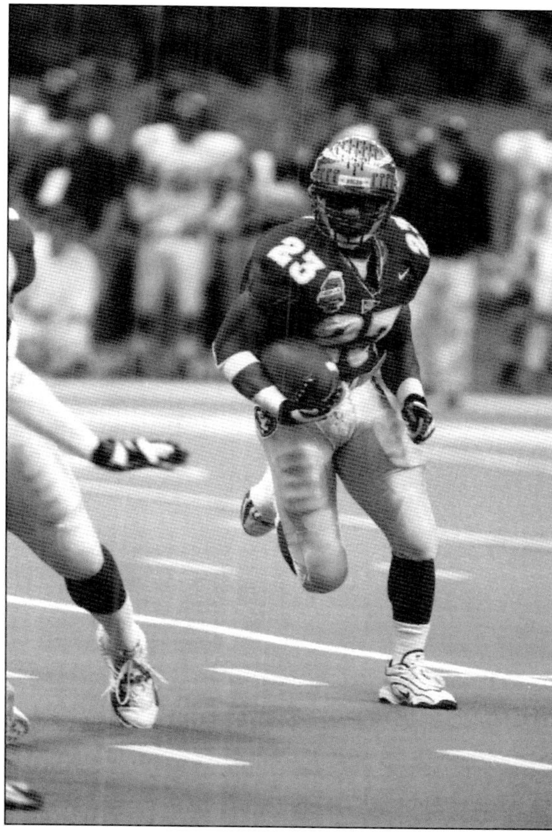

The Florida State University College of Medicine was created in June 2000 with the mission of serving the unique health needs of Floridians. It was the nation's first, new, fully accredited public allopathic medical school in 25 years. The college was granted full accreditation in 2005, the same year its state-of-the-art John Thrasher Building was dedicated. At that time, the new education and administration building was the largest single capital improvement FSU had ever taken on in terms of scope and overall cost. (FSU Photography Services.)

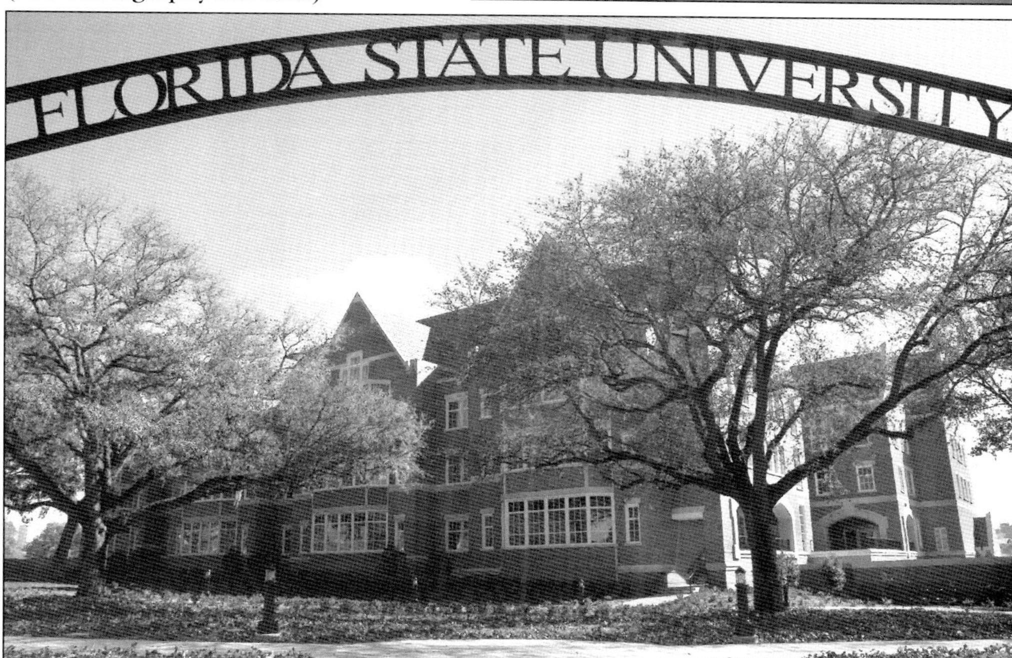

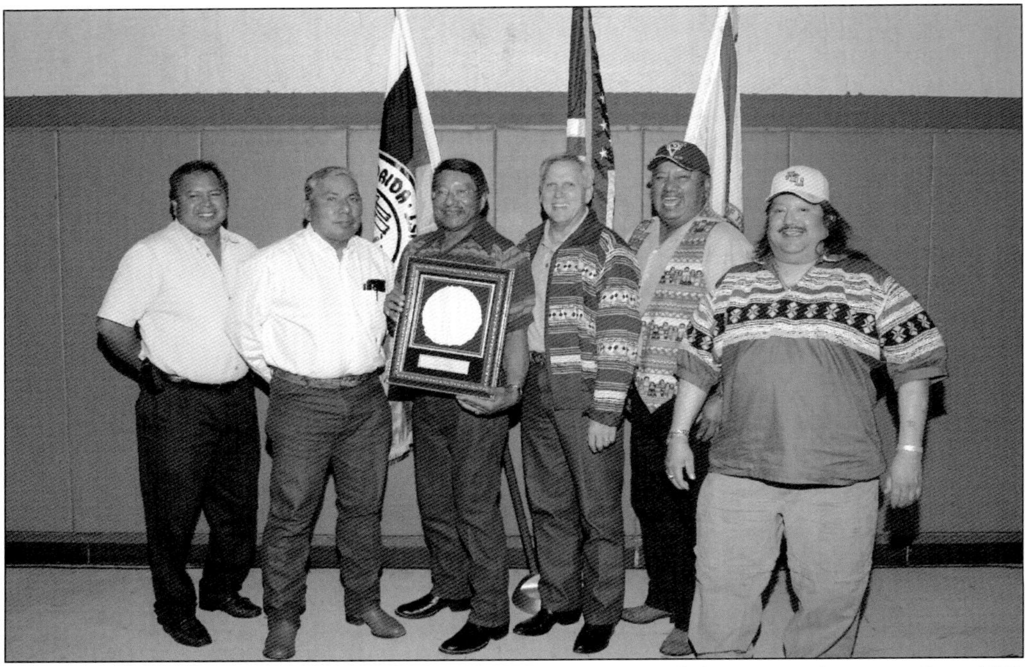

In 2005, during the NCAA's scrutiny of the university's use of the Seminole name, Pres. T.K. Wetherell accepted a historic resolution affirming the Seminole Tribe of Florida's commitment and relationship with the university. The action was crucial to the NCAA's withdrawal of its objection. Pictured here, tribal council members appear with Wetherell, from left to right, as follows: vice chair/president Moses Osceola, Andrew Bowers, chairman Mitchell Cypress, Wetherell, Max Osceola, and David Cypress. (FSU Photography Services.)

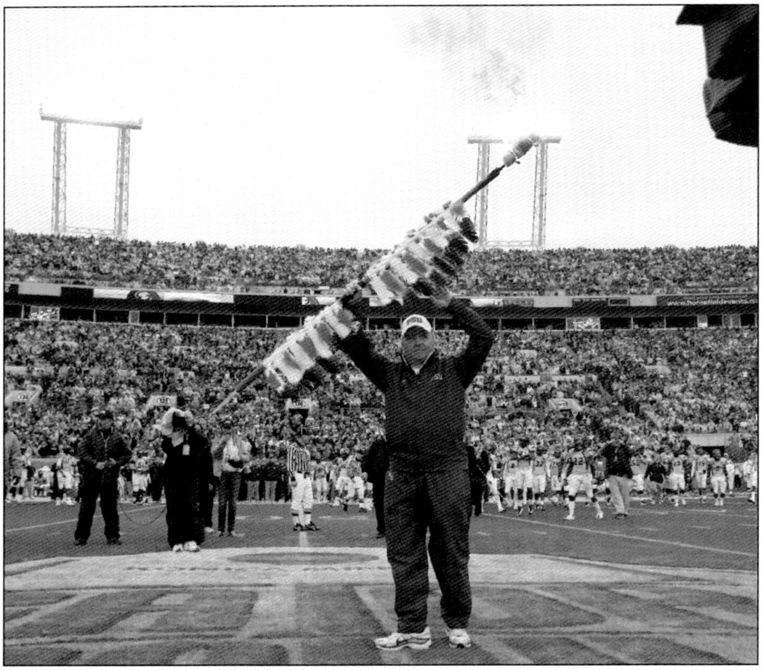

To commemorate his last game as head football coach—the 2010 Gator Bowl—Bobby Bowden took the flaming spear from Osceola, hoisted it upward to the cheering crowd and slammed it into the turf. During his 34 years as head coach, he had only three losing seasons. In an incredible run from 1987 to 2000, the Seminoles finished every season with at least 10 wins and scored two national championships. (Ryals Lee.)

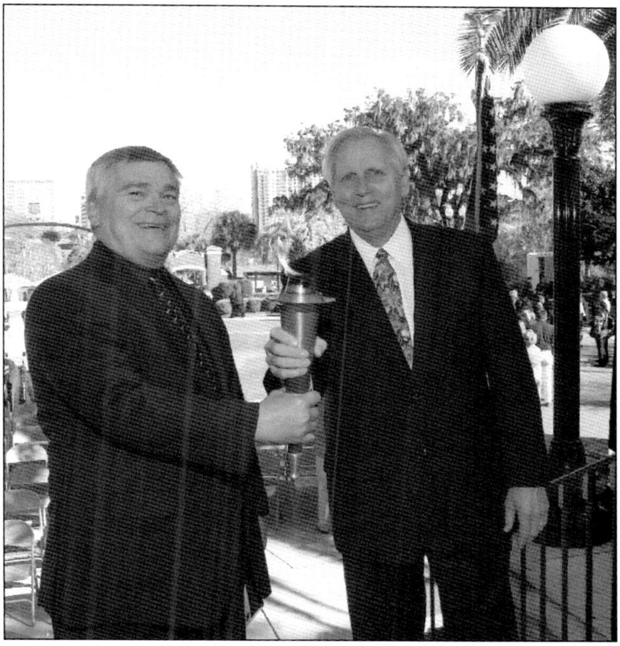

At FSU's 2010 Heritage Day Celebration, Pres. T.K. Wetherell (classes of 1967, 1968, and 1974) passes the torch of leadership to his successor, fellow FSU alumnus Eric Barron (class of 1973), the 14th president of the university. He and Wetherell are the only alumni ever to serve in this capacity. President Barron has worked aggressively to increase private funding, and despite budget challenges, his aims remain firm: to preserve the quality of an FSU education, maintain faculty-student ratios, sustain the university's impressive retention and graduation rates, and continue to provide access to highly qualified students. (FSU Photography Services.)

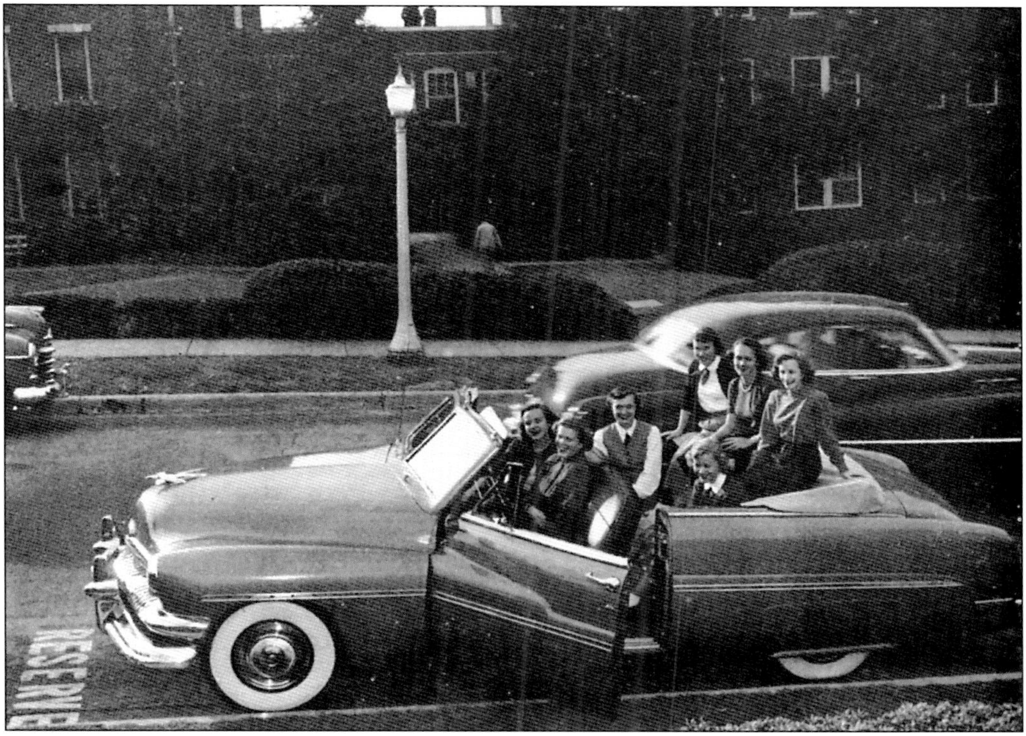

The mission of Heritage Protocol is to identify, acquire, catalog, and preserve items related to the institutional history and cultural heritage of Florida State University and its predecessor institutions. To offer financial support or to donate FSU-related artifacts or memorabilia, please visit the Heritage Protocol website at heritage.fsu.edu.

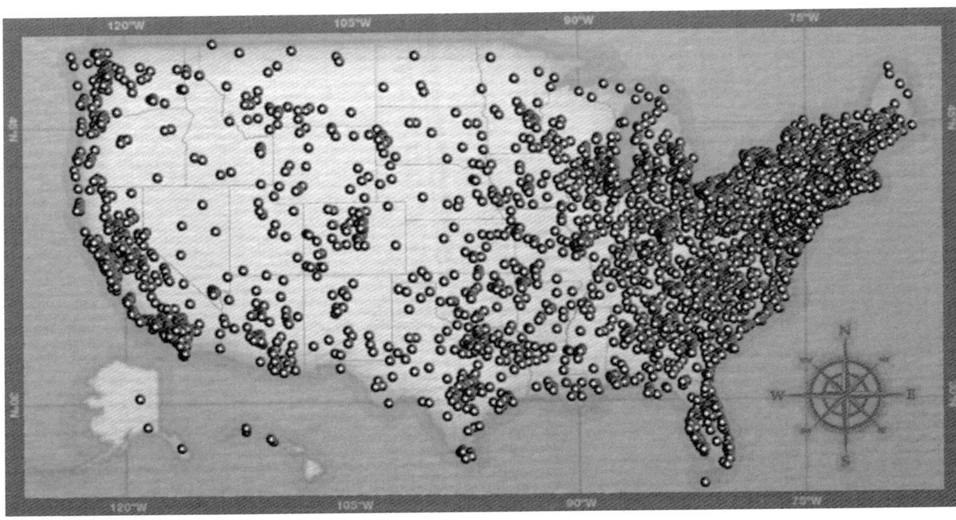